Barbara Kingsolver's World

Barbara Kingsolver's World

Nature, Art, and the Twenty-First Century

Linda Wagner-Martin

BLOOMSBURY

NEW YORK · LONDON · NEW DELHI · SYDNEY

Bloomsbury Academic
An imprint of Bloomsbury Publishing Inc

1385 Broadway	50 Bedford Square
New York	London
NY 10018	WC1B 3DP
USA	UK

www.bloomsbury.com

Bloomsbury is a registered trade mark of Bloomsbury Publishing Plc

First published 2014

Library of Congress Cataloging-in-Publication Data
Wagner-Martin, Linda.
Barbara Kingsolver's world : nature, art, and
the twenty-first century / Linda Wagner-Martin.
pages cm.
Includes bibliographical references and index.
ISBN 978-1-62356-628-9 (hardback : alk. paper) – ISBN 978-1-62356-446-9
(pbk. : alk. paper) 1. Kingsolver, Barbara--Criticism and interpretation. I. Title.
PS3561.I496Z95 2014
813'.54–dc23
2013049296

ISBN: HB: 978-1-6235-6628-9
PB: 978-1-6235-6446-9
ePub: 978-1-6235-6031-7
ePDF: 978-1-6235-6736-1

Typeset by Integra Software Services Pvt. Ltd
Printed and bound in the United States of America

For Paul, Carly, and Jessica Wagner
William and Evan Duff
Tommy, Elizabeth, and Isabelle Wagner

Contents

Preface

*I think people go to literature in search of wisdom, and ideally you
obtain wisdom the way you get scar tissue—by living in the world. It
accumulates ... I have an allegiance to my people, whom I consider to be
the un-fancy, the unpresumptuous. And I have an allegiance to community,
which includes both my human community and the biological community
that surrounds me in this habitat. And I have an allegiance to the possibility
of their collective, maybe even collaborative, survival into the future.*

Kingsolver in Fisher 30

In Kingsolver's closing interview for the 2011 "Barbara Kingsolver
Conference," held at Emory and Henry College deep in the Appalachian Blue
Ridge, she reiterated her belief that the human community and the biological
world are part and parcel of both identity and spiritual existence. Her
insistence on what she terms a "collaborative" survival marks her as one of
the scientifically informed positivists of literature in the twenty-first century:
while Kingsolver and her writing have for years been illustrative choices for
readers interested in various strands of ecological criticism—ecocriticism,
ecofeminism, ecopoetics, what E. O. Wilson terms *biophilia*, as well as ecology
itself and environmentalism—it is with her 2012 novel, *Flight Behavior*, that
her belief becomes both instructive and passionate. It is also unmistakable.

Criticism of her writing from the 1990s and the earlier twenty-first
century has pegged her *Animal Dreams* (1990) and *Prodigal Summer* (2000)
as classically ecocritical works; obviously, her non-fiction *Animal, Vegetable,
Miracle: A Year of Food Life* (2007) belongs in that category. Very recent
criticism has returned as well to Kingsolver's first novel, *The Bean Trees*
(1988), often now considered a pair novel with *Pigs in Heaven* (1993), to
address the issues of ecofeminism as well as the multiculturalism and class
that both books present. Critics have also realized that within Kingsolver's
essays (many of them grouped in her two essay collections, *High Tide in
Tucson* [1995] and *Small Wonder* [2002] and her short stories—only one
story collection has appeared, *Homeland and Other Stories* in 1989, as has one
poem collection, *Another America/Otra America* in 1992) she consistently
emphasizes that reciprocity between the human and the natural. Perhaps
overlooked because it is not fiction is her lucid and moving prose commentary
in *Last Stand: America's Virgin Lands*, a text that accompanies Annie Griffiths
Belt's inspiring photographs (2002). Even though her recent novel *The*

Lacuna (2009) won England's Orange Prize in 2010, and her worldwide bestseller remains the novel about American religious patriarchy transplanted to Africa (her 1998 *The Poisonwood Bible*), these books have been primarily treated geographically, historically, and politically, with commentary more focused on gender than on ecocriticism. It has taken her newest work, *Flight Behavior*, to clarify one of the primary directions of Kingsolver's aesthetics, which is the congruence of human life with the natural—and with all the problems that today accompany that classification.

The attempt to place Kingsolver's *oeuvre* geographically has also been insistent. First identified as a Southwestern writer (because *The Bean Trees* and her next two books were partially set in Arizona), she became linked with various myths about Westerners and the frontier. Her use of women protagonists seemed to embroider a different kind of gender emphasis onto those familiar mythic landscapes. Later, reinforced by her powerful essays, Kingsolver's identification seemed to be with the American South. In the words of critic Robert Brinkmeyer, Kingsolver changed the notion of the expansive and perhaps brutal frontiersman to one of the character as "a refugee, being displaced." The author also repeated her conviction that *race* and sometimes class played major roles in the theme of "dispossession" (Brinkmeyer 98–9). Seeing throughout her work that Kingsolver believed optimistically in what he calls "the miracles of human community," Brinkmeyer found that the presence of Kentucky and Appalachia was more significant to her and her work than was the exotic, arid Southwest.

Admittedly, Kingsolver's own statements in interviews and essays, as well as her implicit beliefs expressed through her fiction, underscored her dedication to the natural world—regardless of geographic description. As she wrote in *Last Stand*,

> I am one of those lucky ones, whose best memories all contain birdsong and trees. In the long light of summer, on every consecrated Saturday of spring and fall…my compatriots and I carried out our greatest accomplishments in the company of hickory and maple…We had no idea we were living at the edge of an epoch…We knew just enough of our world to eat it alive, swallowing wildness by the mouthful. (*Last Stand: America's Virgin Lands* 11)

One recent dimension of ecocriticism has become the study of wildness, that is, wilderness studies, and Rinda West's readings (in her current *Out of the Shadow*) emphasize the ways in which Kingsolver uses metaphors of animals living in the wild (the foxes in *Animal Dreams* and *Prodigal Summer*, for instance) to explore human reactions to natural catastrophes. West brings her seemingly separate study into alignment with an ecofeminist theme by making statements like this: "Kingsolver seems to me principally interested in exploring the relationships among psychological growth, intimacy with place, and political activism. Activism requires narratives of hope, both personal and political" (West 151).

West uses as illustrations of this point Hallie's passionate activism in Nicaragua and the ways in which the community of women in Grace, Arizona, with equal passion, saved the polluted river: she comments that *Animal Dreams* shows clearly "political action as both effective and celebratory" (West 151). Readers remember as well Kingsolver's quoting Edward Abbey's landmark statement, "The idea of wilderness needs no defense. It only needs more defenders" (*Last Stand* 187). And in Linda Hogan's lament, "Even wilderness is seen as having value only as it enhances and serves our human lives, our human world. While most of us agree that wilderness is necessary to our spiritual and psychological well-being, it is a container of far more, of mystery, of a life apart from ours… It is something beyond us, something that does not need our hand in it" (Dwellings 45).

West's critique of wildness and the value of returning to wilderness, like Hogan's, increasingly suggests that the human and the natural must be paired. West states several times, "Wilderness is not a place to live. It needs protection so that animals other than humans will have habitat and safe migratory routes and so that biological diversity can continue on the planet" (West 120). Similarly, in an essay comparing Kingsolver's writing with that of Rachel Carson, Richard T. Magee seconds West's conviction, noting that although both Carson and Kingsolver were trained as scientists, both women see that "nature is not merely a separate entity… but also an integral part of human community" (Magee 75).

This book is not a study of the ways in which ecocriticism differs from ecofeminism, or the way love of science and its accumulation of details differs from narrative patterns that inscribe both human and natural behaviors. Rather, it attempts to fuse discussion of Kingsolver's use of different lines of scientifically based knowledge with readings of her 14 books. Today's theoretical concern with ecocriticism has many spokespeople: at its simplest formulation in Scott Knickerbocker's statement that "the mission of *environmentalism* is to help us gain a meaningful relationship with the nonhuman world and to encourage more ecologically concerned behavior" (2), to Lawrence Buell's sense that *place* becomes one of the touchstones for viewing and describing human behavior (56), to Leonard Scigaj's poetically based responses to what he calls "the worldwide despoliation of nature at the hands of humans" (5), through Timothy Clark's myriad divisions within *The Cambridge Introduction to Literature and the Environment* (a book in which he begins with large assumptions such as our human concern with the "degrading environment of the planet" (xiii), to Barbara Bennett's 2012 definition that *ecofeminism* "approaches the subjects of science and nature, politics, human and animal rights, spirituality, and feminism holistically rather than in isolation" (5). Bennett resists Clark's tendency to isolate separate critiques so that she can assume what she terms "the interconnectedness of all things" when readers are faced with the continuation of human life amid global concerns.

A few years before Bennett, Christine M. Battista had said emphatically that "Kingsolver illustrates how we can and must give voice to those who have been 'disproportionately' harmed—namely, women and ecology" (in Austenfeld 54). Kingsolver herself has stated that her work as author comes from the *whole* vision she finds within herself, and then inscribes. As she said in the Perry interview,

> I'm only going to write a book if it's addressing subjects I care about. Otherwise, why write a book? It's not worth the time, and it's not worth the reader's time, and it's not worth burdening the world with another pile of pages. It surprises me constantly that almost everybody else in the United States of America who writes books hates to be called a political writer. As if that demeans them. (Perry 154)

Responding to the issues of place, and more definitively, of "home place," Kingsolver is repeatedly on record as identifying with "the vernacular of the South and [that] of Appalachia ... I suppose this question of accessibility goes back to that question that is asked in this part of the country whenever a group of people get together in a room and that is 'Who are your people?' Always, that question comes first. Then you talk, and you talk, until hopefully you find a relative in common, or an in-law, or someone you know who knows someone they know. Then you relax and move forward because you've established who we are as people. I can't disregard who I am ... I still belong to the people who made me" (in Fisher 26).

Since 2008 and following, Kingsolver has been even more adept at merging her love of intricate social history with the biology of the natural world: in the 2011 interview she repeated, "Certainly an appreciation for nature is an important feature of my work, and it arose in part because I grew up running wild in the woods with little adult supervision and I studied biology as a college student and then went to graduate school in biology. I am one of thousands of species that live in this place, and I don't ever forget the other ones are there. Species diversity is a biological fact. I think a lot about the world out there beyond the artifice that human beings have created" (in Fisher 27).

Critics have used *Prodigal Summer* as a touchstone for all the love, and the knowledge, that Kingsolver brings to any mention of the natural world. More recently, in her 2009 novel, *The Lacuna*, the mysterious inversion of space that occurs in the ocean depths provides the key to plot elements as well as dimensions of character. Although *The Lacuna* seemed more invested in Russian, Mexican, and US politics than in natural occurrences, there were many scenes of natural elements that were ocean based, or ocean bordered. But to clarify the centrality of the natural world to Kingsolver's philosophy, it took *Flight Behavior* to give the author the means of allowing her readers to see that the increasingly precarious state of the global world was—and is—everyone's responsibility—just as it is likely to become everyone's miasma: Kingsolver's 2012 novel leaves a shriek of silence in readers' minds as they see how inevitable, how unavoidable, the natural disaster of flooding in the Tennessee farmlands has become.

As she said recently, when asked about the themes of the then as yet unpublished novel, *Flight Behavior's* fundamental theme is interrogative:

> How is it possible that many people can look at the same body of evidence—for example on climate change—and draw different conclusions? It's not about the evidence, it's about something else. That's the question this novel is pursuing; How do people decide what to believe when it comes to important matters? All of us like to believe we've made our minds up based on the sum of the evidence, but in fact we're mostly looking at the same evidence. So do we believe as we do because of fear of alternatives? Do we decide what to believe by investing our trust in other people who make those decisions for us? What does this all mean, in a time when there are certain very large looming problems that have to be addressed, problems which some of us are simply deciding not to believe in? (in Fisher 30)

Flight Behavior, most readers would say, is "about" global warming. The ways in which Kingsolver makes the reader move into, and sometimes away from, stable positions about the state of the ecological world is the crux of her artistry—the proof of her authorial identity—in this new and strangely foreboding work of fiction.

Flight Behavior:
Dellarobia's Bildungsroman

Return is what we are banking on as we attempt to put back what has disappeared, the songs of wolves in Yellowstone, the pale-edged wings of condors in California sky, the dark, thundering herds of buffalo to Indian country, the flamingoes along the River of Hope.

Linda Hogan, *Dwellings* 90

As its title suggests, this novel stubbornly holds the reader to the notion that *flight* is possible. As she often has, Kingsolver here fixes on a metaphor that seems to be central to many of the novel's events. In the case of this 2012 book, however, readers who wish for the protagonist's escape from her husband's small Tennessee farm are led to crushing disappointment. Not only can Dellarobia Turnbow not escape her life as farmwife to move to a nearby town, so that she can attend college—and consequently change the direction of her personal story; she cannot even take the first step out of the flooded farmland.

> The ground was spongy with snowmelt and sank strangely under her feet…the whole mountain of snow was melting in a torrent. Every channel gouged in this slope by a long wet winter was now filled to overflowing. (Flight 429)

Whether people called it a "freak storm" or a "sudden flood," the *fact* that Dellarobia saw—that had created within her an "inflated edginess"—was that the walls of pouring water were covering not only the land but also the cars, the farm implements, and the corner of her small frame house. The unquestionable *fact* was that she "was alone out here." At first the water had reached her knees, as "the current pulled in a way she understood to be dangerous. This was where she lived."

Instead of positing ecological disasters in remote countries, Kingsolver here stresses that the disaster facing Dellarobia Turnbow is swamping her very yard. The way the author makes this frightening water both visible and palpable is to create Dellarobia's time line of recognition. With her two small children at school and at her mother-in-law's house, she knows she cannot even use her cell phone: why would she bring her husband into this kind of danger? What could another adult do in this terrorizing threat? Soon, Kingsolver gives the reader this description: [Dellarobia] "was stunned to see the water had now risen level with the porch and doorsills of her house. Its foundation and cement steps were no longer visible and the yard had eerily vanished, its embankment dissolved into the road, all memories of her home's particular geography erased" (Flight 431).

As Dellarobia accepts the power of the flooding water and the unrecognizable state of the previously abused land, she has learned in working for the Monarch butterfly project that those thousands—millions, numbering perhaps fifteen million at the start—of the butterflies have come to her Tennessee woods after having found their Mexican habitat destroyed (by flooding, wind storms, aberrant weather of all kinds): now the butterflies are being forced from these protective woods by a similar kind of immensity— the snowmelt that finds no natural boundaries to stop its progress. The deft descriptions that Kingsolver creates show the reader that Dellarobia has learned the lessons of a nature in outrage—she watches the frantic birds, she ferrets out the remnants of the Monarch colony, she eventually finds a fragment of personal tranquility in the midst of the destroying waters. By the end of this effective description, Kingsolver has created a haven for Dellarobia as well as for what Monarchs remain. As the author writes matter-of-factly,

> She'd come out here to see the butterflies. Since yesterday she had watched them leave their clusters in the dead peach orchard and scatter downhill into cedars and tangled brush along the roadsides. Now they dotted every small muddy rise that was not yet swamped. Wherever she looked she saw their aggregations on the dwindling emergent places: forming bristling lines along tree branches and the topmost wire of the fence, clustered on driftwood, speckling even the distant, gleaming roof of her car. Orange clouds of the undecided hovered in the air space above them. (Flight 432)

Because much of the biological surveying of the Monarchs had been given to counting the dead, focusing on how many butterflies remained alive during and after the inimical weather, the reader does not expect to find this almost euphoric description of living butterflies. (Many, far too many of the butterflies have died.) The paragraph continues, "The vivid blur of their reflections glowed on the rumpled surface of the water, not clearly defined as individual butterflies but as masses of pooled streaky color, like the sheen of floating oil, only brighter, like a lava flow. That many" (Flight 433).

Subject to the human curiosity that motivates not only the scientists who have come to work at Dellarobia's farm—*and* Dellarobia herself, *and* the reader—the most pressing question here on the last page of *Flight Behavior* becomes, how many *are* left? How many *is* "That many"? Thinking that the novel has been a traditional account of a woman character's growth through education as well as life experiences, the reader may be momentarily confused: *Flight Behavior* in Kingsolver's deft hands, however, does *not* give the reader Dellarobia's outcome. It does not explain how she likes her college courses, or how much influence she will be able to maintain over her smart young son Preston. Most strikingly, it does not even explain whether she lives or dies. Instead, the narrative's focus moves entirely to the Monarchs as they shroud the remaining protective trees. The book's two final paragraphs are Kingsolver's choice to force the natural world to become integral to the human one, a feat that is accomplished without Dellarobia's name ever being mentioned.

> She was wary of taking her eyes very far from her footing, but now she did that, lifted her sights straight up to watch them passing overhead. Not just a few, but throngs, an airborne zootic force flying out in formation, as if to war. In the middling distance and higher up they all flowed in the same direction, down-mountain, like the flood itself occurring on other levels. The highest ones were faint trails of specks, ellipses. Their numbers astonished her. Maybe a million. The shards of a wrecked generation had rested alive like a heartbeat in trees, snow-covered, charged with resistance. Now the sun blinked open on a long impossible time, and here was the exodus. They would gather on other fields and risk other odds, probably no better or worse than hers.
>
> The sky was too bright and the ground so unreliable, she couldn't look up for very long. Instead her eyes held steady on the fire bursts of wings reflected across water, a merging of flame and flood. Above the lake of the world, flanked by white mountains, they flew out to a new earth. (Flight 433)

Avoiding outright didacticism, Kingsolver draws the reader back into the metaphor of the fragile, lost Monarch butterflies. It is the natural world, even in chaos, that provides information for the reader. Intent on continuing their new lives on some "new earth," the butterflies—the countless living organisms that are truly facing extinction—have managed to find a place of unexpected life in the midst of disastrous global changes.

The ambiguity Kingsolver creates is itself almost flooded away in these closing scenes. How wide is the implication of "They would gather on other fields and risk other odds, *probably no better or worse than hers.*" At first, the reader thinks the reference is to *Dellarobia's* terrain, the farm, her land. Grammatically, however, it becomes clear that that is far from the author's intent. Kingsolver is talking about *chances.* Chances and risks. Just as Dellarobia was about to chance going to college, moving away from the limitations of the Turnbow family and its farm, she is forced into a life-and-death struggle with her own natural world. Her learning about the Monarchs and their defiant processes has brought her, along with them, into a flight path that seems only destructive.

From the earliest scenes in *Flight Behavior*, Kingsolver has given readers vocabulary that equips them to understand the science of good observation. Early on, when it appeared that this novel was to be a feminist story of Dellarobia's escape from too-early marriage into ways of learning about life important to her and her questing intelligence, this protagonist's relationship with her girlhood friend, Dovey, is described as choosing a "flight path." In one instance, when the women are still in high school, Kingsolver points out their united purpose—to escape their small town lives. Dellarobia and Dovey had "sworn onto a flight plan, older guys with vocabularies and bank accounts, men from anywhere but here" (Flight 41). (The ultra feminine name "Dovey" matches the somewhat ornate "Dellarobia" in creating *difference* within the female population of the town: these two are prestigious women, beauties worth owning, women who wear unusually fashionable clothes, even if cheap ones, and smoke cigarettes.)

In one of the few positive scenes between Dellarobia and her husband Cub, the author echoes the phrase. Cub, depressed over his father's desperate need for money, has taken refuge in the loft of his father's barn. When Dellarobia joins him there, his desperation touches her also and she moves—in a useless search for answers—to the propped-open door at the end of the loft. "A person could just run the length of the haymow and take a flying leap ... she could see perfectly well how a person arrived in that flight path: needing an alternative to the present so badly, the only doorway was a high window" (Flight 41). Just as her recklessness here terrifies her, she sees how the financial ruin of the once-prosperous Turnbows marks every member of the family.

The butterflies have also managed to shape Dellarobia's life in unexpected ways. She has first discovered the bevy of butterflies too numerous to count as she treks up the mountain to meet Jimmy, a young "telephone man": conventionally, Dellarobia thinks that a new and forbidden romance may bring life to her existence. Instead, stunned by the beauty of this inexplicable mass that covers the trees with its orange and black constancy, she watches it, bemused, and then returns home. She avoids meeting the boy/man who has been flirting with her. Kingsolver's imagery as Dellarobia absorbs the beauty of the massed insects leads the reader, like her protagonist, to a complicity in the relentless closing scene that is unsurprising: as the would-be-runaway wife watches the spectacle before her, she gives language to that astonishing view, "It was a lake of fire, something far more fierce and wondrous than either of those elements alone. The impossible" (Flight 16).

Metonyms for life and death, beauty and a fearful kind of ugliness, the Monarchs and their several conditions take on Biblical overtones as they become the chart for readers' judgments about Dellarobia and her personal attempts to escape. Can twenty-first-century readers find fault with Cub, the bumbling teenager who chooses to marry Dellarobia when she becomes pregnant? Can the Turnbow family itself—so typically middle-class, religiously conformist, and hard working—be made to seem threatening? Can the sexy Dellarobia, still defining herself through her physical and sexual appetites, be seen primarily as a sympathetic young mother? Can Hester, her mother-in-law, win the reader's empathy by finally telling Dellarobia the story of her own unwanted first pregnancy? Kingsolver has chosen less than conventional characters as she works out her own *flight plan* for the narrative of a human world peopled by flawed and confined figures, a world eventually subordinated to the happenings of the natural world that surrounds them.

The ostensible plot of the Monarch butterflies' searching for refuge is only one layer of Kingsolver's narrative of ecological changes, all of them dire. In a sense, the glorious color of the huddling butterflies is a bright spot both literal and figurative: the rest of the Appalachian hillside is greyed into a sameness that seems, to Dellarobia, to match the tenor of her days.

No wonder the Monarch colony has attracted so much attention. In a world of financial strain like this one, the luxury of such color—and such abundance—is rare. The awe that tinges Dellarobia's description of "air filled with quivering butterfly light" (53) stems partly from her unfamiliarity with sheer beauty.

The ecological drift that has taken over the farmers' lives since Cub's father, Bear Turnbow, built the modest house for Cub and Dellarobia more than a decade earlier has landed all these farmers into straightened times. Poverty that seems to be unmanageable has arrived: plans must be changed, neighbors must admit to needing help from each other, the patriarchal structure of the Tennessee families has been shaken. Without explanation, Bear Turnbow has more often been supporting his family from the profits of his metal working shop than from the farm. This summer, the crops have failed once again—this time from unrelenting rains. It is for those machine shop tools that he has taken on the balloon note. The note is now due. If he does not log (or, more accurately, *clear cut*) the hillside forests, he will lose the bulk of his mortgaged tools and once more be dependent on the whimsical weather patterns that have already driven some of his neighbors into bankruptcy. With his farm as collateral for the note, its failure may also take his farm.

At the start of *Flight Behavior*, Kingsolver makes the reader attend to the visible effects of this killing rain. When Dellarobia begins her climb up the mountain, she works to avoid stumbling over an uprooted tree, intact but dislodged by the wet surround: "After maybe centuries of survival it had simply let go of the ground, the wide fist of its root mass ripped up and resting naked above a clay gash in the wooded mountainside...The ground took water until it was nothing but soft sponge, and the trees fell out of it" (Flight 5). Later, one of the visiting scientists would tell her, "there are unstoppable processes. Like the loss of polar ice. White ice reflects the heat of the sun directly back to space. But where it melts, the dark land and water underneath hold on to the heat. The frozen ground melts. And that releases more carbon into the air. These feedback loops keep surprising us" (Flight 279). Even if the farmers most affected by the heavy rains are content to talk about the "unusual" extent of the damages, the scientific world already knows that the rains—and their effects—are irrevocable. They are just one illustration of the constant changing of the natural world. Even in her conversations with Cub, climate change is apparent: he has more work delivering gravel because roads have washed out and people's driveways are bare of cover under the pounding rain. And, if Dellarobia had been listening, she would have known that "Trees were getting new diseases now...The wetter summers and mild winters of recent years were bringing in new pests that apparently ate the forest out of house and home" (Flight 12).

In their frantic need for more and more money to replace farm income, the Turnbows have learned to raise sheep; this part of their existence has become Hester's responsibility (and her authoritative bossiness has cost her friends). A secondary plot concerns both the critical shearing of the 90 ewes and their lambs, and the ewes' giving birth to increase the herd. Every new lamb is important. Even though it is Cub and Dellarobia who are a month behind in their mortgage payments, the financial pressure on Bear and Hester is so great that the younger Turnbows cannot comprehend that stress. It is a noticeable victory for Dellarobia when Hester agrees to let her oversee the birthing of the pregnant ewes. The animals are moved to the land behind Cub's smaller farm, and Dellarobia uses her oversight responsibility as a means of including Preston in the process. It is clear by this point in the novel that Dellarobia lives to teach Preston. Young as he is, Preston has already defined himself as a scientist, and he hungers for information about all parts of the world.

Dellarobia's ability to save the lamb that is born dead, encased in a caul, shows that she may be critical to the family's survival. Because she had filled her house with books about lambing, she knows about the swinging technique that pulls the still born lamb from its shroud: Kingsolver here provides another instance of the validity of scientific information used in the actual world. Although Hester jealously guards her knowledge—gained through years of experience—Dellarobia is able to save this one small life. Kingsolver refers to it as "the puddle of a lamb" inside its milky caul; it definitely is not breathing. The violent swinging motion, however, brings it back to life (Flight 414). When she and Cub rejoice, it is one of the novel's rare moments when they are happy together. Tempered by recognition of the larger situation, they quickly realize "It was all impermanent, the square white corners of house and home, everything. This one little life signified nothing in the long run" (Flight 419).

Juxtaposed with the knowledge Dellarobia is gaining from her work with the scientist Ovid Byron, the practical matters of trying to keep the farm alive illustrate the often abstract comments Ovid makes. When he tells her, after the heavy snowfall, that there is no way the Monarch butterflies can live, she does not want to believe him ("Survival wasn't possible … given the mortality under the snow" (421)). Ovid had claimed his superiority earlier when he told Dellarobia, who admired learning but also remained somewhat romantic about what sheer effort could achieve, "I am a doctor of natural systems. And this looks terminal to me" (Flight 282).

He later showed his deep sorrow when he explained, "Not everyone has the stomach to watch an extinction" (Flight 319). His pain as he sees how few Monarchs will live belies his apparently calm demeanor as he watches the weather change. And for Dellarobia's part, accepting the inevitable began to have some allure; her temperament starts to change from romantic to more nearly objective. As she said to herself, "The hard part is letting go, she could see that. There is no life raft; you're just freaking swimming all the time" (Flight 394).

Narratively, Kingsolver has seeded the novel with many descriptions that help the reader understand the complicated progress of the planet's warming. When Dellarobia describes the sheep shearing day, for instance, she mentions that the "nonstop rain" that had ruined their crops has given way to sunshine. At times she takes on a kind of editorializing voice: at one point she explains "The world of sensible seasons had come undone." Again, she tells the reader, "Ground water was rising everywhere" (Flight 20, 49, 123).

Other descriptions are given in a voice that approximates the idiom Dellarobia would use: She speaks in third person of "another family's bled-out luck" in the same passage where she describes the farmers' constant poverty: "A life measured in half dollars and clipped coupons and culled hopes flattened between uninsulated walls" (Flight 17). This is a culture where people drive old cars as a matter of course (Dellarobia drives her deceased mother's silver Taurus station wagon; Cub has an old truck, as do his parents), and where they shop at Second Time Around, or comparable used clothing stores, for both their clothes and their children's. (When Dellarobia heads for her tryst, she wears a suede jacket that she has borrowed from Dovey and a pair of ill-fitting cowboy boots which she paid $6 for at the second-hand shop and then hidden so that Cub does not see them.) Early in the book Kingsolver chose to have Dellarobia covet—prompted perhaps more by her poverty than by her marital unhappiness—"Something of her own... every other thing got snatched from her hands: her hairbrush, the TV clicker, the soft middle part of her sandwich, the last Coke she's waited all afternoon to open" (Flight 6). She also must allow the science team to pay her electric bill, using Ovid's credit card: the team, housed both in her barn and beside it, has used a great deal more electricity than the Turnbows have expected (Flight 242).

Studding the novel and adding poignance to the recitations of poverty are the excitements and yearnings of her older child. At one point, from Santa Claus, Preston asks for a watch like that of Mako, one of the graduate assistants (Flight 173); he is thrilled to have the iPad that Dellarobia has spent her assistant's earnings for (they are sharing this since it will also become her phone; she has no other computer technology) (Flight 428); he also is the family member who reaches out to new kinds of friends. It is Preston who knows the Mexican child, Josefina Delgado, another kindergartner in Miss Rose's class. When Josefina brings her parents—Lupe and Reynaldo—to the Turnbow house to visit the butterflies, it is clear that the parents know no English: Josefina is their "ambassador" (Flight 98).

The Delgadoes' visit is a key plot device. They are refugees from Angangueo in Michoacan, Mexico, which was the site of the Monarch colony's overwintering before catastrophic flooding and mudslides wiped out both the village (along with more than 30 lives) and the Monarch refuge. There, Josephina's father, Reynaldo, was a *guia* on horseback, a guide to the butterfly colonies, who also did scientific duties such as counting the insects; her mother, Lupe, cooked for the tourists. Coincidental as their presence in Tennessee is—their having come to this location because of their relatives who work in the tobacco fields—it gives Kingsolver the opportunity to describe radical climate changes that force living things to change habitats. (As she explains further in the book's non-fiction postscript, in February 2010, "unprecedented rainfall brought down mudslides and catastrophic floods" on Angangueo in the Mexican mountains. Although thousands of people lost their homes and their livings, the butterflies did not leave—and still overwinter in that area (435).) Preston's obvious kindness to and interest in Josefina mark him as a most unusual child, but perhaps the bonding through both families' poverties evens out differences in language and culture.

Kingsolver also gains the pathos of having Josefina's mixed Spanish/English language convey the story. As the child tells Dellarobia, "Gone. Everything is gone…The water was coming and the mud was coming on everything… *Un diluvio.*" In answer to Dellarobia's question, What was gone, she continues, "The houses. The school. The peoples. The mountain. And the *monarcas* also … Some childrens did die" (Flight 102).

A clear foreshadowing of the fate of *Flight Behavior's* butterflies, Josefina's narrative also illustrates the difference in vocabularies between the scientific community that Dellarobia quickly absorbs and that of the farmers who live in these mountains. "King Billies" the residents call the Monarchs, and the legend is that each of the butterflies represents the soul of a child who died young. Strikingly germane to the loss Dellarobia and Cub experienced, when Dellarobia's first pregnancy (the reason for their marriage) ended in miscarriage, this belief keeps her reaction to the butterflies from becoming entirely objective. Late in the book, she muses as she watches the surviving butterflies, still alive after the snowstorm, "For the souls of dead children, they were good at planning ahead. She thought of Josefina's small hands fluttering out from her chest. And the little black lamb blinking its eyes open, drawing its breath, taking hers away" (Flight 423). Language becomes one of the mysteries of enduring. More significantly, life itself is the greatest of these mysteries.

As *Flight Behavior* progresses, the book's religious underpining becomes more and more important. Praised by the congregation of their homey church and held in a kind of reverence by her naïve spouse, Dellarobia—thanks to the presumptions of reporters on several television shows that have come to film the Monarchs—is changed into the sainted viewer of the natural miracle, "Our Lady of the Butterflies." She has been chosen to see this miracle. Although not a religious person—and embarrassed by this attention within the church community—Dellarobia understands the terms of this notice. In some ways, the attention of her home community is more significant than the scientific recognition brought by Professor Ovid Byron and his graduate assistants.

The Turnbows' participation in their church is a stable, consistent link with the author's belief that saving the earth and its people, its animals, its living organisms is a spiritual act. As she wrote in her preface to Norman Wirzba's *The Essential Agrarian Reader,* "The decision to attend to the health of one's habitat and food chain is a spiritual choice. It's also a political choice, a scientific one, a personal and a convivial one. It's not a choice between living in the country or the town; it is about understanding that every one of us, at the level of our cells and respiration, lives in the country and is thus obliged to be mindful of the distance between us and our sustenance" (in Austenfeld 52–3). Throughout Kingsolver's *oeuvre*, much community-building as well as many humane activities are located in churches, although protagonists themselves may not be church members. In *Flight Behavior*, for instance, Dellarobia uses the interval of the morning service to smoke a cigarette or two, while Preston and Cordie are in Sunday school. Similarly, her father-in-law spends the time with other men in a separate meeting room. For Hester and Cub, however, prayer is meaningful. They listen to Reverend Bobby Ogle, and they respect him for his plain-spoken wisdom. Accordingly, to be pastor to a Protestant congregation that numbers 300 people on most Sundays is to wield great influence. Later, they turn to him for mediation when Bear Turnbow insists on logging the farm's forest areas.

Kingsolver's descriptions of Reverend Bobby provide the sense of a pastorate marked by its humility. Dressed in a plaid shirt from Target, the minister speaks without notes, simply, directly, humanly. He made "all things seem possible." For this Sunday's sermon, he draws from Corinthians: "Take captive every thought to make it obedient to Christ," with references about "disobedient thoughts" to Jeremiah 79 (Flight 64, 67). The author sets the minister's words in the midst of a six-page section of Dellarobia's widely varied (and non-Christian) thoughts, always creating the sense of her questioning of outright religion. The minister's lead statement is that "we can look something straight in the eye and give it a different name that suits us better": the way tough problems divide people, an issue that is playing havoc in the Turnbow family. Again, the Reverend Bobby, "We all have the special talent of believing in a falsehood, and believing it devoutly, when we want it to be true" (Flight 68).

Kingsolver creates an unlikely power dynamic in the minister's role in this important family financial decision, whether or not to clear cut the forest. For Cub, who has seldom argued against his father's decisions, preserving the Monarchs and putting off the logging (or, more likely, returning the initial deposit from Money Tree Industries), and taking a stand against his father's financial decision is unexpected—and brave. For Hester, whose marriage to Bear had depended on her giving her first baby (an illegitimate child) up for adoption while Bear was in the service in Europe, her dependence on Bobby is a revelatory act. Bobby *is* that illegitimate child, adopted by an older couple who had the wealth to educate him—but no one else in the community knows this. Nor does Bobby.

Dellarobia describes Cub, Hester's other son and her own husband of a decade, as "an immense sad man in boxers" (Flight 399). In contrast, she has become so admiring of Professor Ovid Byron that she can scarcely stay away from him, and once she inadvertently sees him naked in the trailer the scientific group uses—parked as it is beside the Turnbow barn—she reverts to her teenage patterns and literally lusts after the tall man of color. Happily, toward the end of their stay, Ovid brings his strikingly beautiful and well-educated folklorist wife, Juliet Emerson, back with him and gives Dellarobia insight into what a loving marriage might be: she learns that marriage was not the "precarious risk she'd balanced for years against forbidden fruits, something easily lost in a brittle moment by flying away or jumping a train to ride off on someone else's steam. She was not about to lose it. She'd never had it" (Flight 398).

In addition to the countless metaphoric uses Kingsolver gives to the Monarchs, she punctuates the text with parables that align with her larger description of this book in her pre-publication interview: *Flight Behavior* becomes a means of showing the differences possible as people avail themselves of factual information, even though they still differ radically as they attempt to discern *what* that information means.

For example, when Dellarobia watches little Cordie play with her yellow plastic telephone, she must admit that the toddler has no idea that the toy was supposed to model the telephones of Dellarobia's own childhood. For Cordie, telephones looked nothing like this toy. "She'd seen something so plainly in this toy that was fully inimical to the child, two realities existing side by side. It floored her to be one of the people seeing the world as it used to be" (Flight 134). Similarly, the views held by Bear—always in opposition to those of Cub, his son Burley, Jr.—can be negotiated as evidence of the same kind of dual realities.

Kingsolver often uses short dialogue scenes to describe the complicated differences of opinion she is dealing with. Dellarobia, for example, adopts a condescending attitude toward Cub and his parents—probably stemming from her adolescent friendship with Dovey, when they were the elite, popular girls—and her speech patterns still reflect those attitudes. When Cub is trying to fight against his father's insistence that they clear cut the forests, he explains to Dellarobia, "Dad says they wouldn't log up there if there was any risk to it," she replies tersely, "The hell they wouldn't" (Flight 172).

One of the novel's pivotal scenes fits this pattern. Trying to explain the role of science in the lives of these Tennessee farmers, Kingsolver creates an argument about DDT so that Cub can argue against his father's attitudes. As the Turnbow family watches the butterflies in their shrouding clusters, Bear comments,

'I've got some DDT saved in the basement.'

'You've got 3-D in your basement?' his friend asks.

'DDT,' Cub told him. 'Dad, that stuff has been against the law for more than my whole life. No offense, but it must be something else you've got stored.'

'Why do you think I saved it up? I knew it would be hard to get.'

'That stuff's bound to go bad on you,' Hester argued. 'After this many years.'

'Woman, how is poison going to go bad? You reckon it will get *toxic*?' Bear laughed at his own joke. No one else did. Cub normally cowered like a cur under this tone from his father, but was strangely unyielding now ... Bear's eyes were the color of unpainted tin, and exactly that cold. (Flight 55)

More than a dialogue between scientifically based knowledge and the nonscientific, this scene shows the fundamental and pervasive anger that has usurped Bear's humanity. His usual unkindness to Dellarobia is no different than his attitudes toward many in the community, and it takes both Reverend Bobby and Ovid to have any impact on his stubborn ignorance.

In keeping with the notion of parable, in this novel Kingsolver uses Biblical references to cement a point. Early in the novel, as Dellarobia is enroute to her tryst, she thinks of Lot's wife turning to salt because she has disobeyed, looking back at the destruction of the city; in later sections of the novel, she thinks of the Monarchs' staying alive as "the resurrection and the life," grimacing to herself that thinking in those terms created "a natural hazard" in itself (Flight 420). She also gropes for ways to refer to Job—in one scene describing the deaths of all his children as a roof collapses, in another picturing herself as depleted as he, "lying on the ash heap wailing, cutting his flesh with a husk" (Flight 228, 232). More comically, apologizing to her children for their having to live with "second-hand smoke," she wonders, "What would Mrs. Noah do?" (Flight 124). She also draws on Biblical phrases to shape her more random thinking:

The times seemed Biblical. *Save me, O God, for the waters have come up to my neck*: that line in particular she remembered, from the Psalms, because it sounded like something Dovey would say. (Flight 123)

Perhaps used more obviously to create a focus is this description of the frightening storm, "When the storm broke, the world was changed. Flat rocks dotted the pasture with their damp shine ... The receding waters left great silted curves swaggering down the length of the hill, pulled from side to side by a current that followed its incomprehensible rules. *Washed in the blood of the lamb* were words that came to mind when Dellarobia ventured out, though it wasn't blood that had washed this farm but the full contents of the sky, more water than seemed possible from the ceiling of any one country" (Flight 134).

For all the scenes given to church attendance, or to the Reverend Bobby's visiting Hester in her kitchen, there is little religious rhetoric. In fact, Dovey's text messages (mostly based on the ineptly-worded religious sayings on church announcement boards) keep Dellarobia comforted: most of the real world does not believe in the literal Bible. When Dovey sends her the texts, "Come ye fishers of men: You catch, God will clean" (Flight 65) and "Get right or get left" (Flight 286), her humor sparks her endurance of her family life. Interestingly, it is Cub's language—though spare—that often conveys the sense of religious empowerment; it is Cub who speaks of Dellarobia's "foretelling" the "miracle" of the butterfly colonies. And it is Cub who speaks proudly to the large congregation about his wife's having been chosen to do this work (Flight 54). In his mother's words, Dellarobia has been given *grace*.

More of Dellarobia's internal arguments focus not on religion but on money. Early in the book as she thinks of her own possible marital infidelity, she muses, "Heartbreak. Broken family. Broke, period. What she might do for money if Cub left her was anyone's guess. She hadn't been employed … since the Feathertown Diner closed" (Flight 9). What Dellarobia learns as the narrative takes her into a province of learning that she had not known existed—even though, as she points out to Ovid, she was the only student in her class who drove, alone, to take the ACT test in order to go to college—is that the world itself provides all the metaphoric knowledge she needs to express the wisdom she trusts.

In those later scenes, she is actively learning from both the work Ovid sets her to do, and from listening to him describe scientific existences. She does not understand why his graduate students are so impressed that he has won a MacArthur "Genius" grant, years of funding for his research; she is not familiar with the accolades education furnishes. But she does know that Ovid is a leader in these fields and that his graduate students are honored that they are allowed to work with him. She also knows that she has become well trained already during these brief months—that she understands parts of the global climate changes, that she understands the cyclic nature of the butterflies' reproduction and existence, and that she is capable of learning a great deal more than she already knows. She subconsciously repeats Ovid's words, "We are seeing a bizarre alteration of a previously stable pattern … A continental ecosystem breaking down … due to climate change." "It's not a happy scenario: climate change has disrupted this system." Ovid's discussion of the migration of the Monarch butterflies from Mexico to Tennessee includes the fact that in Mexico, there remains only "a catastrophically diminished population." Referring to the butterflies on the farm, Ovid explains, "*This* population is about all that's left" (Flight 227–8). She daily recalls his three-part explanation for the possible reasons the butterflies may have settled here: first, perhaps, the scarcity of herbicides, coupled with the fact that the parasites they have picked up may have shortened their ability to fly long distances. There is also the issue of winter and spring nectar sources (Flight 348–50). Ovid also emphasized regularly that the cycles of species reproduction were inviolable: the butterflies do not lay eggs until spring, and they lay those eggs only in the milkweed. Scientists have only patience; they cannot change patterns. In Ovid's final anger, he said testily, "the damn globe is catching fire, and the islands are drowning" (Flight 226, 231).

An anonymous *New Yorker* reviewer comments in a 2012 critique that *Flight Behavior* "lurches toward the scientific sermon" (139), while Karen Holt in *Oprah* says flatly that Kingsolver's "environmental message" is "anything but subtle" (135). The significant reason for Ovid's language of scientific explanation becomes clear: he does not know how else to express his knowledge. By the later pages of the novel, he endears himself to Dellarobia because he has taken some of her ideas seriously—even if she does not know the appropriate scientific words to use. In the dinner table conversation with Cub and the children, and with Ovid's wife Juliet, the scientist explains to Juliet that he has been scouring his scientific journals to find restatements of Dellarobia's theory about noneducated observers' hostile behavior in the face of obvious global change.

Listened to for perhaps one of the first times since her high school classes, Dellarobia is surprised that Ovid thinks her ideas are worth discussing with his wife. The reader has come to accept her self-identification, largely because of the comic descriptions through the early segments of *Flight Behavior*, when Dellarobia's character is, in Kingsolver's words, "a stay-at-home mom," and is described by the author with outright humor. She calls this profession "the loneliest kind of lonely, in which she was always and never by herself. Days and days, hours and hours within them, and days within weeks, at the end of which she might not even have gotten completely dressed or read any word longer than *Chex*, any word not ending in –*os* or formed a sentence or brushed her teeth or left a single footprint outside the house" (Flight 59).

Ovid has observed Dellarobia's life intently, as he has all aspects of life on the Turnbow farm; he sees her as untapped potential. Just as Mako has given her his watch so that Preston may have his Christmas wish, Ovid works earnestly to create better circumstances for Dellarobia and her family.

The interchange about observers' hostility occurs after the meal is finished. Ovid uses the term "the territorial divide," and Dellarobia, confused, does not at first see that *this* is her idea:

> "climate-change denial functioned like folk art for some people, he said, a way of defining survival in their own terms. But it's not indigenous, Juliet argues. It's like a cargo cult. Introduced from the outside, corporate motives via conservative media. But now it's become fully identified with the icons of local culture, so it's no longer up for discussion.
>
> 'The key thing is,' Juliet said, resting her elbow on the table, ... 'once you're talking identity, you can't just lecture that out of people. The condescension of outsiders won't diminish it. That just galvanizes it.'
>
> Dellarobia felt abruptly conscious of her husband and her linoleum. 'Christ on the cross,' she said without enthusiasm. 'The rebel flag on mudflaps, science illiteracy. That would be us.'
>
> 'I am troubled by this theory, Dellarobia,' Ovid said, 'but I can't say you are wrong. I've read a lot of scholarly articles on the topic, but you make more sense.'
>
> 'Well, *yeah*,' Juliet said, 'that's kind of the point, that outsiders won't get it. ... '" (Flight 395)

Rather than deploring Kingsolver's creation of a scholarly scientific language for the character Ovid to use, reviewers might instead comment on how frequently the author adds humor to scenes in order to soften the effects of the scientist's erudition.

What is an appropriate language to discuss the fact that towns are sinking, cataclysmic storms are wiping out areas (Montana's Glacier National Park will likely lose its glaciers), and the warming of the earth increases the volume of waters in oceans, resulting in rising sea levels and "acidified oceans." People will have more asthma and allergies, as well as heat strokes. Flooding everywhere will destroy bridges, swamp subways, and close airport runways. Whole villages in Alaska may have to relocate. The concentration of heat-trapping carbon dioxide emissions is higher than anyone has ever measured. The parameters of what constitutes global climate change are wide. As Ovid says in one discussion, "Ecology is the study of biological communities. How populations interact. It does not mean recycling aluminum cans" (Flight 324)—and it is not the entire environment.

In some scenes, it is as if Kingsolver were returning to her early essays about ecology. The reader is reminded of her saying (in "The Forest in the Seeds") that "Evolution can't be explained in a sound bite ... the things we will have to know—concepts of food chain, habitat, selection pressure and adaptation, and the ways all species depend on others—are complex ideas that just won't fit into a thirty-second spot" (High Tide 241). Again, "Last May, I saw a dragonfly as long as my hand—longer than an average-sized songbird. She circled and circled, flexing her body, trying to decide if my little lake was worthy of her precious eggs. She was almost absurdly colorful, sporting a bright green thorax and blue abdomen. Eventually she lit on the tip of the horsetail plant that sends long slender spikes up out of the water. She was joined on the tips of five adjacent stalks by five other dragonflies, all different: an orange-bodied one with orange wings, a yellow one, a blue-green one, one with a red head and purple tail, and a miniature one in zippy metallic blue. A dragonfly bouquet. Be still, and the world is bound to turn herself inside out to entertain you. Everywhere you look, joyful noise is clanging to drown out quiet desperation. The choice is draw the blinds and shut it all out, or believe" (High Tide 267).

Aside from difficult scientific language, Kingsolver also tackles the problem of skepticism within the community. She creates a flow of believable people who understand environmental change—the British knitting women, who make orange and black textile butterflies; the representatives from 350. org, with Bill McKibben, who care about the thermal stability of the planet (they understand how hurricanes can reach a hundred miles inland, why the deserts are on fire). As Ovid explains, the name of the group signals "350 parts per million, the number of carbon molecules the atmosphere can hold, and still maintain the ordinary thermal balance." Pointing to the reason for some of the dramatic change, the organization tries to give people information through their Web address. Ovid adds, "This has not happened before" and therefore, there is no evacuation plan (Flight 277–8). Other representatives appear, some to volunteer to help Ovid's group with their work, others to protest what they have heard will be the clear cutting of the land. The latter, a group from CCC, the community college in Cleary, chants outside Dellarobia's home, "Stop the logging, stop the lies! Save the monarch butterflies" (Flight 235). Some members of this latter group became volunteers for at least a time.

It may be anathema to Feathertown that the butterfly mass has impinged on community existence, but the television producers have been right in at least one respect—viewers are interested. Through social media as well, news of the Monarchs has circled the globe.

Still heavily invested in letting the world know about Ovid's research-oriented life, deeply impressed with his knowledge and his aplomb, Dellarobia has looked for ways to involve him in the publicity that attends the butterfly colonization. The single most interesting point about Ovid and his assistants is their devoted attention to their work—living with few human comforts, they spend long hours charting the Monarch activities. Dellarobia in turn wants to learn how to give that seamless concentration to something worthwhile. Kingsolver makes Dellarobia's smoking a kind of signal to the reader. Not only is smoking a costly pastime; it diverts Dellarobia from paying attention to life around her. It keeps her rooted in unfulfilling patterns. She finds some solace in remembering her high school English classes: she has chosen science at this stage of her life. She will take on life's crucial and transforming events. In her quasi-comic musing, she decided "You couldn't stand up and rail against the weather. That was exactly the point of so many stories. Jack London and Ernest Hemingway, confidence swaggering into the storm: Man against Nature. Of all the possible conflicts, that was the one that was hopeless" (Flight 245).

Now, however, Dellarobia finds focus for her energy. She creates a field trip for Preston's kindergarten class—knowing that such a visit will entrance her son and Josefina, and assuming that all the children will be interested. She smiles to herself at Ovid's wearing a tie and a dress shirt for the occasion. Even though she does most of the talking to the children, he is pleasantly involved—and spends a great deal of time with Preston.

A few days later, however, the television interviewer, Tina Ultner (the woman who has aired parts of her interview with Dellarobia after she had promised not to—including the suggestion of the young mother's possible suicide) reappears at Dellarobia's door and this time (given that Ovid had seemed to enjoy the kindergartners) Dellarobia took the crew directly to Ovid's province. Unfortunately, Ultner's questions there were not appropriate. She asked Ovid to put his explanations into "nutshells" or to answer "briefly." She clearly knew nothing about scientific issues, and his manner, accordingly, became more and more defensive, and often rude. (The interview, which Dovey quietly films on her phone—and then distributes on YouTube—goes viral because there are many people who understand what Ovid is saying, and how dismally the mainstream media covers scientific "news.")

In response to Tina's vapid comments about the Monarch colony's being "a beautiful sight," Ovid replied that he was "distressed" because they were seeing a great deal of death and, even more important, evidence of a "disordered system." The message should be "damage," not beauty. He continued, "This is a biological system falling apart along its seams" (Flight 364–5).

The interviewer would not let him discuss global warming accurately. *She* explained to *him* that their viewers wanted pleasant news. *She* told *him* that scientists cannot agree about these natural disasters, that their conclusions are ambiguous. Ovid then scathingly replied, "If you were here to get information, Tina, you would not be standing in my laboratory telling *me* what scientists think." The interview continued but Ovid was not backing down. He accused her television station of being in Exxon's pocket, of avoiding any semblance of the truth. He said "You are letting a public relations firm write your scripts for you ... You are allowing the public to be duped by a bunch of damned liars!" (Flight 367–9). Remorseful, he later apologized to Dellarobia as Tina and her photographer spun out of the drive and it was then that Dovey confessed that the entire interview was already on YouTube. And when Juliet arrived several weeks later, she explained that—a world away—she had seen the footage almost upon its posting, alerted by many friends to its location.

As readers, we are with Dellarobia and her family facing the disastrous flooding that the relentless rains will bring. Once Juliet and Ovid leave the farm for an interlude away, the Turnbows go about their business: and midway through the novel, Kingsolver has provided a brief set of sentences about Preston that could easily be moved to close *Flight Behavior*. She says explicitly,

> Preston would go far ... For all her worry about his lack of advantages, Preston would be like Ovid Byron. Already he seemed set apart by a devotion to his own pursuits that was brave and unconforming. (Flight 266)

It is in the penultimate scene of the novel that Dellarobia keeps Preston from getting on the school bus so that she can talk with him about the next stage of their lives. It is the day before his birthday; she chooses to give him his present early so that she can explain why it remains partly hers (because it will become her phone as well as his computer). As they sit together in the damp grass, the boy's face filled with "happy eagerness," she knew all too well that what she was about to tell him would change his life irretrievably.

First she explained about his brother, never born and now buried in the graveyard. Then she told him about his iPad, all the while explaining that she would need to have the use of it because she and he and Cordie would be living with Dovey in Cleary, while she went to college there. As she told Preston, "Dr. Byron did this totally amazing nice thing and talked to professors over at CCC ... They set me up with a job and stuff." But to his inquiry about where Cub would be, she had to explain that while he and Cordie would live part time with their dad, she would remain with Dovey in Cleary. Saddened, not understanding the range of this information, Preston asked simply, "What if I want everything to stay how it is?"

With all the knowledge that has come with her introduction into the world of science, Dellarobia must answer him honestly: "It won't ever go back to how it was, Preston" (Flight 425, 429).

Sequentially, the next and last segment of *Flight Behavior* expands on another early scene. Midway through the novel, after the lumber estimators have taped off portions of the forest that they will be cutting, the flagging tape unhooks and lands further down the hillside at Dellarobia's feet. "That was a shock. From way up there it had traveled to here, this was the path of the flow. Next stop: her house" (Flight 137). Now a part of what Ovid had termed "a sickness of nature" (Flight 149), the flooding that she looked out upon, and that she was drawn to enter, covered *her* yard, *her* land. The opening pages of this chapter recreate that immense roil of water, and Dellarobia's sure movement through it to various small points of safety. But as she continues out into the unstoppable flood, thinking meditatively of Columbus on the edge of his own known world, Kingsolver tells her readers, "Insofar as a person could understand that, she could." As Dellarobia watched the starlings fly higher and higher in their attempts to escape, she remembered Job again—"'Man is born into trouble as the sparks fly upward,' she thought, words from the book of Job, made for a world unraveling into fire and flood. 'Among the dark birds were wavering flints of light, the same fire that had unsettled her so drastically on first sight. Now it was irresistible'" (Flight 430–2).

In answer to an interviewer for *Time* magazine, Kingsolver explained in her customary laid-back way that *Flight Behavior* was written "Because I wanted to write about that particular culture war [global warming]. I live in southern Appalachia and I'm surrounded, literally, my home is surrounded by farms and by coal mines. Our agriculture here has gone through one disaster year after another, so climate change is not some kind of abstract future threat here. It is literally killing our farm economy. We've had record heat years. We've had record drought years. So the people most affected by climate change already are people among whom I live: rural conservative farmers. And it strikes me that these are the same people who are least prepared to understand and believe in climate change and its causes. Our local politicians are quite deliberately misinforming us and fighting every kind of environmental regulation that could possibly slow down the release of carbon for the very obvious reason that they're beholden to the big player in this region, which is the coal companies. Here we are, caught between the devil and the deep blue sea. What can I do but write a novel?" (Time, Walsh).

Flight Behavior as a totality exists as if it defines the sentence with which Kingsolver closes her concluding "Author's Note," "The biotic consequences of climate change tax the descriptive powers, not to mention the courage, of those who know most about it" (Flight 435). Kingsolver's 2012 *Flight Behavior* inscribes and enacts the author's years of concern about climate change: it sobers us all.

2

The Innocence of *The Bean Trees*

… it's interesting to me that our traditionally patriotic imagery in this country celebrates the individual, the solo flier, independence. We celebrate Independence Day; we don't celebrate We Desperately Rely on Others Day… It does strike me that our great American mythology tends to celebrate separate achievement and separateness when in fact nobody does anything alone.

Kingsolver in Fisher 27

Several years earlier than the 2012 publication of *Flight Behavior*, John Nizalowski wrote a prescient essay about Kingsolver as a political author. As clear as the fact that *Flight Behavior* fuses numerous ecological and political themes, Nizalowski's commentary is both predictive and summarizing. He begins with the assertion that "Barbara Kingsolver is a political author." He continues that she intends to be "the progressive social conscience of her times, and her political interests are largely rooted in her personal experiences. Therefore, such thematic concerns as environmentalist, class structure, race, feminism, labor rights, immigrant rights, American Indian rights, U.S. foreign policy, post-colonialism, organic agriculture, and ecological diversity all arise from a life lived in the pursuit of wisdom, social justice, and creative fire" (in Austenfeld 17). To this critic's use of the word "political" might be added Meredith Sue Willis's more expansive comment that for her, agreeing as she does that Kingsolver does write political fiction, her definition of the term is "the world of relationship of people in society"—a kind of treatise about "citizenship." Willis calls attention as well to Kingsolver's focus on "the labor of ordinary people" (Willis Iron 13–14).

This commentary about politics evolved through Kingsolver's 20 years of successive novels, but when she published her first novel, *The Bean Trees*, in 1988, the world seemed to be a simpler place. It also seemed to be a sturdier place, one intent on taking the care of Taylor Greer and her illegally adopted Indian daughter Turtle as seriously and as calmly as possible. Readers accepted the book at face value, echoing Margaret Randall's positive critique in *Women's Review of Books*, which described *The Bean Trees* as a book that tells "the story of ordinary people ... as they touch their own ... a story about racism, sexism and dignity" (Randall 1).

The book appeared without fanfare. Before its publication, Kingsolver had not published so much as a single story. The novel unexpectedly took off, after the agent she had arranged to work with on the publication of an academic book about a copper mine strike—Frances Goldin—sold it to HarperCollins. Readers who found the book liked the humor, the natural sounding idiom of the young Kentucky woman trying to escape the small town of her childhood as she drives west into a more exciting, more beautiful, part of the United States. That idiom convinced them that Taylor Greer was an authentic questing woman. Somewhat lacking in material resources, she still had the spirit of a conqueror—until the abused Indian girl is handed to her as she gets into her aging Volkswagen in a parking lot.

With no planning by anyone, in 1988 *The Bean Trees* sneaked into the dynamic company of Gloria Naylor's *Mama Day* (1988) and Toni Morrison's *Beloved* (1987). In those works, readers' attention—sometimes grudgingly—was fixed on stories of generations of women in families that were trying to survive both poverty and classic patriarchal power structures. Even though first-wave feminism was said to have ended, Erica Jong's *Fear of Flying* (1973) and Marilyn French's *The Women's Room* (1977) were being taught across the United States—if not in English Department classes, then in the newer courses linked to women's studies (or, more likely, hybrid classes labeled "women's literature"). What Kingsolver's *The Bean Trees* accomplished was that it drew from the provocations of women's novels published during the 1970s, women's novels by white writers, and yet satisfied readers' growing interest in other, different cultures. Naylor and Morrison, for example, wrote from their African American backgrounds; so too did Maxine Hong Kingston introduce the otherness of Asian American life in her memoir novel *The Woman Warrior*, 1976. In contrast, Kingsolver was a white writer, creating a white woman protagonist—but adding into the mix the abused Native American child Turtle as well as the Guatemalan refugees Estevan and Esperanza and Lou Ann Ruiz's absent Mexican husband. In both this novel and its sequel, *Pigs in Heaven*, Kingsolver portrayed a number of Sanctuary (middle American) refugees and Native American issues as part of the fabric of the primary narrative. Politically aware readers consequently felt that their interest in "the other" was being satisfied. Later criticized for her relatively comic use of Taylor's mother's attitude about the fact that she and Taylor were themselves part Cherokee, Kingsolver made amends for her flippancy in *Pigs in Heaven*. She repeatedly commented, as she did in her 2011 interview, that "Cultural differences are really exciting territory, not just for literature but for learning in general because sparks fly when there's friction among different viewpoints" (in Fisher 27).

Readers liked Kingsolver's characters. Stubborn as Taylor Greer was, the small Turtle, even as an inarticulate child, would prove herself to be even more tenacious: "The most amazing thing was the way that child held on. From the first moment I picked it up out of its nest of wet blankets, it attached itself to me by its little hands like roots sucking on dry dirt. I think it would have been easier to separate me from my hair" (Bean 22).

Humorous in word choice, this passage leads to what follows, as Taylor remembers her training as a medical laboratory tech and creates a description of both her exhaustion and her underlying stability. "It's probably a good thing. I was so tired, and of course I was not in the habit anyway of remembering every minute where I had put down a child, and I think if it had not been stuck to me I might have lost it while I was messing with the car and moving stuff into the little end room of the Broken Arrow. As it was, I just ended up carrying it back and forth a lot. It's like the specimens back at the hospital, I told myself. You just have to keep track. It looks like carrying blood and pee was to be my lot in life" (Bean 22).

Readers no doubt appreciated the somewhat crass description here of Taylor's livelihood. Books from first-wave feminism were filled with discussions of women's autonomy—or lack of that quality. How professional were women allowed to become? Could a woman ever become a family's primary wage earner? What about the male ego in relation to male and female incomes? It comes as a sort of relief—here at the end of the 1980s—that *The Bean Trees* is not focused on Taylor's work opportunities, or on how much satisfaction she finds in earning her living.

The novel also is not didactically focused on the second big question in feminist novels—what is the role of motherhood? One of the reasons for the staying power of Marilyn French's *The Women's Room* was its assortment of women characters, grouped around Harvard University. Some of French's characters were students, some were the mothers of students, and some were stay-at-home moms now free to return to school. Others were deliberating whether or not to have children; still others were causing trouble as they ended bad heterosexual relationships, one after another. Readers during the 1970s were fixated on the problem of becoming mothers: with the average marriage age for women only slightly above the 20.4 years average marriage age of the 1950s, and with a woman's capacity for sexuality having become one of the determinants of female desirability. Issues of fertility, sexual response, and the various prohibitions against abortions dominated conversations. Women readers looked for fiction germane to their lifetime decisions.

The brilliance of Taylor's so willingly and easily becoming a mother to the little girl she named Turtle, the abused child who never gave up and who never let Taylor leave her, was that motherhood in *The Bean Trees* was separate from both sexuality and issues of power within a relationship. Readers found escape from the heavy battles of argumentation that haunted much other writing by women in the 1970s and the 1980s: *The Bean Trees* was a novel to read. It was *not* a tract.

As Kingsolver portrayed her, Taylor was not a woman nervous about what her appropriate role in life should be. She was trying to leave her family's provincial Kentucky farm, although that escape seemed vexed from the start: her car was old, she had little money, and while she had some professional training, it was minimal. One big motivation for her life as a teenager and young adult was that she *not* become pregnant, as had so many of her high school classmates. Kingsolver plays this irony subtly: it is through no desire of her own that Taylor is given the young Indian girl, carried away from her tribal life because of the visible sexual abuse she has endured.

Feminist historian Marilyn Yalom points out that being able to provide for one's children is a particularly female anxiety. Women are marked with the fear of having children and not being able to either support them or to keep them safe. "From the moment of one's birth the potential for maternity sets in motion the biological clock that ticks incessantly within the female form." She expands that relatively simple statement to show different levels of fearfulness: "The maternal possibility forces upon each woman ongoing confrontation with the most elemental aspects of existence ... Motherhood, as reality, possibility, or impossibility, raises questions about the meaning of life, the value of projecting oneself into the future through one's progeny, the eventuality of replacing one's parents, the inevitability of death ... " (Yalom 106). Without drawing overtly on sociology, Kingsolver creates characters within this first novel who illustrate each step of this generic female psychological process.

Lou Ann Ruiz is the fertile young mother, whose disabled husband ("Angel" Ruiz) has disappeared. When Dwayne Ray, her son, is born on New Year's Day, she takes on the role of what Dorothy Dinnerstein termed "the dirty goddess," the woman in charge of "infant and early child care"—accordingly feared by men for her power (Dinnerstein 26). For the interval when Lou Anne's mother and her grandmother come to visit Tucson, traveling three days each way by bus in order to bring water from Tug Fork in Kentucky for Dwayne Ray's baptism, Angel returns briefly to the household (as Lou Ann explains to Taylor, Kentucky people do not divorce). Eventually, compatible in their individual mothering responsibilities, Lou Ann and Taylor combine households and try to manage their ever diminishing finances.

Kingsolver creates several older (nonchild-bearing) women characters as Taylor has driven west. The most prominent of these is Mattie, who owns and eventually hires Taylor to work in "Jesus Is Lord Used Tires." Mattie leaves on trips of three or four days, driving her white Blazer and taking her binoculars. Far from being a birdwatcher, however, Mattie is a key player in the Sanctuary movement, taking political refugees in and out of Tucson. In this novel, she is housing the Guatemalans Estevan and Esperanza, trying to get them from Arizona to Oklahoma.

Two other older women characters are important to the politics of *The Bean Trees*. Given that the darker skinned Turtle, Dwayne Ray, and the Guatemalans blend readily into the population of this poorer section of Tucson, the racism of the genteel neighbors Mrs. Parsons and Edna Poppy might be problematic—but Kingsolver develops Taylor's coming to understand these women's own disabilities and finally makes them into compellingly warm, helpful figures.

The Bean Trees quickly becomes a novel about women caring for their children. It begins, however, with a set of humorous narratives that might seem to disparage Taylor's small Kentucky town, but in reality show the damaging effects of patriarchal anger. Taylor's reminiscence about Newt Hardbine's father being thrown up over the Standard Oil sign after he had overfilled a tractor tire—"He wasn't dead but lost his hearing and in many other ways was never the same afterward"—gives the novel its initial comic voice. But as Taylor's memory continues, it darkens considerably. During her first week as a laboratory tech working in the hospital emergency room, she sees Newt brought in, dead, and his wife Jolene bleeding from someone's shotgun fire, "a wet tongue of blood from her right shoulder all the way down her bosom, and all the color was pulled out of her lips and face, her big face like a piece of something cut out of white dough. She was fighting and cursing, though, and clearly a far cry from dead" (Bean 7). Jolene had married Newt when she became pregnant in high school; now she would be caring for their baby and Newt's father for the rest of her life.

Admonitory though the Newt Hardbine incident was, Taylor worked more than five years longer to accumulate money—and nerve—to head out on her own. Her plan was to drive until the decrepit car simply stopped and in effect, with the addition of Turtle, that was what happened. Working first as a waitress and a cleaning person, she finds her job at "Jesus Is Lord Used Tires" satisfying and responsible.

More of her attention has gone to the fact that Turtle cannot yet speak, but eventually the little girl begins acquiring her own noun-based language: *bean* is her first word, followed by *humbean*. She recognizes vegetables from Mattie's garden, and feels safe in communicating through those names. Within a few days, Turtle is making the single nouns into sentences: "Corn, 'tato, bean." "Cabbage, cabbage, cabbage," she said (Bean 98, 100, 111). Looking at the ducks in the zoo, Turtle finds one of the peanuts that could be purchased for feeding them. "'Bean,' she said." 'This is a peanut,' I told her. 'Beanut.' She made trip after trip, collecting peanuts and mounding them into a pile" (Bean 127). Turtle's resourcefulness makes Taylor understand that Mattie was right: Turtle had created her own language.

Kingsolver shapes a key metaphor from the physical presence of Mattie's garden. Representative of the willed creativity of a woman who produces satisfying food from her efforts in the cast-off debris of her culture, Mattie's garden might well prompt Turtle's efforts to speak. "Outside was a bright, wild wonderland of flowers and vegetables and auto parts. Heads of cabbage and lettuce sprouted out of old tires. An entire rusted out Thunderbird, minus the wheels, had nasturtiums blooming out the windows like Mama's hen-and-chicks pot on the front porch at home. A kind of teepee frame made of CB antennas was all overgrown with cherry-tomato vines" (Bean 45). Women who garden, women who work magic with the earth, themselves spring from a set of ancient matriarchal myths about the female power to engender.

Setting *The Bean Trees* in Arizona gives Kingsolver reason to lavish descriptions of the dry lands that are exotic to Taylor, who is herself more familiar with the lush growth of Kentucky. Just as she uses the story of Buster the Crab in her *High Tide* essay collection, here she casually describes the vicissitudes of life in the natural world. "There was a cactus with bushy arms and a coat of yellow spines as thick as fur. A bird had built her nest in it. In and out she flew among the horrible spiny branches, never once hesitating. You just couldn't imagine how she'd made a home in there" (Bean 124). The reader transfers the metaphor of this kind of seemingly impossible effort to Taylor and her accomplishments as she makes Turtle's life safe, comfortable, and normal. Without therapy, without medical attention, and often without childcare, she and Turtle do the best they can—always together. Taylor loses one waitressing job because the play area in the mall where other women leave their children is public and open; the place is in no way a day-care and she cannot tolerate its risks. With double irony, Kingsolver has placed the description of the spiny cactus harboring the bird's nest immediately after the scene of the doctor's changing his assessment of Turtle's age from two years to three; seeing her x-rays, he concludes that as a baby she was so often abused that she developed "failure to thrive" syndrome and therefore still seemed small and fragile.

Kingsolver set *The Bean Trees* in Arizona largely because she was living there, working as a scientific grants writer and journalist after she had dropped out of a doctoral program in ecobiology. But metaphorically, the desert setting was congruent with many of Taylor's hardships. In the words of Edward Abbey, living in arid lands mandates "a fierce resourcefulness." Deserts are regularly viewed as "places of exile and emptiness," habitats for people who may be unwanted, those "pushed out of greener pastures." Deserts are unpredictable, ruled by "forces we can't control" (Last Stand 156–7). As Mattie might have said, it takes toughness to live in Tucson.

Making Taylor equal to the need for such toughness might have been easier than Kingsolver's actual choices—to make Lou Ann Ruiz a woman with the lowest possible self-esteem, and to give Taylor herself countless insecurities.

Part of Kingsolver's development of Taylor is the character's growing sense of inadequacy. She is learning that providing for Turtle is different from keeping herself alive, and she comes to admit that she had had "no business just assuming I could take the responsibility for a child's life." When she asked Mattie what that wise woman had thought when Taylor and Turtle had arrived, Mattie replied honestly, "I thought you seemed like a bewildered parent. Which is perfectly ordinary. Usually the bewilderment wears off by the time the kid gets big enough to eat peanut butter and crackers, but knowing what I do now, I can see you were still in the stage most mothers are in when they first bring them home from the hospital" (Bean 177). Kingsolver explained her handling this theme prominently in her Beattie interview, Taylor's "terror of becoming a parent, the emotional inadequacy we feel facing the possibility of raising a child ... became a bigger and bigger part of the book" (Beattie 160). Part of the reason *The Bean Trees* rang so true to readers, particularly women readers, was Taylor's recognizable fear of the huge undertaking of being a parent.

Expressed in Taylor's seemingly natural idiom, the issues Kingsolver was emphasizing did not seem "political." Her quick-moving scenes kept readers involved in the narrative; few reviewers of the novel used the word *didactic*. Yet in her "Letter to My Mother," Kingsolver pointed out that she *was* as didactic as she thought she could be, and still attract readers: "I've explained everything I believe in, exactly the way I've always wanted to: human rights, Central American refugees, the Problem That Has No Name, abuse of the powerless, racism, poetry, freedom, childhood, motherhood, Sisterhood Is Powerful" (Small Wonder 170). By returning to Betty Friedan's 1963 *Feminine Mystique* for her "Problem That Has No Name" reference, Kingsolver tied this modest fiction to the sometimes overpowering feminism of works of the 1970s. Her connection with "Sisterhood is powerful" makes that link even stronger: the relationship between Taylor and Lou Ann, which gets little attention in reviews, creates an instructive perspective. It is Taylor's advice about Angel that keeps her Southern friend stable, as Lou Ann and Dwayne Ray meld with Taylor and Turtle to create that other element Kingsolver found so fascinating—the creation of new kinds of "families."

As she had said in several early interviews, "[d]ivorce, remarriage, single parenthood, gay parents, and blended families simply are ... Families change, and remain the same. Why are our names for home so slow to catch up to the truth of where we live? ... [I]t's probably been suggested to you in a hundred ways that yours isn't exactly a real family, but an imposter family, a harbinger of cultural ruin, a slapdash substitute" (High Tide 136). Magali Michael's 2006 study explores what she terms "alternative models of kinship" as Kingsolver draws them in both *The Bean Trees* and *Pigs in Heaven*. She calls them "alternative nonhierarchal familiar communities that respect but do not privilege blood ties as positive" (Michael 73). The way this reconsideration of important concepts of "family" plays out for Michael is that two key changes are occurring: members may well represent mixed race characters. Also, the economies of class will be reconsidered. Otherwise the poor and middle-class will have to feel failure, because they will not climb the economic ladder that propped up social class. Michael points out that because Kingsolver's concept of class is not market based, her early novels give the reader characters that are not judged. Instead, her books "reconceive agency" as she shows the individual character "having a stake in the collectivity [family, community] in terms of the common good" (Michael 77).

Kingsolver, too, frequently worked to expand the concept of *family* into that of *community*. As David King Dunaway remembers, the author told him

Everything that I write really comes down to an exploration of community. What is community? How do we fit into it? How do we hold our place and lose ourselves to something bigger in time? I think that is the only question I am ever going to try and answer ... When I studied literature in high school, I learned that there are three great themes in literature: man against man, man against nature, man against himself. So it was all 'man against' and so much of my life has no 'against' in it, whatsoever. It's mostly 'with.' ... Doris Lessing wrote about such women, whose goals in life were not to escape from connectedness with humanity, but to become connected; and to find a way not to lose themselves at the same time. I think that's what a lot of us women write about—'connectedness' instead of 'againstness.' (Dunaway Foreword xii–xiii)

Coming as the author did from a kind of idealized family—her father the doctor, intent on working across borders to help the indigent (taking his family to both South Africa and the Caribbean); her mother the patient, good-humored support for her three children; and her brother, who joined with Kingsolver for hoydenish games in the natural world, accompanied by their younger sister. Isolated to some extent in the rural milieu that they did not care to emulate, the Kingsolver family read a great deal—often, together—and for some periods, did without television. They did not participate in the culture of consumerism that had already blanketed American towns. They wore second-hand clothes, if necessary; they grew their own food, where possible; they created a loving unit that was indestructible, comparatively immune to outside influences.

Kingsolver also wanted to write about class in ways that did not allow readers to, simply, pity the poor. When she created the Tucson neighborhood of people who lived in modest circumstances, she wanted to signal readers that concepts of class could wrongly identify people. The mixture of races and nationalities that originally bothers Edna Poppy and Mrs. Parsons allows Turtle and Dwayne Ray, as well as Estevan and Esperanza, to fit in. As Kingsolver said in the Beattie interview, "What I needed was an outsider's take on this place that most people would consider a bad piece of real estate, but, really, it's this rich, lively, symbiotic, interconnected community of women" (Beattie 160). Such an explanation allows the reader to align Kingsolver's comments with the single most important rationale for her choices throughout her fiction, "I think our first responsibility, and also our first treasure as writers, is to represent ourselves. So women are always dead center in my novels. And my novels are about the things women think most about, like keeping our children fed, and how to manage on not very much income" (Epstein 34).

With apt purpose Kingsolver brings together her interests in women's stories (particularly the stories of mothers), her fascination with other cultures and their customs, and her broad definition of "community" to write the novel's Chapter Nine, which is titled "Ismene." This is the narrative of Esperanza's attempted suicide, as told to Taylor by the grieving husband. It enables Taylor to start to understand the fearful circumstances the refugees have faced. Even though Mattie had explained why both a physician and ministers were necessary to help the refugees in the Sanctuary movement—specifically mentioning the burns from cigarettes and electric telephones, instruments of torture applied to both organs and skin—Taylor could not comprehend the endurance of the Guatemalan refugees.

In this chapter Kingsolver makes clear that even greater damage can occur emotionally: the reason the chapter carries the name "Ismene" is that Estevan and Esperanza's only child, a daughter about the age of Turtle, has been kidnapped in Guatemala. "Ismene" signifies knowledge (the child as knowledgeable), daughter of Oedipus. Here it is used in part ironically because her *parents* have the knowledge her captors demand: the names of 17 members of the teachers' union, which is considered a subversive political force. To reclaim their beloved child, Esperanza and Estevan would have had to give her kidnappers those names.

Esperanza's brother and two other members of the union, however, have already been murdered by the group in power. Were they to give the names of the 17 unknown members, they would be sealing death warrants. Estevan, who teaches English in Guatemala, might himself be executed. There is no way these parents can reclaim Ismene. Fleeing the country, saving themselves, is the only action they can take. Again, Kingsolver uses irony to name Esperanza (Hope, Waiting) but the woman's desperate suicide attempt shows how inconsolable she is in her grief. Another irony is that the aspirin she had taken to cause her death was "baby" aspirin.

Mattie has discovered a clinic which will serve illegals, so she drives Esperanza to that location: Estevan has come to Taylor's for sympathy, and because he trusts her. Mattie had earlier told Taylor how difficult it was to find medical attention (beyond that of red-haired Doctor Terry) for these Sanctuary refugees; one man who was working as a lemon harvester had cut off his thumb in the machines. He "bled to death because the nearest hospital turned him away" (Bean 131).

Kingsolver draws the character of Mattie as rescuer, Mattie as source of useful information, to supplement the image of Mattie as creator of her garden. She is the constant figure in what Loretta Martin Murrey terms a "matriarchal community" (in Austenfeld 114). Mattie is also intuitive. She explains to Taylor that she is nervous about the Guatemalans' precarious situation; she explains that "Immigration is making noises. They could come in and arrest them, and they'd be deported ... " (Bean 159). It is inconceivable to Taylor that the United States and federal authorities would enter Mattie's home, and that they would deport people into such fearful situations. Mattie explained that people who are fleeing often do not bring documentation, and that no American court would act only on verbal reports.

Structurally, *The Bean Trees* usually moves through paired events, alternating positive experiences with more discouraging ones. We have seen the way Esperanza's suicide attempt and Taylor's coming to understand the terrors of political life in Guatemala, however, lead the reader from negative to negative. The positive alternation of those scenes, however, is Estevan's coming to trust Taylor. His belief in her inherent goodwill accordingly empowers her to take a more active role in their rescue. Before the narrative takes on an explanation of that rescue, however, Kingsolver creates an unexpected lyric moment, suitably based in the natural world—free from the machinations of human politics.

Working from her deep knowledge of desert life provides Kingsolver one of the most sustained descriptions of the arid terrain. Adopting the Indian custom of calling the day of the first summer rain "New Year's Day," Mattie on July 12 closes shop and drives Taylor, Esperanza, and Estevan to a high plateau so that they can watch the coming of the first warm rain. She, in effect, creates a joyful ceremony for them. "The whole Tucson Valley lay in front of us, resting in its cradle of mountains. The sloped desert plain that lay between us and the city was like a palm stretched out for a fortuneteller to read, with its mounds and hillocks, its life lines and heart lines of dry stream beds … A storm was coming up from the south, moving slowly. It looked something like a huge blue-gray shower curtain being drawn along by the hand of God. You could just barely see through it, enough to make out the silhouette of the mountains on the other side. From time to time nervous white ribbons of lightning jumped between the mountaintops and the clouds. A cool breeze came up behind us, sending shivers along the spines of the mesquite trees" (Bean 161).

Everything was alive: "The birds were excited … spadefoot toads" burrowed out of the ground—"all the things that looked dead were just dormant." "As the storm moved closer it broke into hundreds of pieces so that the rain fell here and there from the high clouds in long, curving gray plumes. It looked like maybe fifty or sixty fires scattered over the city, except that the tall, smoky columns were flowing in reverse. And if you looked closely you could see that in some places the rain didn't make it all the way to the ground. Three-quarters of the way down from the sky it just vanished into the dry air."

"That was when we smelled the rain. It was so strong it seemed like more than just a smell. When we stretched out our hands we could practically feel it rising up from the ground" (Bean 162–3).

The alternation of mood here—from Taylor's joy in these natural surroundings to fear—occurs when Taylor returns home and sees the somber faces of Lou Ann, Edna Poppy, and Turtle. She learns then that a man has attacked the small Turtle as she played in the park with the blind Edna Poppy—the two were awaiting Mrs. Parsons' arrival. Edna Poppy heard the skirmish, and swung her white cane, high, so as not to hit Turtle, and she did hit something.

Taylor, however, knows without any verbal explanation: she is looking into Turtle's bleak, black eyes, the same eyes the child had turned to her when her aunt gave her to Taylor. And too, in this scene, Turtle does not speak. The horror has returned her to those earlier powerless days.

Yet, despite help from the social worker, the police, and the community, *Taylor* is the person most affected by Turtle's having been attacked. Eventually, Turtle speaks again, telling the story of the way Ma Poppy "popped" the "bad man." But for Taylor, the incident reinforced all her fears about the great responsibility of parenting; she was convinced she could never become a good mother. When social services questioned her about her claim to for Turtle, she was prompted into more direct action. She volunteered to drive Mattie's Lincoln to Oklahoma, the location that would be safest for Estevan and Esperanza; while there, she would try to find Turtle's Cherokee relatives and see whether or not she could obtain legal rights to her daughter.

Again, Taylor's innocence of the power of law over the illegals protects her. As she drives off toward Oklahoma with Esperanza and Turtle in the backseat and Estevan beside her, she has no idea that Immigration will soon be stopping every car on the freeway. The Border Patrol stopped Mattie's car a hundred miles from New Mexico. When the officer asked if they were all United States citizens, Taylor said *Yes* and showed her driver's license, explaining that Estevan was her brother and Esperanza, her sister-in-law. The officer's next question was, "The kid yours or theirs?" and then, when Taylor froze, Estevan said calmly, "She's ours" (Bean 191).

That was the only inspection stop. Though the ride took several days, Turtle kept herself occupied by telling Esperanza a long story ("a vegetarian version of Aesop's Fables") and playing with a homemade doll Mattie had given her (which she named "Shirley Poppy") (Bean 196). They slept enroute the first night and spent the second night at the Broken Arrow Motel, learning there of the death of Mrs. Hoge, who had befriended Taylor and Turtle.

Searching through the restaurant-bar where she had been given Turtle, Taylor learns that that business had also changed hands. She has no way to find the family of origin so she goes to Plan B. She entreats Estevan and Esperanza to pretend to be Turtle's parents, and to sign their supposed daughter over to her in front of the local judge, Jonas Wilford Armisted. Esperanza's tears at giving up Turtle are convincing, and Turtle—who has been calling her "Ma" for most of the trip—in fact seems to be the child of the Guatemalans. The "adoption" is successful, and Kingsolver concludes that "we filed out, a strange new combination of friends and family" (Bean 216).

Taylor then continues the drive to the Pottawatomie Presbyterian Church of St. Michael and All Angels, the next stop for the Sanctuary rescue. Sorrowful to be leaving Estevan, Taylor feels as if she has buried her good Guatemalan friends. She and Turtle (now named *April* Turtle, an attempt to recover her birth name) must wait for the processing of the official adoption papers, so they spend the time visiting the city library.

Looking at an encyclopedia that includes pictures of vegetables, Turtle finds the wisteria pods that she labels "bean trees" and the novel meanders to its satisfying end. Kingsolver creates a far-reaching metaphor for the library scene: "wisteria vines, like other legumes, often thrive in poor soil, the book said. Their secret is something called rhizobia. These are microscopic bugs that live underground in little knots on the roots. They suck nitrogen gas right out of the soil and turn it into fertilizer for the plant. The rhizobia are not actually part of the plant, they are separate creatures, but they always live with legumes: a kind of underground railroad moving secretly up and down the roots." In Taylor's translation, the scientific gloss becomes "'It's like this,' I told Turtle. 'There's a whole invisible system for helping out the plant that you'd never guess was there.' I loved this idea. 'It's just the same as with people. The way Edna has Virgie, and Virgie has Edna, and Sandi has Kid Central Station, and everybody has Mattie. And on and on.' The wisteria vines on their own would just barely get by, is how I explained it to Turtle, but put them together with rhizobia and they make miracles" (Bean 227–8). No reader is surprised that Kingsolver uses this rhizobia concept to also anchor the notion of family in Taylor and Turtle's world.

The Bean Trees had barely been discovered and used in classrooms when the critical attacks on Kingsolver's so-called misuse of Native American culture began. For all the interesting anthropological concepts—kinship families, motherhood that is nonbiological, fused communal interests— what some critics stated emphatically was that the novel showed the author's ignorance of Indian customs. Kathleen Godfrey accused Kingsolver of "playing indian" (Godfrey 270); Karen Karbo said the author "completely ignored" the question of Taylor's taking (i.e., removing) Turtle (Cohen 146). For Robin Cohen, the possible slight to Native American customs was ameliorated by Kingsolver's showing that "childrearing is a communal activity," and that the attitudes of *The Bean Trees* present "a thoughtful attempt to suggest the need for a hybrid society, favoring feminism and tribal forms of community over the lone masculine individualist" (Cohen 147). This critic sees the adoption ceremony in Oklahoma as "part of a larger pattern in which Kingsolver engages other stereotypes such as the universal Cherokee grandmother, Indian country as wasteland, the alcoholic Indian ... in order to deconstruct them. In incidents ranging from the minor to the more consequential, Kingsolver exposes the racism [toward Indians] embedded in the very language and culture of mainstream American and suggests an alternative" (Cohen 147).

Catherine Himmelwright wrote that the fact that the Cherokee culture was matrilineal may have reminded Kingsolver to emphasize that tribal identification (in Leder 35). She also noted that the author stressed the ongoing tragic consequences of the Indian removal (the Trail of Tears), suggesting that the people's economic and social problems stemmed from a history they were not responsible for creating.

In a more comprehensive assessment, Himmelwright notes that even in *The Bean Trees* Taylor allows some of the Cherokee beliefs—about the family, children's rearing, and the spiritual—to impact the mother–child dynamic she creates with Turtle. To such a positive reading of Kingsolver's first novel, however, came general opposition (Ryan 77–82, Owens in Bataille 11–25, Sokolowski in Leder 157–73, and others). It may be that, as a result, Kingsolver studied the Native American culture which she had assumed she already knew: when she later wrote *Pigs in Heaven*, the novel now considered the sequel to *The Bean Trees*, she addressed the Native American culture as a primary subject.

3

Pigs in Heaven and Its Interrogation

People invest themselves differently in the same set of truths. Because of my training as a scientist, I'm always looking at the dialectic between the truth we believe exists outside ourselves and the truth we invent for ourselves.

Kingsolver in Fisher 27

Here in the twenty-first century, Kingsolver's efforts to create multiethnic characters and to meaningfully juxtapose varied cultures may be seen as *vigorous, vital*: American culture is increasingly diverse and complex, and the so-called *globalization* of both US life and narratives about it has been acknowledged for decades. As literary historian Frank Shuffelton wrote years ago, ethnicity "is a process—a dynamic relationship of assimilation and alienation—and not a product" (Shuffelton 7–8). All readers know that the best writers take on an immense number of complex issues—social, religious, financial, political, racial, gendered, historic—and use their own base of wide knowledge to help readers follow clear paths through labyrinthine situations.

As Kingsolver approached writing a further story about Taylor and Turtle, she was surprised, as she commented in an early interview, to realize "that I'd already set up the situation perfectly with *The Bean Trees*" (Beattie 170). In some respects, her comment is accurate. Readers had asked to follow the story of the tenacious Turtle and the increasingly capable Taylor, so both the author and her publisher knew that there would be good markets for a sequel. The opening of *Pigs in Heaven*, however, suggested important changes in the narrative. One of the lead characters in *Pigs in Heaven*—whose lengthy section opens the book—is Alice Greer, Taylor's mother, the grandmother that Turtle has seen only once, a likely rendering of the spirited mother who dominates some families within US culture. Alice has been introduced carefully at the close of *The Bean Trees*, talking to Taylor by pay phone as Taylor celebrates having adopted Turtle. In that segment, Alice speaks about her own antipathy to class differences. (She has just remarried, and so will be able to stop working as a cleaning lady for the wealthier families in town. Her animosity toward those privileged women who have employed her comes through in her commentary to Taylor.)

> All these years, you know, these ladies get to thinking that they own you. That you wouldn't dare breathe a word for fear of getting fired. Now I think they're all scared to death I'm going to take out an ad in the paper...
>
> Alice Jean Greer Elleston wishes to announce that Irma Ruebacker has fifty-two pints of molded elderberry jelly in her basement; Mae Richey's dishes would be carried off by the roaches if she didn't have hired help; and Minerva Wickentot's boys read porno magazines. (Bean 222)

Never ashamed of working for a living, Alice now recognizes how often her fellow townswomen lorded their circumstances over her. By the time *Pigs in Heaven* opens, several years into Alice's second marriage, she has come to see that physical comforts are less important than they had once seemed.

Titled somewhat ominously "Queen of Nothing," the opening of Kingsolver's novel shows Alice waking up beside her quiet husband Harland, whose idea of marriage "is to spray WD-40 on anything that squeaks." Living in her wordless union, a union "that has failed to warm her," Taylor's mother realizes that "Women on their own run in Alice's family" (Pigs 5). About to declare her own independence from convention, from both her marriage and the town in which she has lived, Alice thinks of her "tall, fierce" mother, Minerva Stamper, who single-handedly ran her own hog farm for 50 years. Rejecting her own tendency to stay put, Alice thinks as well of her favorite cousin, Sugar Boss Hornbuckle, who was the often-photographed beauty queen of Heaven, Oklahoma, in 1955. It is Sugar, living a native life in Oklahoma, who reminds Alice of their families' small portion of Indian blood, the Cherokee inheritance that began with Grandmother Stamper, Minerva's mother, and was seldom valued in Kentucky (Pigs 6–7).

Kingsolver's early novels benefited from new feminist literary theories. The year after *The Bean Trees* had been published, critic Marianne Hirsch called for more attention to women's stories, what she termed "women-centered mythologies" (Hirsch 5). Asking where women characters *are* in male-authored novels, this critic insisted—somewhat unfashionably for the time—that the stories yet to be told, and explored, are those of mothers who are simultaneously daughters. By using Alice's story as a legitimate introduction to the Taylor–Turtle narrative, and by including yet other women—Alice's own mother and grandmother—in the family history, Kingsolver created a genealogy of Stamper-Greer women. Hirsch stresses that writers need to create the matriarchal line in fiction by pointing out that the great and beloved women novelists of England seldom did this. She notes that "mothers tend to be absent, silent, or devalued in novels by Jane Austen, Mary Shelley, George Sand, the Brontës, George Eliot, and Kate Chopin" (Hirsch 12, 14). To that list one might easily add the names of Edith Wharton, Willa Cather, and Ellen Glasgow; however defined, Hirsch's statement found hungry acceptance among late twentieth-century critics and readers, and allowed the initial interest in Kingsolver's novels to continue growing. This author frequently introduced the concept of women's lineage; to open Chapter Twelve, for example, she noted "All three generations of Alice's family have been lifted into the air for the first time this summer" (Pigs 125).

As she had in *The Bean Trees*, Kingsolver adds in a number of strong— and often single—women characters. In effect, the genealogy of the Stamper-Greer line blurs into other women's histories. Part of the reasonableness for Kingsolver's focus on women characters also stems from her attention to the role of native cultures, many lines of which are traditionally matriarchal.

By keeping the focus on the Native American cultures of Oklahoma, Kingsolver is doing much more than extending narrative. She could easily have charted Alice's helpfulness to Taylor without taking her characters to Heaven (despite that town's connection with the somewhat awkward title of this novel). As if to supplement Alice's early comments on social class and poverty, Kingsolver's descriptions of fictional Oklahoma life write an extreme script: readers have seen the kind of genteel poverty that Taylor, Turtle, and Jax enjoy in Arizona. Oklahoma poverty, however, shows a different kind of need, one rooted in the "Trail of Tears—The Trail Where They Cried—where one quarter of the Cherokee people died ... I imagine that: Children frozen to the ground each morning; mothers struggling to raise their faces from hair locked in ice while babies cry at the starved breast. At least four thousand Cherokees dead. Obviously many survived, but at what cost?" (Owens Mixed 195). In the words of native critic and novelist Louis Owens, the lives of many present-day Indians are the result of the trail, where no real choices existed, to "abandon Mississippi homelands or stay in Mississippi and starve, scratch survival from removal lands, remember stories, and nurture or abandon their children. They suffer inconceivable hardships and survive" (Owens 154). Speaking eloquently of pervasive survivor's guilt, he sets that guilt against the simple belief in the American Dream of success: "For many, success means we leave family and relations, and often the only selves we know, behind. Authentic selves hang tattered on berry vines somewhere back there beside the trail, we think." Owens, who was himself a suicide, provides a scathing contrast to the restrained sociological understanding of the historic trials of that removal, and, similarly, in her characterization of the mixed blood families that Taylor and Alice represent, Kingsolver tries to reclaim some of that poignance.

The very fact of the plotline of Turtle's having been given away to Taylor comes from Oklahoma history. Again, Owens speaks of his aunt, "the baby given away at that country dance," expanding that reference to take the space of full-blown story: "In Oklahoma one night at a country dance—a moment and a place I imagine in stark light and shadow, the whirring of insects around kerosene lanterns, the shuffling and musty smells of patient horses standing amidst rattletrap cars, and the shouting of children backed by barn music—my own mother, uncle, and aunt were given away by their mother. Given away easily, in the told story, each to a different country farming family who could use another pair of small hands or even an infant who might grow into useful labor" (Owens 140). Oklahoma reeking of poverty, this writer describes the state as "a brown, black, and white place of awkwardly hewn log or piled-stone houses, desperate-looking families of differing complexions, and seemingly despoiled landscapes from which those families sought a living." In another segment, he describes the state as "a place of unimaginable horror" (Owens 145, 142).

Given that one strand of contemporary ecological focus is land and landscape, stated in the words of Lawrence Buell as "There never was an is without a where," Kingsolver's steady insistence on place becomes a part of the fabric of her characters' lives. Buell notes that this significance of location draws from issues of poverty and wealth, of a kind of appreciation as ownership: "The more a site feels like a place the more fervently it is so cherished, the greater the potential concern is at its violation or even the possibility of its violation" (Buell 55–6). Linda Hogan, an Indian writer who says explicitly in *Dwellings, A Spiritual History of the Living World*, that the land has power, here writes about a cave-like healing site:

> Evening arrives at the mouth of the cave and the earth turns blue. A soft mist is raining, the kind some call a female rain. Clouds rise up from where it touches ground. A creek moves through this place; it smells of iron and tastes of earth's blood. The land is open, receptive, and it is very young in terms of geological age, having just begun to move and shift. The elements of earth are patient and take their time to grow and collapse.
>
> In earlier days, before the springs and caves were privately owned, they were places of healing for Indian people, places where conflict between tribes and people was left behind, neutral ground, a sanctuary outside the reign of human differences, law, and trouble ... (Hogan 29–30)

None of today's ecologists of earth has ever denied the great significance of native ritual that determines the force of the land, but sometimes the comparatively romantic language used to describe human connections with landscape obscures what Hogan refers to here as "earth's blood" and what Owens limns as a consistently disastrous backdrop—in the country's far-reaching poverty—for survival. As Kingsolver herself wrote in "Knowing Our Place," "just like in real life, all these things happen in some *place*" (Place 15). She continues, "fiction is nothing but a collection of details piled carefully upon one another until they resemble a universe. If you leave out the details, you have a black hole . . . Whether we are leaving it or dealing with an outsider coming into it, it's *here* that matters . . . storytelling is as old as our need to remember where the water is, where the best food grows." She continues, "Story is our grand explanation for ourselves, and it grows from place, as surely as carrots grow in dirt." More personally, she notes, "I write about people, but I believe I am a writer because I grew up among trees" (Place 17–19).

Known for a surprising number of essays that express a great human love for place and the earth that embodies it, Kingsolver's attention to the places she uses in her fiction is never, simply, mechanical. In *Pigs in Heaven*, what appears to be a somewhat artificial plotline—Turtle's seeing the large figure of Lucky Buster fall down the Hoover Dam spillway—enables Kingsolver to create both the Grand Canyon and its environs and the small village where Taylor and Turtle drive in order to return Lucky Buster home. The novel also takes the reader to Heaven, Oklahoma, and its environs during the struggle over Turtle's custody.

In this novel, Kingsolver rapidly alternates chapters, setting in motion the plotline that brings the child Turtle to the world's attention. It is spring break, and Taylor has driven with Turtle to the Grand Canyon—leaving Jax, her boyfriend, at home. It is Jax who answers the phone when Alice Greer calls there, thinking that she has seen Taylor and Turtle on a news feed from the Hoover Dam: Alice is right, although Jax does not yet know about Turtle's adventures. In the growing dark, Turtle had seen Lucky Buster slip under the dam; nobody else saw the man's accident. Taylor does not understand what Turtle is describing until they have gotten back in their car and driven away; once she comprehends what has happened, she takes Turtle back and they eventually rouse a night watchman. But it takes another long day before a search begins: no one will believe that this small Indian child has been the only observer. (Taylor refuses to lie and say that she also had witnessed the event.) Later, when Taylor describes her frustration to Jax, she says, "They took one look at this skinny Indian kid and said, 'Well, ma'am, we don't actually have a witness'" (Pigs 41).

The attention of the news camera brings Turtle's bravery to not only her grandmother's attention, but also to the crew of the *Oprah Winfrey* show. In order to appear on Oprah's show about children who have saved lives, Turtle and Taylor fly to Chicago for the filming. The story of not only *Turtle's* saving Lucky Buster but also of *Taylor's* "saving" her child Turtle makes national news, and the plot involves more residents of Heaven, Oklahoma, who watch *Oprah's* afternoon show. Viewed by Annawake Fourkiller, a novice Indian lawyer, this episode triggers her interest in what Taylor had called the "adoption" of Turtle, and the novel begins its real narrative, a political one. Focused on the 1978 "Indian Child Welfare Act," the story becomes a tug-of-war between Turtle's rights as an Indian child, as expressed and defended by Annawake, and Taylor's compelling love for the abandoned, abused child—regardless of Turtle's ancestry—that she has—admittedly—used trickery to adopt.

Pigs in Heaven plays out in its matriarchal way, but Kingsolver uses prominent extensions from *The Bean Trees* to link the two novels. The books are connected through the matriarchal patterning (Annawake Fourkiller's relationship with her mother Bonnie parallels Taylor's with Alice), as well as the author's emphasis on existing well in the natural world. In *The Bean Trees*, for example, one of the most compelling scenes is the literal vision that Edna and Mrs Parsons share with Taylor and Turtle, Lou Ann and Dwayne Ray. The children are asleep when they knock on the door, and invite the Taylor–Lou Ann household to watch the night-blooming cereus, which shares its flowers only once a year. As Kingsolver had in her description of the first summer rains, she here devotes a lengthy description to the impact of nature—set in the communal, female world of observation.

Enormous blossoms covered the plant from knee level to high above our heads. Turtle advanced on it slowly, walking right up to one of the flowers, which was larger than her face. It hung in the dark air like a magic mirror just inches from her eyes. It occurred to me, that she should be warned of the prickles, but if Lou Ann wasn't going to say anything I certainly wasn't. I knelt beside Turtle.

There was hardly any moon that night, but gradually our eyes were able to take in more and more detail. The flowers themselves were not spiny, but made of some nearly transparent material that looked as though it would shrivel and bruise if you touched it. The petals stood out in starry rays, and in the center of each flower there was a complicated construction of silvery threads, shaped like a pair of cupped hands catching moonlight. A fairy boat, ready to be launched into the darkness.

"Is that?" Turtle wanted to know. She touched it, and it did not shrivel, but only swayed a little on the end of its long green branch.....
"Cereus," I said. Even its name sounded silvery and mysterious.
"See us," Turtle repeated. (Bean 185–6)

Kingsolver creates a similarly metaphoric scene in *Pigs in Heaven* when Taylor and Turtle drive Lucky Buster back to Sand Hill. Exhausted from his ordeal at the dam, Lucky understands that his mother has his favorite foods waiting at her restaurant, Angie's Diner. Members of the community also appear there, greeting Lucky and sharing Angie's joy at his return.

In this scene, the natural world has been replaced with the enclosed communal "home" that surrounds Lucky. His mother's gratitude extends to her feeding both Taylor and Turtle—the people who have saved her son. In two places during the creation of this scene, Kingsolver describes Lucky's obvious retardation in the gentlest possible terms. As Taylor parks her car in Sand Hill, she awakens him and Turtle: "He and Turtle both rub their eyes, equally children." And in the mealtime scene, the author notes, "Lucky leans so eagerly over his mashed potatoes that Taylor has to look away. This must be what people dislike about the retarded: they get straight down to the animal business of life, revealing it for what it is" (Pigs 33–4).

Given that this abundance of food also emphasizes the matriarchal power of survival, and the positive force of matriarchal control, this scene undercuts whatever false sentiment might naturally appear. When the weekly newspaper's photographer insists on taking a photo of Lucky and Turtle, we see how integral Angie's Diner and her son are to the community of Sand Hill: just as members of the community help in tying yellow ribbons on trees and bushes (signifying that Lucky is lost once again), so they claim a share in his happy return.

What faces Kingsolver as Taylor and Turtle leave Sand Hill, however, is the problem of conflict. The narrative stops so that the author can introduce Annawake Fourkiller, the Indian lawyer. What *Pigs in Heaven* must become is an assessment of the rights of Indian children: what kinds of scenes can convey those rights—or the struggle over them—to the reader? As Priscilla Leder acknowledges in her introduction to her essay collection, this novel makes Kingsolver deal with real conflict, and working it out creates the novel per se ... The "'working it out' takes place through a series of confrontations, a hearing, and finally a compromise" (Leder 12).

Always upfront about her personal feelings as she writes, Kingsolver admitted in her Perry interview that writing *Pigs in Heaven* gave her "knots" in her stomach because she saw no possible compromise. As she explained, "In all my other books the villain is offstage: it's the community against the bad mining company or it's the woman against poverty" (Perry 164). In this novel, in contrast, the conflict was between two interesting women characters—and their point of argument was the proprietorship of the innocent child, Turtle. Admitting that her HarperCollins editor had pointed out that she tended to avoid conflict, Kingsolver agreed: "You know, raise your voice and I'll be under the desk in an instant... It was very hard for me to write about direct conflict between characters" (Beattie 170).

Argumentation, no matter how well done, is not great theater. Because Taylor and Annawake "are both right" (Mendes 31), Kingsolver used an omniscient narrator who could present the two women "equally." But readers of the novel thought differently. They would consistently side with Taylor; even though Annawake had lost her young twin brother Gabriel, her appeal to have Cherokee children returned and kept safe had little force beside the day-to-day and hour-to-hour experiences that Taylor was living with Turtle.

Kingsolver, however, tried several strategies to even out the struggle. She uses Annawake's history of losing her brother and her personal history of leaving home to study law: there is sorrow in Annawake's confession to her boss that "People thought my life was so bleak. And I guess it was, so far from home, hearing the ambulances run by all night to the hospital, somebody cracked up or beat up or old and dumped out by their family, and laws jumping up and down in my head. But I always dreamed about the water in Tenkiller. All those perch down there you could catch, any time, you know? A world of free breakfast, waiting to help you get into another day. I've never been without that" (Pigs 67).

Kingsolver also uses a barrage of facts, always coming to the reader through Annawake's voice. Speaking to Alice, she rehearses the Cherokee history—its high rates of literacy; the first public education system in the nation; its city planning; its use of the telegraph. She describes a golden culture which disappears once the railway reaches Oklahoma and the federal laws begin to change. Even her descriptions of the Trail of Tears seem rote: "It was just a wall of people walking and dying... There was smallpox and just exhaustion. The old people and the nursing babies died first; mothers would go on carrying dead children for days, out of delirium and loneliness and because of the wolves following behind." She closed her impassioned argument to Alice that one quarter of all Cherokee children have been taken from their families and their culture (Pigs 282–4).

Alice becomes the intermediary between Annawake and Taylor: she flies west to be with Taylor and Turtle. When they meet her at the airport, a relieved Taylor thinks "Alice always knows what you need. Being near her mother makes Taylor aware of all her inside parts" (Pigs 131). Her observant mother also sees changes in Taylor: "Alice realizes something important about Taylor at this moment: that she is genuinely a mother. She has changed in this way that motherhood changes you, so that you forgot you ever had time for small things like despising the color pink" (Pigs 138).

Perhaps most damaging to Annawake's credibility is her creation of a flimsy romance plot that involves Alice Greer with one of the Cherokee widowers. In this attempt to bring Taylor's family into alignment with the native culture, Annawake shows little originality: she tells friends of Cash Stillwater's that Alice thinks he is handsome, and she tells Sugar that Cash thinks the same about Alice. In reality, neither of them has seen the other person. What appears to be the gullibility of both Alice and Cash makes all the book's characters except Taylor, Turtle, and Jax look either opportunistic or stupid.

This ill-chosen subplot also means that Kingsolver must make Cash Stillwater (named for his mother's favorite singer, Johnny Cash) more than just a returning widower. To do this, Kingsolver moves the narrative to Jackson Hole, Wyoming, Cash's new city, where he has gone after the deaths of his beloved wife and Alma, his older daughter. The only work he can find is as a bag boy (at fifty-nine years of age) at the freshfoods market, and then doing beadwork nights for his younger lover Rose, who is supposed to be the Indian.

In an attempt to draw Cherokee life reliably, Kingsolver weaves in elements that could be given native meanings (the bothersome pigeons, geese, and other birds that the townspeople plan to hunt, various feathers, discussions about music—whether native or non-native). She introduces Cash, for example, watching the white birds "shining outside his window. They make their circle again and again, flaunting their animal joy" (Pigs 109). As the citizens of Jackson Hole prepare to shoot the misplaced pigeons, Cash understands that "The balance of nature is upside down" (Pigs 118). He also realizes that he has left the only place that could make his remaining years worth living.

Then, to keep the narrative in motion, Mr. Crittenden, Rose's boss—who talks occasionally with Cash about native beadwork, and about his own rescue of a python as well as a nearly extinct Australian bird—commits suicide. It is the grasping Mr. Crittenden, who counted every bead that Rose took home for her night work, that teaches Cash that having wealth is sometimes difficult: "It must be hard work, that business of mistrust" (Pigs 111).

Death sobers both Rose and Cash; in the early morning they find Crittenden's body. Whereas Kingsolver does not tell readers what becomes of Rose, soon Cash Stillwater returns to Oklahoma.

The chapter set in Jackson Hole seems digressive; so too do the sections in which Annawake talks with Franklin, the half-Cherokee head of her law firm. Resonating throughout these seemingly nonessential sections is the description of Taylor and Jax's Arizona house, warmly modest and comforting. "Suddenly, noticeably, the failing sunlight turns golden and benevolent. The cacti lit from behind glow with halos of golden fur ... the sun touches the mountains. The horizon is softly indented as if the landscape had been worn down right there, like the low spot in the center of an old marble step, by the repeated tread of sunset. The red ball collapses, then suddenly hemorrhages into the surrounding clouds" (Pigs 82–3). Even with Taylor gone as she runs away with Turtle, so fearful that Annawake will return at the close of her conference, the house—with Jax maintaining it—becomes a beacon of comfort. As Taylor struggles in her on-the-run poverty, losing jobs because she has no adequate childcare, she carries the memory of her good house along like a talisman.

Phoning Jax in her misery, she announces, "I'm going to make this work here. I have to. I'm not stupid, and I'm not lazy. I'm working so hard ... but we never quite get caught up." And Jax is correct when he tells her, "It's not your fault, Taylor." She has not been poor for long; she cannot accept his comfort,

> Well, whose is it? I should be able to keep a roof over my own head. If I work at it ...
> "That's just a story. You're judging yourself by the great American cultural myth, but Horatio Alger is compost, honey. That standard no longer applies to reality." (Pigs 245–7)

She will not allow him to send her plane tickets (and of course he has no idea of her address). She dreams of being able to eat real food as she and Turtle exist on peanut butter. Even the milk she tries to get Turtle to drink sickens the child (the native antipathy to milk has begun to trouble her). Taylor is paying $390 a month for rent, but she cannot keep the utilities paid. Finally, in an honest confrontation with both Cash Stillwater and Annawake, Taylor admits "I've let her down too. In different ways. I made her drink milk even though I should have seen it was making her sick ... Since all this came up, we've been living on the edge of what I could manage. I had to leave her alone in the car sometimes because I couldn't afford a sitter. We didn't have enough money, and we didn't have anybody to help us ... That's why I finally came here. Turtle needs the best in the world, after what she's been through, and I've been feeling like a bad mother ... Turtle deserves better than what she's gotten, all the way around. I love her more than I can tell you, but just that I love her isn't enough, if I can't give her more. We don't have any backup. I don't want to go through with this thing anymore, hiding out and keeping her away from people. It's hurting her" (Pigs 320–1).

Far in Turtle's past history is the abuse—the sexual violation, the broken arms—as Taylor admits that she is only one person, with such limited funds that she cannot stretch enough to give her beloved Turtle decent food and care. As Amanda Cockrell said early on, "Children are always at the heart of Kingsolver's fiction: lost children, children regained, children found and adopted" (in Austenfeld 190). And from the hidden recesses of *Pigs in Heaven* itself, the single set of lines describing what Turtle remembers whenever she is once again surrounded by fear: "Everyone here is afraid. Turtle feels the old place coming, with him and no light and you can't get air" (Pigs 93).

Showing firm restraint not to sensationalize the child's abuse, Kingsolver gives the reader comparatively little description about its effects on Turtle. When Alice talks to Annawake, she says, "You don't know what that child goes through. She's still not over it. Whenever she feels like she's done something wrong, or if she thinks Taylor's leaving, she just … It's like her body's still there but her mind gets disconnected some way" (Pigs 223). In contrast to Annawake's "lawyer-speak" about "the chain of caretaking" that native families are known for—with relatives stepping in for missing parents—these comments that both Alice and Taylor make, rooted in the hiddenness of Turtle's unforgettable pain, strike fire.

Obliquely, then, Turtle herself identifies her abuser as an adult man. When she is surprised to see Cash Stillwater in the lawyer's office in Oklahoma, she "stares. Suddenly she holds up her arms to Cash like a baby who wants to be lifted into the clouds. She asks, 'Pop-pop?'" Later, more talkative, she exonerates her grandfather by explaining, "The bad one wasn't Pop-pop" (Pigs 321, 326).

At the tribal hearing, when Andy Rainbelt, the appointed representative of Child Welfare Services, and Annawake meet with members of the tribe and Taylor and Turtle, their decision is that Cash Stillwater will become Turtle's guardian (with whom she must spend three months each year), and that that responsibility is to be shared with Taylor Greer, with whom the child is allowed to live. It is difficult not to feel the fall into the sentiment that has plagued the novel throughout, but Kingsolver tries by giving readers Cash's suggestion that he and Alice marry (so Turtle can spend her summers with her grandmother as well as her grandfather), as well as closing the novel with the scene of Cash's shooting and destroying his television set (so that Alice will not ever again be married to a man who lives in a fantasy world). Financially, the point is made that Turtle's expenses, such as counseling costs, will be assumed by the tribe. This section of outcomes might partly bring Annawake back to the reader's good graces, but she instead remains the stern legal voice rather than the warm loving representation of Taylor's caring for Turtle.

Aside from the legal commentary that Annawake professes, Franklin, her boss, says to himself that he never could think of any generalizations about white people—but he could think of a dozen generalizations about the Cherokee: "They're good to their mothers. They know what's planted in their yards. They give money to their relatives, whether or not they're going to use it wisely" (Pigs 63). Between Franklin's quiet wisdom and the conversations that Alice has with Sugar and Cash, Kingsolver creates an approachable and relatively dynamic native culture.

Criticized once more for her inability to "do" Cherokee, Kingsolver replied in yet another interview, "What I really wanted to do in that book was not necessarily write about Indians. I wanted to introduce my readers to this completely different unit of good and have them believe in it by the end, have them accept in their hearts that that could be just as true as the other" (Epstein 37). Because *Pigs in Heaven* follows *Animal Dreams*, the most "native" of Kingsolver's books, however, she might be underplaying all she had learned since writing *The Bean Trees* about a culture more native than her own.

Deny her interest in native cultures as she did, Kingsolver yet created an underlying thematic strain that somehow did make that connection: the economics of Taylor's poverty seems more germane to an uneducated, uncommercialized culture (which could well be native) than to mainstream Midwestern living. Among Indian writers of recent times, Louis Owens, for one, considers what being one of nine children meant in Mississippi:

> with nine children and a third-grade education, what could my father do? And with nine children and a third-grade education, what could my mother do? Work was not enough. Shame covered us like the green woolen army blankets we slept under and the commodity peanut butter, raisins, lard, canned 'meat,' rolled oats, and butter we gathered from the government each month to supplement the deer, rabbit, quail, fish, and mountains of potatoes and beans we consumed ... we children knew that somehow being who we were meant that our parents had virtually no way of supporting us, and that my father would ride a bicycle twelve miles to work to stand for hours in water in a laundry—unable to afford either a working car or rubber boots—until his feet rotted and the flesh fell away when he removed his shoes at night. (Owens Mixed 197, 200)

It is Maureen Ryan who is most harsh about Kingsolver's use of native cultures. She admits in her critique that the author has been "aggressively politically correct," but tends to weave in a condemnation by stressing that even as Kingsolver deals with complex and controversial issues, she remains "fundamentally conservative." Her fiction, says Ryan, stems from realistic descriptions, and her characters are driven by their own morality (and it is that morality that makes her conservative): Kingsolver is not writing a postmodern or minimalist literature (Ryan 77). It remains for Charlotte M. Wright to try to soften that criticism by stressing that this author's work is "complex," never simple, and that she usually creates "a multicultural, political and passionate place" (Wright 510). That there is something of a struggle between criticism and acceptance stems, I think, from the pat ending of the controversy over Turtle.

One of the other difficulties that prompts a mixed critical response is that the poetry that Kingsolver tries to embed in *Pigs in Heaven* falls short. Twice in the text she has Annawake tell the story of the constellation of stars, the Pleiades, the *six* pigs (replacing the *seven* sisters in mainstream lore), the little Indian boys punished for their lack of obedience (especially to their mothers). Perhaps emblematic of the cultural divide of white mainstream culture from Cherokee, the difference in the stories does not convince a reader—even though the novel also plays humorously with the Biblical story of King Solomon dividing the baby in order to please the warring mothers. (The Cherokee medicine man, Uncle Ledger, claims that this is a native tale; Annawake knows it is from the Bible.) But no such irony surrounds the recounting of the six pigs (in heaven) story.

When Annawake first tells Jax the tale, he is impressed with her eloquence—and with the aptness of the story as a parable of difference. But when she tells it once more to Alice, whose acceptance is more questioning, the very repetition costs the reader some empathy:

> "Law … They must of felt awful," says Alice. "They did. They tried to grab their sons by the tails, and they begged the spirits to bring them back, but it was too late. The pigs ran so fast they were just a blur, and they started rising up into the sky. The spirits put them up there to stay. To remind parents always to love their kids no matter what, I guess, and cut them a little slack."
>
> Alice looks up for a long time. "I swear there's seven," she says … .
>
> "Maybe so," Annawake says. "The Six Pigs in Heaven, and the one mother who wouldn't let go." (Pigs 314)

Whether intentionally or not, Annawake's parable valorizes Taylor and her stubborn intensity as she tries to keep Turtle safe—despite her inadequate finances.

Robin Cohen emphasizes Taylor's role in her reading of *Pigs in Heaven* as "a thoughtful attempt to suggest the need for a hybrid society, honoring feminine and tribal forms of community over the lone masculine individualist" (Cohen 147). Similarly, Magali Michael uses both *The Bean Trees* and *Pigs in Heaven* to illustrate her contention that Kingsolver is more interested in "alternative" familial communities than in creating recognizably Indian narratives (Michael 73). For this critic, the author seems to have intentionally avoided giving her main characters the kind of visible ethnicity that a reader might expect. It is Jax, for instance, the white musician with whom Taylor lives, who understands without question why Taylor runs away from their home to protect Turtle: Jax says, simply, why Taylor runs is "not an answerable question." If comprehension is supposedly tied to a difficult ethnicity, Kingsolver does not give her readers stereotypes (Pigs 155).

Michael anticipates the power of both Jax and Cash in this novel by writing about the way Kingsolver's interest in class permeates her characterizations. She notes that, in especially these early books, "class dynamics intersect with gender, race, and ethnic cultures. This class analysis leads not only to a critique of the American ideal of self-interested individualism, particularly in the ways ... of the marketplace, but also in the construction of an alternative model of the individual within and as a function of the community." In making this assessment, Michael also redefines the term "agency," saying that in *Pigs in Heaven*, agency is seen as "a process of ongoing negotiation that requires stitching together a patchwork of interests and traditions in ways that both respect those interests and traditions and rewrite them by forcing them to enter new dialogues" (Michael 76–7). Annawake's difficult role—and one of the reasons for her garnering little sympathy from readers—is to do most of that rewriting.

Perhaps Kristin Jacobson's insistence on the effectiveness of Kingsolver's structure in these early novels provides more answers than do the critics mentioned here. Jacobson sees the author writing "a blend of at least three genres" (in Leder 180). The first is *utopian fiction* (since readers comment on the author's ability to create hopeful endings); the second and third tropes, however, stem from realism. The second, in Jacobson's terminology, is the *domestic novel*, set at "home" and peopled with commonplace, often familial, characters. The third is the *political novel*, with a clear directive to be understood—and perhaps implemented.

Adopting this tripartite and focused structure takes the novel away from romance, so that the reader does not question the absence of either Harland or Jax (although Kingsolver relents toward the end of *Pigs in Heaven* and shows Alice, at least, that Taylor does care for Jax, her housemate).

In Jacobson's explanation of the dominance of the domestic coupled with the political, "These realist traditions share the political goals of transforming the reader. Both traditions frequently rely on sentiment to achieve their aim to reform the reader. Kingsolver blends the domestic novel's focus on the domestic sphere with the political novel's activist stance. She describes her troubling of these generic boundaries in her essay 'Knowing Our Place': 'I write about the likes of liberty, equality, and world peace, on an extremely domestic scale'" (in Leder 180, "Place," 37).

Pigs in Heaven might speak consistently for a larger responsibility— something far past one individual's care for another individual. Kingsolver calls it "connectedness" and relates it to community (Pence 20). When it becomes clear that the focus for all human efforts in both the Taylor–Turtle novels will be the care of the child and her well-being, Kingsolver takes readers step by step through Turtle's development. Signaled by the idiosyncratic vegetable-based language in *The Bean Trees*, *Pigs in Heaven* is dominated by Turtle's returning memory. The burial of her mother surfaces repeatedly in the child's timid fascination with cemeteries and in her attempts to dig holes and place objects under the earth. Just as Kingsolver questioned the literal definitions of *home* and *family*, and *animal* and *human*, she makes the reader conscious of the fact that to *bury* (or *plant*) may result in *growth* and *fruition*. Turtle's life has come to illustrate that flowering. One of the climactic scenes in *Pigs in Heaven* is Taylor's telling Turtle, "That's what *home* means, Turtle. Even if they get mad, they always have to take you back" (Pigs 289). Another such scene is the child's recognizing Cash Stillwater as the *good* grandfather. Memory, too, helps a life grow.

Led initially by the fact that her third novel was to be a continuation of her first, Kingsolver drew a set of characters and a plotline that emphasized a strong relationship between women as individuals and community, a relationship that was new to not only novels written by women but also to most fiction written in the closing years of the twentieth century. And as Mary Ellen Snodgrass points out, readers' reception for these books was overwhelmingly positive. *The Bean Trees* won notable book awards from both the American Library Association and the *New York Times*, as well as an Enoch Pratt Library Youth-to-Youth Books award. *Pigs in Heaven* was honored by the National Cowboy Hall of Fame and the Western Heritage Museum in Oklahoma City; Kingsolver was awarded a John D. Free sculpture (Free was an artist of Cherokee-Osage heritage). The novel won a *Los Angeles Times* Fiction Prize, Publishers Weekly Audio Best of Year, *New York Times* Bestseller and Notable book, and Mountains and Plains Booksellers Award— as well as the American Booksellers Book of the Year nomination (Snodgrass 16, 22).

4

Animal Dreams,
a Prototypical Ecological Novel

I guess it's a biological way of seeing the world. And I don't understand the
suggestion that interdependence is a weakness. Animals don't pretend to be
independent from others of their kind; I mean no other animal but us. It
seems like something we should get over.

Kingsolver in Fisher 28

After the unexpected success of *The Bean Trees*, Kingsolver set about making
what she saw as a definite literary footprint in the world of American
literature. She did this by publishing the non-fiction work she had long
worked toward (*Holding the Line: Women in the Great Arizona Mine Strike
of 1983*), a collection of her short stories (*Homeland and Other Stories*) and a
collection of her poetry (*Another America/Otra America*). Most importantly,
she began working almost immediately on a large second novel that was not
only inclusive but, in many ways, narratively cumbersome. *Animal Dreams*
was, in the author's words, "about five novels" and Kingsolver later admitted
that she had problems bringing all its themes together (DeMarr 70). The
book dealt with the absence of mothers and mothering, the comparative
coldness of the worlds of science and medicine, the acceptance of the values
of powerful native American cultures, the beauties of the southwestern
natural world, and the decisiveness of educated and self-directed women like
Hallie Noline (contrasted with the indecisiveness of her sister Codi). It is
Codi who grows to become the hero of *Animal Dreams*.

For readers who knew *The Bean Trees*, some of Kingsolver's choices in
writing *Animal Dreams* were startling. The most obvious was her turn from
a definite interest in the role of mothers to a nearly complete absence of that
parent. Because Alice Noline, the girls' mother, dies of kidney dysfunction
soon after Hallie's birth, Kingsolver draws on other women characters
throughout the novel to contrast and compare with the girls' father, Homero
Noline: the scattering effect of this use of a sometimes minor set of figures
adds to the readers' difficulty in locating the seminal patterns in the
development of both Hallie and Codi.

Perhaps more importantly, *Animal Dreams* takes readers past the gendered focus that emphasizing either father or mother creates. In this novel, Kingsolver in her professional role as biologist and ecologist takes center stage. After *The Bean Trees*, the author was clearly thinking of her fiction as stemming from a more scientific model. In interviews, she begins telling readers that she shapes her fiction in order to answer life's important questions. For example, about *Animal Dreams*, she muses, "I celebrate dependency," and continues, the animal world is integral to the human: "everything kills something else in order to live" (Perry 146). In the novel itself, Kingsolver writes, "We're born like every other mammal and we live our whole lives around disguised animal thoughts" (*Animal* 118). As her title suggests, identifying the animal in the human was one thrust of this 1990 book.

A few years later, Kingsolver asks about the omnipresent discussions between Annawake and Taylor/Alice, "In this dialogue, is there any point of intersection?" (Beattie 170). By the time of *Pigs in Heaven*, the author had pared down descriptions of characters. Pruning her style so that the *questions* and not *characters* were emphasized gave the 1993 novel some of its didactic tone.

In *Animal Dreams*, however, the author's focus on the differences between Codi and Hallie as they have developed becomes a key narrative strategy. In Kingsolver's words, "Why is it that some people are activists who embrace the world and its problems and feel not only that they can, but that they must, do something about the world and its problems, while other people turn their back on that same world and pretend that it has no bearing on their lives? Why is it, moreover, that these two kinds of people can occur in the same family?" (Beattie 164).

Setting up the novel so that these characters' intimate differences carry much of the weight of the story mandated some juggling of technical choices. The tactic of juxtaposing Codi Noline's voice with that of Doc Homer effectively creates a fluid kind of dialogue: the author may not explicitly mention "interrogation," but the novel's structure provides a question and answer framework. The dialogue between Codi and her father, however, is based on the revelations of their characters' memories, a technical difficulty for the doctor's character because his memory has been crippled through the losses of his encroaching Alzheimer's disease.

It was in Kingsolver's 2011 interview with Stephen Fisher that she used "interrogative" to describe her writing: "Literature is not mandative. It is interrogative. I don't even know who you are, as my reader, so I wouldn't dare presume to tell you what to do. What I would like to do is invite you to have a conversation with yourself. I would like you to review the evidence in a new way ... " (Fisher 29).

At the time Kingsolver began writing *Animal Dreams*, in 1989, she was intent on giving her readers help in deciphering her own authorial motives. Early on she said candidly that the Noline sisters related to herself autobiographically. "When I began to write the story I understood it was a triangle of Codi, Hallie, and Doc Homer, and it was going to be about the ways that memory creates a family and creates a culture ... Hallie would have been very easy because Hallie is me ... Codi's motivations mystified me, and her personality scared me because she's so detached; she's so wounded and she's so cynical ... I didn't like Codi much, and I didn't want to get close to her" (Perry 159–60).

The novel differs from *The Bean Trees*, then, in that Kingsolver's identification with Taylor Greer there is clear—and remains consistent, through both books of the narrative. *Animal Dreams*, however, creates a broader canvas of meaning. In this book, Kingsolver takes the Homer Noline family and places them in the stunning, almost other-worldly Arizona landscape. As she drew the village of Grace, Arizona, with its mixed Spanish, Mexican, Caucasian, and Native American population, she did not sentimentalize the power of community. (In *The Bean Trees* and *Pigs in Heaven*, community provided both a governing ethos and a means of survival for characters who were alone.) The elaborate circumstances of the settling of the village of Grace—descendants from the nine Gracela sisters, all marked at birth by their marble-eyed photos (a surprising manifestation of recessive genes)—creates a magical atmosphere: Krista Comer comments about the fact that Grace, Arizona, is integral to what she calls Kingsolver's "origin myth." The sisters and their accompanying peacocks, settling in the fields of fruit trees, populate what Comer calls a "fantasy topography" (Comer 229–30).

Just as her first two novels moved from state to state, with characters living in unrecognizable parts of unrecognizable cities, here Kingsolver pushes the limits of literal geography to make her readers attend: the novel underscores the point that "home" has never been "home" to Codi, partly because of Doc Homer's denial that Grace was their family's place of origin. (Shamed by his ancestral ties to Grace, Doc argued that they had hailed from Illinois.) Adopting an outsider mentality, despite being included in the life of Grace by many of its mothers and grandmothers, Codi drifts away from the community and the people who love her. Even when she returns, ostensibly to care for her ailing father, she does not live with Doc Homer; instead she lives in a guesthouse on the property of her girlhood friend, Emelina Domingos, her husband, and their five children. That the author works hard to build a plausible village, giving it natural characteristics—the mountains, the polluted river, the cemetery, the streets—belies the fact that

Codi does not see Grace, Arizona, as any meaningful part of her existence. She has wandered through life, and through its landscapes, and she has so far—despite ten years in medical school—failed to accomplish anything significant.

The strident reality of place in *Animal Dreams* occurs in connection with Hallie, whose mission—to take agricultural information to Nicaragua—removes her not only from Grace but also from the United States. That setting emphasizes another villainous spectre in Grace itself, the big business that corrupts, first, the river and then, as a result, the land. Unreal as Grace may seem to be at times, what *is* real is pollution, waters that have little ability to bring nourishment to trees and plants (and people), and a kind of lethargic disdain for the capacity of human beings' power to change the corruptible landscape.

Kingsolver chooses to draw Hallie as a shadow figure, existing in infrequent letters to Codi and then in the sorrowful event of her murder in Nicaragua, and the ceremony of her memorial in Grace, arranged by her numbingly bereaved sister. Kingsolver makes clear that Hallie looks up to Codi, seeing her older sister as the mother figure in her life, as when Emelina tells Codi that Hallie "copied you like a picture" (Animal 31). Codi, however, contrasts herself with the brave Hallie to her own detriment. Codi's first section of *Animal Dreams* opens, "I am the sister who didn't go to war" (Animal 7).

Half a decade before the designation "trauma studies" came into the average person's vocabulary, and before the acronym PTSD (Post Traumatic Stress Disorder) was widely used, Kingsolver had created a vivid portrait of the talented but sadly underdeveloped Codi. Stifled by her father's bereaved misunderstanding of what his role should be in rearing his daughters, and caught in the image of her mother's unexpected death—the helicopter rising slowly from the field only to land again quickly, Codi turns more and more frequently to the world of nature and what she sees as self-sufficiency. (Kingsolver will wait to add in the miscarriage and burial of Codi's six-month fetus, a supposed secret loss observed, but not ameliorated, by Doc Homer.) One of the recurring images throughout the novel is Codi and Hallie as children, braving the flooded river as they try to rescue a litter of coyote puppies: the mothering instinct is strong in both girls, but they are betrayed by the frailty of their hands. ("There were seven," she'd wailed over the telephone. "I could carry four but Hallie could only get one in each hand and we didn't want to leave the other one. He would have gotten drowned.") It is Uda Dell's husband who rescues the small girls on his mule, after Doc Homer has called. The bridge is out; he cannot reach his children, who have been crouching for half a day in the small shelter of the gravel bank. Doc

Homer is paralyzed with his fearful grief, asking himself "God, why does a mortal man have children? It is senseless to love anything this much" (Animal 20–1).

The first account of this scene occurs in a Doc Homer monologue. Later descriptions of it are confused—who is the strong sister? Hallie remembers that Codi is always the inventive, caring girl: Codi remembers only her failure. In fact, when she returns to Grace, taking on the job of teaching science at the high school, she finds that she does not either recognize or remember Uda Ruth Dell, the babysitter who had cared so often for them, and whose black-and-red crocheted afghan remains so vividly in her memories.

As she had in her first novel, Kingsolver creates metaphoric scenes that spark memories about earlier life experiences. But for Codi, her memories increasingly differ from those of Hallie. The reader assumes that Hallie's recollections are true. The author is making it clear that Codi is working through the damage that occurred from childhood, and then throughout her adolescence. Lee Ann De Reus discusses the way Codi's remembering her mother's death causes the first developmental crisis—trust versus mistrust. "Feeling abandoned and relegated to the negligent care of their father, Codi and her sister were subjected to the desperate, awkward attempts of Doc Homer to raise daughters acceptable to a community that had previously rejected him" (in Austenfeld 160). De Reus continues that during Codi's more mature years, she behaves toward her father as if she were a "diffused" adolescent, caught eternally within a shell of mistrust.

One of this critic's metaphors for the daughters' behavior is their "game" of playing orphans when they attend school or parties. Never expecting any warmth or visible love from Doc Homer, they watch other people to see if they could pretend that one or another resident of Grace would reveal himself or herself as their real parent. Perhaps they had borrowed this tag from the women of the community—who had often referred to them as "the orphan girls" (*huerfanas*; Animal 43).

Critics in the twenty-first century have given fully informed psychiatric readings of Codi. Sheryl Stevenson, for example, describes Kingsolver's presentation of Codi in this way:

> Characterized by oscillation between numbed inability to remember and sudden overpowering floods of memory and feeling, Codi's sections of the novel constitute a crisis autobiography, uncovering the intensity of her fears and griefs as she faces the possible, then actual, loss of Hallie … Yet both Codi's perspective and her father's show that the present crisis elicits memories of unresolved losses in the past—the death of Codi's mother when she was three and that of a child she secretly miscarried when she

was fifteen, a daughter she frequently dreams about, even as her father is also haunted by memories of this event. (in Leder 89)

Stevenson also points out that the reader must supplement Codi's narration with the sometimes confused memories of her father, but that because Kingsolver sees Doc Homer as an unreliable narrator, he "is not given first-person narration."

Kingsolver has said herself that she was writing about "the way that loss of memory is the loss of self, both for a culture and an individual" (Serendipity 3). The enigma that the author found at first in the character of Codi was gradually resolved. Kingsolver created a generally believable woman, a person slowly folding back into the culture of Grace that had lost its memory place in her mind. Accordingly, the character of Codi tells her story through indirection. As she muses early in the novel, "it takes your sleeping self years to catch up to where you really are. Pay attention to your dreams: when you go on a trip, in your dreams you will still be home. Then after you've come home you'll dream of where you were. It's a kind of jet lag of the consciousness" (Animal 9). As the Noline story reveals more details, the reader learns how many of Codi's inexplicable behaviors are, in reality, plausible. She quits her study of medicine because she cannot deliver the premature baby who will be a breech birth; she avoids choosing where to live and how to earn a living because she thinks of herself as a younger, untrained, person. She writes letters to Hallie that are in themselves timeless, bare of details about what she teaches in the classroom, what her social life has become. Codi's letters fashion an unreal existence because in them she meditates so frequently about her childhood with Hallie. In one of her early letters, for example, she asks Hallie about the litter of coyote pups, an experience that Hallie rehearses for her in vivid detail.

Much of Codi's development occurs because she is surrounded by Emeline and J.T. and their healthy boys. When Codi is able to save the baby Nicholas from choking, she becomes an intimate part of that family. But more of her development stems from her relationships with Loyd Peregrina, the man who, as a high school boy, had unknowingly fathered her lost child. The steady Pueblo, Navajo, and Apache mixed blood, who reveres the Arizona land as well as all parts of his own ancestry, wants to create a deep well of comfort for Codi. He becomes her guide to the native customs and places (the 800-year old pueblo Kinishba, the volcanic hot springs in the Jemez Mountains, his mother's Santa Rosalie Pueblo with its dances, the cock-fighting site); more significantly he guides her without coercion. He is trying to understand what has given her such pain. Even though he has no idea about her becoming pregnant after their love-making, he apologizes for his brief exploitation of her when they had dated years earlier. For critic Robin Cohen, Loyd becomes a model for "a new man, transcending ethnicity, for a new age and a better world" (in Leder 151).

Accompanied by his mongrel dog Jack, an animal half coyote, Loyd like T.J. works on the railroad since the mines have closed. He bears the scars of the death of his twin brother Leander and of his father's life of alcoholism. He also has survived a short-lived marriage. He speaks comparatively little, but Kingsolver makes clear that much of what Loyd expresses runs parallel with Hallie's words in her letters. Hallie writes to Codi, "What keeps you going isn't some fine destination but just the road you're on, and the fact that you know how to drive" (Animal 224). The disillusionment and angst that mark Codi's response to much of life have no place in an active, and involved, participatory life. Hallie had also said, "It's what you *do* that makes you who you are." Loyd's value system is correspondingly brusque: "The important thing isn't the house. It's the ability to make it. You carry that in your brain and in your hands, wherever you go." He somewhat jokingly continued, "Anglos are like turtles, if they go someplace they have to carry the whole house along in their damn Winnesotas." Codi corrects him, "Winnebagos. They're named after an Indian tribe." She then silently rejoins, "Morality is not a large, constructed thing you have or have not, but simply a capacity. Something you carry with you in your brain and in your hands" (Animal 235–6).

Leavened with the dramatic beauty of the deer dance, of the millennia-old pueblos, of the pristine natural farms, of the ceremonial Day of the Dead rites, the discourse between the meaninglessly intellectual Codi and the wise yet proud Loyd draws the reader further and further into the distinction, which the novel shows to be arbitrary, between human and animal. The novel opens with Doc Homer watching his daughters sleep, and equating them with animals: "His girls are curled together like animals whose habit is to sleep underground" (Animal 3). In the assessment of critic Janet Bowdan, one of Kingsolver's strengths as writer is her ability to fuse all parts of a novel. She notes, "Kingsolver uses boundaries but refuses to maintain all of them at all times: the results create new images, overlapping, demanding inquiry into the idea of possession, position, the habitation of a place, a body, a language" (Bowdan 16).

Listening to Loyd and his mother Inez speak together in Pueblo, Codi finds the rhythms of acceptance in what she calls "a steady, musical downpour of language" (Animal 228). Loyd speaks numerous languages, though he has not gone to college. In his various proficiencies, he has been a careful observer. His behavior stands iconically as a model: Kingsolver focuses much of her narrative on the various annual celebrations of The

Day of the Dead—marigold-decorated graves linking family members together while living celebrants revere those who have gone before. On the first page of *Animal Dreams*, in fact, Kingsolver takes Doc Homer back to his memories of the days Hallie and Codi are invited along with the Domingos and other families to partake in the rituals and the feasting. Fearful that they will eventually discover their own relatives in the graveyard, he decides that this will be their last year as celebrants. At the end of this somewhat decisive scene, Kingsolver relents and shows the astute heart of Doc Homero, a man who is no more fooled by his own lies than are the others living in Grace, Arizona:

> They're deep in the corpselike collapse that takes hold of children when they are exhausted, but still he won't risk going in to stand over the bed the way he once would have. He would see the usual things: unraveled braids and the scraped shins hidden from his punishing antiseptics. Tonight he would also see cheeks and eyelids stained bright yellow from marigold pollen. He's spent a lifetime noticing small details from a distance. From the doorway he smells the bitterness of crushed marigold petals on their skin.
>
> There is a deeper draft of breath and they both move a little. Their long hair falls together across the sheet, the colors blending, the curled strands curving gently around the straight. He feels a constriction around his heart that isn't disease but pure simple pain, and he knows he would weep if he could. Not for the river he can't cross to reach his children, not for distance, but the opposite. For how close together these two are, and how much they have to lose. How much they've already lost in their lives to come. (Animal 4)

Pieces of *Animal Dreams*, separated out by content and tone, suggest throughout the book that any happy resolution will be difficult.

The resonance of sorrow clings to both Codi and Hallie—and not only here in Doc Homero's description. Despite the tranquility Loyd brings to Codi's existence, and despite his empathy for her worrying about Hallie in Nicaragua, much of his wisdom accrues from the native culture that is his background and his blood. Just as his mother has referred to Codi as "the Bread Girl" after she has visited their pueblo, the embedded humor of their native philosophy leads Loyd to a kind of healthy complacency. As Priscilla Leder notes, "Among the gifts of other cultures are alternative ways of looking at families and child rearing. The native ways do not so rigidly mark a child's development. Indians see children as part of tribes rather than, first, as individuals" (Leder 11). Cohen too sees cultural change ahead for Codi's existence: "Kingsolver's new America would be less materialistic. Children would not be ridiculed for their lack of possessions. There would be no room for Barbie dolls, human or plastic ... People would have a closer relationship to nature and more respect for the environment." Gender, too, would be "redefined," so that there would be "the demise of rugged individualism and the rise of community" (in Leder 154–5).

At the time of *Animal Dreams'* publication, it was Paul Gray in *Time* magazine who called it "eco-feminist." He saw the novel—in its interest in gender roles and in self-affirmation, as well as in pertinent politics—as "entertaining" for its "fragile landscape, its doughty heroine, and its strong-willed matriarchs" (Time 87). Although he comments somewhat negatively on the novel's "hectoring tone," he sees it as a useful "distillation of eco-feminist materials." Most reviewers did not use the terms that Gray chose. In the *New York Daily News, Animal Dreams* was called "an emotional masterpiece." In *Publishers Weekly*, it became "a well-nigh perfect novel ... brimming with insight, humor, and compassion." For reviewer Holly Holt, this book, like *The Bean Trees*, offered "a fully realized and profoundly moral vision" (Holt 1). None of the reviews would have prepared readers for Kingsolver's steady theme of political corruption in the countries the United States was funding.

This is one of the two dominant political strains Kingsolver repeatedly hammers home. (The other is the ecological theme of the preservation of our natural wonders, a prefatory kind of preview of incipient global change.) The US political involvement in Nicaragua becomes the real text of Hallie's letters back to Codi. Kingsolver creates suspense by the mail delays, and by Codi's ritualistic opening of the letters and her close reading of Hallie's words. But as the necessarily epistolary plot makes its vivid mark on the already grieving Codi, the tragedy of Hallie's murder is clearly foreshadowed.

One of Hallie's letters was "moderately alarming." In it she describes the destruction of four John Deere tractors, "burnt down to scorched metal hulls." Because "of the US embargo, we can't get parts" so each tractor is "like a hunk of gold" (Animal 157). Successive attempts at destruction ensue, but it takes the letter that opens "This morning I saw three children die. Pretty thirteen-year-old girls wearing dresses over their jeans" to awaken both Codi and the book's readers. Out picking fruit in an orchard, the teenagers are strafed by a helicopter—manned, it is subsequently discovered, by "active-duty National Guardsmen ... American citizens." Hallie continues, "Codi, it's a helicopter from the US, guns, everything from Washington." Even though the helicopter was eventually shot down and two of the three men killed, the remaining man was jailed in an upper-class unit and would be allowed to take a week's vacation (Animal 179).

Knowing that horror in the abstract is relatively dulling, Hallie describes "When they brought them into town, oh God. Do you know what it does to a human body to be cut apart from above, from the sky? We're defenseless from that direction ... The girls were alive, barely, and one of the mothers came running out and then turned away saying, 'Thank you, Holy Mother, it's not my Alba.' But it *was* Alba." Asking Codi to watch the news for any account of the murder of the three girls, and the US involvement in their deaths, Hallie continues, "Nobody here can eat or talk. There are dark stains all over the cement floor of the church. It's not a thing you forget" (Animal 180).

In what becomes a closing sequence of four of Hallie's letters, which arrive in the States just briefly before Hallie is kidnapped and taken to Honduras, the first three catalogue various political abuses. The first was positive: Nicaragua "(*our* government, she called it)" planned to take action against the pervasive layers of DDT accumulated over time. The second described a child's dying from drinking poison out of a Coke bottle (in the fourth letter, she reported that little boy's death). The third happily told of five Contras taken captive by armed farmers as they attacked a hydroelectric plant. The fourth letter lit into Codi for her self-pitying attitudes, and then, when Loyd asked her what was new with Hallie, Codi replied simply "Nothing." The momentum of *Animal Dreams* will change abruptly with the news of Hallie's kidnapping—by unknown forces, and despite the villagers' protests and those of the American ambassadorial staff—a sequence that will eventually end with Hallie's murder (Animal 223–4).

Just as in *The Bean Trees* and here, the Sanctuary Movement is both elevated and defended, so in *Animal Dreams*, Hallie's innocent motivation of providing agricultural aid is unquestioned. The novel's dedication to Ben Linder, an Oregon engineering student who, while helping to build a hydroelectric dam in Nicaragua, had been shot in the head by Contras, continues that political thrust. A few years later Kingsolver wrote that actions in novels must be seen to have consequences, and that she wrote *Animal Dreams* as a kind of protest:

> It matters to me, for example, that we citizens of the US bought guns and dressed up an army that killed plain, earnest people in Nicaragua who were trying only to find peace and a kinder way of life. I wanted to bring that evil piece of history into a story, in a way that would make a reader feel sadness and dread but still keep reading, becoming convinced it was necessary to care. So I invented Hallie Noline, and caused her to die. I did it because this happened, not to imaginary Hallie but to thousands of real people ... Ben Linder, whose family I dearly love, and whose death is permanently grieved; *Animal Dreams* is dedicated to his memory. I

would write that story again, because people forget, and I want us to remember. (High Tide 255)

In the words of critic Amanda Cockrell, "All of Kingsolver's books deal in one way or another with her own government's blind determination to run roughshod over the needs and political motivations of other people. But the political here is personal" (Cockrell 178).

The second large-scale political theme that draws much of the action of *Animal Dreams* into focus, and incorporates many of the women citizens of Grace, is the battle to fight ecological pollution. Even though Codi has earlier heard men commenting about the poisoned river and the dying fruit trees, it takes the stupefying results of her science class's experiments with river water—finding that it is literally dead, that is, "the usual things that live in a river aren't there"—to move her to action. As she tells the women who come to the meeting of the Stitch-and-Bitch Club, "Here is the chemistry of it. Black Mountain Mining has been running sulfuric acid, which is a clear, corrosive, water-miscible acid, through their tailing piles to recover extra copper. It combines to make copper sulfate, which is also known as 'blue vitriol.' People used to use it to kill rats and pond algae and about everything else you can name. There's a ton of it in your river. And there's straight sulfuric acid in there too. The EPA finally sent a report saying that kind of pollution is very dangerous, and they can't put it near people and orchards, so Black Mountain is building a dam to run the river out Tortoise Canyon... "

When the women laughed about her comment that the town council planned to sue the mining company, Codi continued, "your trees knew all this way before we did. Watering them from the river is just like acid rain falling on them ... The acid-rain problem here in the West comes mostly from mine smelters. It's the same acid, one way or the other. Sulfuric acid." When discussion began and women asked if the river could be saved, Codi was able to reassure them: "The river could recover. It doesn't *start* here, it starts up on the Apache reservation, in the mountains where the snow melts. As long as that's pure, the water coming down here will be okay" (Animal 176–7).

Further discussion shows the women—many of them elderly—gearing up for action. In the words of one speaker, "We don't know how to use the dynamite, though. And the men, they might be good men but they wouldn't do it. They'd be scared to, I think, do something *right now*. They think the trees can die and we can just go somewhere else, and as long as we fry up the bacon for them in the same old pan, they think it would be ... " she faltered, hugging her elbows in earnest ... "that it would be *home*" (Animal 179).

Animal Dreams changes mood quickly because the women of the sewing club take what action they can mount. They sell handmade piñatas (for $60 and sometimes more) in the larger towns; they achieve the publicity they have aimed to create for their river's dilemma. Codi's high school class helps; the fight against Black Mountain Mining becomes something to notice. It was only 1990, however, and US readers had little interest in the pollution of Western rivers. As Jane Smiley wrote in her *New York Times Book Review* comment, it is difficult "to forge a compelling political vision in our new world where so many systems of social organization have turned out to be either ineffectual or bankrupt" (Smiley 2). The novel, however, won prizes, among them the Edward Abbey Ecofiction Award, as well as a PEN fiction prize. Readers became aware that they were to be involved in caring about both that river and the mining company's abuses of the natural world.

Because so many plot strands needed to be brought into alignment, and then eventually completed, *Animal Dreams* lacks the smooth closing energy readers had come to expect from a Kingsolver work. There is a long, terrifying sequence after Doc Homero receives the phone call about Hallie's being kidnapped, while Codi and others try to find information about her and her whereabouts. During an equally long sequence that bridges the news of Hallie's death, the United States' attempts to retrieve her body, and Codi's memorial service for her sister's burial, the reader is made fully aware of Codi's isolation: she turns away from everyone in Grace, including Loyd. She is more isolated in her sorrow than is even her father.

Positive currents of events do exist although they too seem submerged under this all-too-human grief. In the community's struggle to save their river and their orchards, Kingsolver draws a compelling picture of united effort, and it is in this narrative line that the sense of *Animal Dreams* as an ecological novel resonates. As Kristin Jacobson acknowledges, at times the ecological struggle here may seem simple, but "dreams, memory, history and myth saturate *Animal Dreams* and complicate our understanding of the econarrative" (in Leder 189).

Difficult as the many narrative strands are to sort, the novel's impact eventually stems from its ecological concerns. The incipient health of the river becomes instrumental in washing under the inescapable agony of the Noline family's loss. That the river's health results from the combined actions of the women in Grace, separated by generational difference but fused together through philosophical wisdom, demands sympathetic understanding from readers.

Part of Kingsolver's layered descriptions of the women who comprise the Stitch-and-Bitch Club, and part of the reader's involvement in characters such as Viola Domingos, Norma Galvez, Dona Althea, Lorraine Colder, and others, adds to the intensity: Kingsolver had learned well how to use oral history recordings from her research during the Phelps Dodge Copper

Mining strike in the Arizona towns of Ajo, Morenci, Douglas, and Clifton. It was that non-fiction account of the tough women who "manned" the various strikes that had led to her finding a good agent: throughout *Animal Dreams* she drew from her years of covering that hopeless strike effort where the orchards of pecan, plum, and apple were poisoned out of existence by the sulfuric acid used in the copper mines' leaching operations. When *Holding the Line: Women in the Great Arizona Mine Strike of 1983* appeared (in 1989 with a second printing in 1996), the readers of Kingsolver's novels were very different from the academic (political science and labor) readers interested in this book. Had those readers overlapped, they would have noticed that many of the wise Arizona women from *Holding the Line* had been recast as activists clamoring for change from the Black Mountain mining clan in *Animal Dreams*.

Whatever the source of the book's power, readers *did* notice it. *Animal Dreams* collected laudatory reviews; it won the American Library Association Notable Book award and Best Book for Young Adults, the Pen/USA West Fiction award, the *New York Times* Notable Book, the Arizona Library Association Book of the Year, and, perhaps most significant to Kingsolver, the Edward Abbey Award for Ecofiction (Snodgrass 18).

5

The Fiction of Kingsolver's Non-novels

Art is the antidote that can call us back from the edge of numbness,
restoring the ability to feel for each other. By virtue of that power, it is
political, regardless of content.

High Tide 232

There should be no surprise in the fact that Barbara Kingsolver began and then extended her publishing career by writing many different kinds of works. She grew into her proficiency with non-fiction naturally. She had never been an English major with an interest in writing poetry, drama, or fiction, though she would acquire enough credits in literature to have an English minor.

When she entered DePauw University in Greencastle, Indiana, it was as a music major, and she funded part of those four years with the university's piano scholarship. During the first year, she also played clarinet, bassoon, and recorder. She lived on campus. But her sense that she would have a career as a concert pianist was fading, so when she returned for her sophomore year, she prepared to become a biology major. She accomplished this by studying the textbooks for a number of introductory science courses, and then taking those course examinations. By the second semester of her second year, she was allowed to enroll in an upper-level organic chemistry course and laboratory, and her music scholarship was changed to an academic one. (Wagner-Martin interview). Living off-campus, she supported herself by cleaning houses, typesetting, and modeling for art classes at $5 an hour.

Her changing to a biology major was more than a pragmatic decision. As she explained to an early interviewer, "I think biology is my religion. Understanding the processes of the natural world and how all living things are related" (Perry 147). She was fortunate that DePauw had a fine science program, and that Preston Adams treated her as if she were an advanced student: reading E. O. Wilson independently, she was planning to do graduate work in kinship studies in ecology. She also hungered for a range of other courses—"East Asian history and anthropology and psychology and computer sciences and math and physics and chemistry" (Beattie 156). She took literature courses, but only one creative writing class. In the latter she began work on the story that—a decade later—would become "Homeland," drawing on her family's Native American bloodline, her sense of the land as integral to self-identification, and her eventual method of crafting personality through choices in language and idioms.

Kingsolver took advantage of DePauw's Junior Year Abroad program— living in France and Greece—and the next year graduating *magna cum laude* with her science degree. But when she returned home to Carlisle, Kentucky, she was struck with a wanderlust that sent her back to Europe for the next year. Then she applied to several graduate programs, was admitted to all of them, and headed for the University of Arizona, where she would study biology, ecology, and kinship systems. As she spent years in Tucson (working for the Sanctuary movement as well as toward her graduate degree), she still felt a kind of dissatisfaction. When a position opened at the university in scientific grant writing, she took the M.A. she had already earned, and put her Ph.D. dissertation on hold.[1] She became a technical writer, a person specializing in science writing—and she married Joseph Hoffman, a chemistry professor at the university. Among her publications then were chapters in the books *Arid Lands: Communities and Legacies* and *Phytochemical Adaptations to Stress.* (See also Kingsolver's web bibliography, Technical and Scientific Writing.)

Clearly interested in becoming a journalist, Kingsolver also began covering the Phelps Dodge Copper Mine strike. The long hours driving to and from the several sites of protests paid off in the friendships she was able to form with the women who shaped the heart of the strikers' resistance. In 1986 she won the Arizona Press Club Award for journalism. Her three years of immersion in the copper mining strike gave her a less erudite, less academic language, as well as the capacity to endure hours and hours of work toward nonspecific ends (she interviewed more than 75 people during her visits) (Holding xii). Whether or not her journalism would ever see print was less important to Kingsolver than the fact that she had found, collected, and organized the material for a book about the struggle of these previously unknown laborers. As she wrote in the introduction to the book her research was to become, "*Holding the Line* was a watershed event for me because it taught me to pay attention: to know the place where I lived ... the

---

[1] Kingsolver described her dissertation as being about the kin selection systems of eusocial insects, the newest area of sociobiology. The area was heavily mathematical and more theoretical than would have been works in field biology. She said that she was "studying a species of termite whose reproductive strategies (sexual vs asexual) could be predicted with a mathematical model I developed based on the relatedness of individuals within the colony, and how it changed over time ... It was highly mathematical work, relevant to ideas about kin selection that were on the forefront of evolutionary theory work at the time" (Wagner-Martin interview).

project quietly changed my life" (Holding xiii). As she worked among the laborers and their spouses (it was the women who stood on the picket lines), Kingsolver was able to hear all levels of the stories they told, in English inflected with Spanish, Spanish with Spanglish, both in person and on tapes. She was able to identify with their lives. Being friends with the poor and the hardworking was no longer something she felt morally compelled to do; it was something she *wanted* to do for she liked—and admired—those strikers and their families.

As critic Sandra Ballard points out, Kingsolver treated the small Arizona mining towns as if they were her small Kentucky town. She drove in often, and was excited when people referred to her as "that gal that's writing the book about us." As Kingsolver had said about small towns, "Rule One is that nobody stays a stranger very long. A newcomer has two options: become known, or else become a stranger…I cared too much in the long run to pretend I didn't. Clifton declared me the biographer of a place and time" (Holding xii in Ballard 20).

At first, Kingsolver began as if this book would be cultural anthropology. She studied the copper mining industry and the economics of production, including the fact that Phelps Dodge brought in a number of workers from Mexico to take advantage of their willingness to work for very low wages. She studied the history of company towns in the Southwest, with a particular focus on company housing and stores. (Management was housed on the upper mountainsides, laborers—both Mexican and white—in flood areas, and, further down the elevation, Native Americans in shacks and tents rather than houses (Holding 65).) But once the strike began on July 1, 1983, Kingsolver's research became personal. She watched men leave their homes and move elsewhere because they could not live on the $40-a-week strike pay; she heard the anguish in their wives' voices as they coped with raising children with so few resources.

On the day the strike began, Phelps Dodge trucked in 1,400 extra workers. For the first time in US strike history, the mines were not shut down. As the scabs crossed the picket lines, throwing pennies at the strikers and their children, the media talked about the violence and anger of the strikers (then non-existant). Within a few more weeks, Governor Bruce Babbitt sent in nearly 700 state troopers and the National Guard to protect the scabs.

Within a month, events had turned in a way I'd never seen before, nor heard of happening in my lifetime…People were being jailed for infractions no larger than picking up the phone and calling a neighbor "scab." Helicopters and squads of armored men with tear gas and large automatic weapons were storming tiny, bucolic Main Streets, and strike supporters were claiming their right to hold the line with extraordinary resistance. The faces and hands of this resistance mostly belonged to women. (Kingsolver, Holding xiii)

Kingsolver was no stranger to prejudice based on class, but the attention to ethnicity (particularly to the Mexicans and Native Americans—which divided union membership) was new to her. As she wrote the book, she connected the ethnic women characters she was drawing with Emile Zola's novel *Germinal* (about women laborers) and Maxine Hong Kingston's *Woman Warrior* of Chinese legend. Kingsolver wrote, "This is the fortune of the woman warrior, too frail to defend her nation in battle but sturdy enough to take her nation's gunfire in a strike. Every tradition has its price, and most have been bought and sold many times over—history often decides that a woman's place is to do the work of men for half the pay" (Holding 10).

The organization of *Holding the Line: Women in the Great Arizona Mine Strike of 1983* is character based. As her title emphasizes, this is writing about *any* mine strike (not necessarily copper, and not specifically Phelps Dodge), and it is focused on the lives of *women*—whether they are workers, strike supporters, or financial victims. Without much attention to the politics of historical study, Kingsolver was proving herself to be a specialist in recording women's lives. Rather than being organized chronologically, this book begins with the story of Flossie Navarro, a woman nearly 70 years of age who chose to work in the Morenci mine because it was closest to her beloved Arkansas. The Navarro story anchors much of the book. Kingsolver also includes the narratives of Jamie Ramon, employed for a decade at Ajo; of the slight Betty Copeland, who weighs 92 pounds; and of Jean Lopez, from Bisbee, whose reply to Kingsolver during her interview was that she was "Nobody really, just a mom" (Holding 4).

Within that first chapter, titled "The Devil's Domain" because women are supposed to jinx any mine, Kingsolver discusses gender roles, corporate practices, and the subordination of women workers, no matter how skilled they are. In Chapter Two, she provides a history of unions in the mining industry, as well as of mining itself. She also discusses racism within the industry and emphasizes the kinds of work non-white people are expected to take on. In Chapter Three, she mourns the destruction from the San Francisco River flood during the late summer when one third of the area's 1,800 houses vanished in either the flood itself or in the masses of mud that followed. Even though members of the National Guard were there—to protect the strike breakers—they offered no help to the homeless, who had the choice of living in caves or in Red Cross shelters, existing on minimal food. When Kingsolver asked the strikers why they were enduring these circumstances, Carmina Garcia (among many others) replied, "Leave? Where else can you go?" (Holding 65). As *Holding the Line* made clear, what gains did occur came from the actions of united women. It was the economy of the kitchen that kept families afloat.

Kingsolver published her first essay from this material, coauthored with union member Jill Barrett Fein, in *The Progressive*. There they included quotations from Jamie Ramon: "Suddenly, six cars pulled up and state troopers jumped out with machine guns. Not one of us had any weapon other than a baseball bat" (Fein 15). The authors kept to this technique, as did Kingsolver in the book. Her later chapter titles are often drawn from the literal words of the strikers: "We Go with Our Heads Up," "My Union and My Friends," "Just a Bunch of Ladies." Although the copper industry would never change, nor did it pay attention to Kingsolver's journalism, in the *oeuvre* of her own work, the skills that she developed in bringing this impassioned story to print equipped her to find success in many ways. She had come to see how important stories of injustice could be, and how significant a writer's work could become in the whole scheme of human life. As she would state repeatedly, "I check my facts obsessively when serving the journalist's or essayist's trade" (High Tide 261).

Kingsolver's first book to follow *The Bean Trees*, however, at the suggestion of both her agent and her publishing house, was not *Holding the Line*. It was rather a collection of her short stories. In *Homeland and Other Stories*, there is only slight evidence of the author's involvement with the copper mine strikers. "Why I Am a Danger to the Public" uses the idiomatic voice and language of a striking Mexican mother, living in New Mexico and working for the Ellington mine. She explains at the start, "You can't get away from it because Ellington don't just run the mine, they own our houses, the water we drink and the dirt in our shoes and pretty much the state of New Mexico as I understand it" (Homeland 226). Comparatively good humored, the narrator Vicki Morales discusses the strike ("There has never been one that turned so many old friends *chingandose*") and her very active role as, first, an employee and then, a strike leader. The focus of Kingsolver's story, however, falls on Vicki's struggle against Vonda Fangham, the pharmacist's daughter; and her recounting is both class based and ethnic. Since Vicki is from the working class, and she now raises her two sons alone after her husband's having left them, she has no way to compete against the rich Vonda. The most poignant moment in the story occurs when Vicki says, "My son couldn't go to Morse with his baseball team Friday night because they had to have three dollars for supper at McDonald's. Three damn dollars" (Homeland 229).

Vicki recounts the sexual insults both her male boss and the elite women in town give her, based on her working in the mines and supporting her children. She also recollects that when she was a (dark-skinned) child she was not allowed to sit at the counter in Vonda's family drugstore. The crux of the story, however, is that Vonda asks for Vicki's help to rescue her boyfriend, Tommy, a scab said to have been injured and hidden away in a distant hospital. So Vonda agrees to come to the picket line to get union support for her plea for information about Tommy.

When Vonda appears, wearing her idea of casual and cheap strikers' clothes and carrying a baseball bat, Vicky and the other picketers explain that having such a weapon is against their practices. Vicki takes and keeps the bat. Eventually, when it becomes known that Vonda is picketing, Vicki is arrested and jailed (she tells her story from jail), charged with a $500,000 bond. The explanation is that she, Vicki, kidnapped the wealthy Vonda and forced her (by using the bat) to pretend to be on the picket line. Obviously farcical, "Why I Am a Danger to the Public" recounts an all-too-typical story from the copper mining strike, with the intentional misreading of class affecting all elements of the judicial system. That the ironic title does not create humor is evidence of the seriousness with which Kingsolver continues to take the struggles of the strikers.

Unlike nearly all Kingsolver's stories, this one *is* didactic, and her attempts at humor do not modify that affect. And also unlike nearly all Kingsolver's fiction, this story does come more directly from her own experiences—but she wages war on the notion that she writes autobiographically. She states, "I never use my own family and friends as the basis of fictional characters, mainly because I would like them to remain my family and friends. And secondarily, because I believe the purpose of art is not to photocopy life but distill it, learn from it, improve on it, embroider tiny disjunct pieces of it into something insightful and entirely new. As Marc Chagall said, 'Great art picks up where nature ends'" (High Tide 258). Kingsolver has long admitted to using places that are familiar to her: "I've photographed my home town in its undershirt," she admits modestly (High Tide 39). More recently, she has described the importance of location:

> The writing of fiction is a dance between truth and invention. Pittman, Kentucky, the starting point of *The Bean Trees*, resembles any number of small towns in east-central Kentucky where I grew up. I didn't invent its weathered look, its party-line phones, its inclination to rally around good gossip or a neighbor in need. Those things I described from experience in a real place. The same is true of other small towns in my novels, from Grace, Arizona to Isla Pixol, Mexico. They are genuine, but

not identified... Cities are different. I've set parts of novels in Tucson, Mexico City, Atlanta, Seattle, Chicago, and Asheville, North Carolina, to name a few. These places are large enough to absorb events and people... (Web 2013)

The ingredients of fiction, however, seem to remain secondary to the process of creating story. Kingsolver writes in that same essay, "It's a curious risk, fiction... The part of my soul that's driven to make stories is a fierce thing, like a ferret: long, sleek, incapable of sleep, it digs and bites through all I know of the world" (High Tide 43).

Most of the stories included in *Homeland and Other Stories* are less successful than "Why I Am a Danger to the Public," or "Rose-Johnny," or the title story. Most seem driven by Kingsolver's interest in her characters' language choices. For instance, a dark story from the book is the domestic-based "Extinctions," the account of a multigenerational family's memory of painful, dangerous child abuse.

Their references to Grace's experiences when she was a child insult her, now a mother who has driven her two children "home" in order to celebrate the Easter holiday. The story begins with a television program about extinct or nearly extinct animals such as the panda, and Grace's conversation with her husband about the fascination their older son Matt has developed with the whole problem of vanishing or endangered species.

Sitting at the dinner table and hearing the group of family members laugh about her near-death experience when she was small creates in her an unquenchable anger. The next morning, Grace says to herself, "The easiest thing... is if this rage she feels could just be drowned, like an orphaned cat" (Homeland 180). She knows that trying to explain how much she has been hurt by the family's callousness will be futile (Kingsolver does a fine job of re-creating the ignorance and racism that dominates the earlier conversation). So she tells her boys *not* to dress for church, but instead to get ready for the road; and they drive home, one presumes for an indefinite absence. Looking at the rainy highway, Grace yet feels relief: she "braces herself for the road and drives for the light" (Homeland 181).

More than a few of Kingsolver's stories in the collection deal with the existence of children—or with parental decisions of whether or not to have children—and while these stories are not so dark as "Extinctions," they are somber. In "Covered Bridges," the late-married couple, Lena and her unnamed spouse, take care of a friend's little girl for the weekend; they have not made having children a priority because they are both professionals (the spouse, a professor of botany; Lena, a toxicologist). During the weekend, Lena has a frightening reaction to a hornet sting and ends up hospitalized with anaphylactic shock. Even though the toddler Melinda makes great progress with them and in their care (she has not yet walked even though she is 20 months old), they decide that they are happy in their childless state. Lena comments, "You know what I think? Immortality is the wrong reason … Having a child wouldn't make you immortal. It would make you twice as mortal. It's just one more life you could possibly lose, besides your own" (Homeland 59–60).

Similar effective uses of idiom dominate "Survival Zones," "Quality Time," "Stone Dreams," and "Blueprints." In the first, Kingsolver uses the small town of Elgin, near Cincinnati, to discuss the fact that decades earlier, Elgin would have been a "survival zone" if Russians would have attacked. Here the farmers' idioms are used to represent kindly people, parents and a teen-aged daughter who still watch black-and-white television. When family members come for Thanksgiving dinner, the conversation is lax and dull, with no irony or malice anywhere—nothing evil transpires. Underlying the family's rapport, however, is the undercurrent of Roberta's concern that her beautiful daughter Roxanne, a high school senior, is going to have to decide whether or not to marry her boyfriend so that he can accept a football scholarship in Indiana. Roberta worries that marrying young is not a good choice, but when the young couple argues about Roxanne's decision, Roberta takes a quilt out into the yard to cover the white azalea bush that her mother-in-law had years earlier brought from Virginia. A comparatively long story about preservation and aging, "Survival Zones" brings little new to Kingsolver's skills with short fiction.

It is not that the author patronizes the speakers in these stories—both "Quality Time" and "Stone Dreams" approach the timeless themes of the need for good childcare and the weary mothering that results from searching for it. Miriam in the first story picks up her beloved Rennie from day care and the plot of the story unrolls in their discussion about what to eat for supper: Rennie is five. Guilty as most working mothers are, Miriam tries to balance her life between Rennie's desires and her own needs—but the latter get increasingly short shrift. The natural sounding dialogue is this story's primary strength. Contrastingly, in the case of Diane in "Stone Dreams," she balances her energy between her lover Peter and her daughter Julie. For all the time Kingsolver spends on the mountain-forest setting, the reader sees Diane's life as a study in relinquishment. The prompting Julie feels compelled to give her mother occurs when the young teen sends along a note in Diane's coat pocket, which reads "Mom, I know you love Peter. Whatever you want to do about Dad is okay. Just you and me is okay. I (heart) you" (Homeland 98). This permission to remarry is not what Diane needs, however, and she knows that marriage to Peter is not her personal answer. With less dialogue than most of Kingsolver's fiction, "Stone Dreams" sets the adults on their camping trip in an almost unreal location, and creates a confusion of existence instead of supplying final answers.

In "Blueprints," Whitman and Lydia, with their dog David, live together in a tiny cabin in Blind Gap—after nine years of their having lived more sensibly elsewhere in a house. The cramped circumstances have a surprising effect on their relationship. Lydia has taken a job in Blind Gap Junior High, where she teaches science; it is because of her new position that they have moved. One of Kingsolver's more ecologically themed stories, "Blueprints" shows Lydia looking forward to her daily walk home from school ("she takes a dirt road that passes through town, winds through a tunnel of hemlocks, and then follows Blind Creek up the mountain to their six acres") (Homeland 26). Getting to know their neighbors allows Lydia to understand the community's fear of global change. For example, during a long rainy spell, she notices "The old people in Blind Gap are saying it's because of those bomb tests, the weather is changing. It's too warm. If it were colder it would have been snow, rather than rain, and would come to no harm." School closes for a week, since bridges have washed out and busses cannot safely transport children (Homeland 36).

School eventually resumes, and Lydia realizes that she and Whitman cannot live in those cramped quarters any longer. But before they discuss this problem, as she walks through the mud to reach the cabin, she sees Whitman lying as if injured half way down the mountain, and because of the flooded river, she cannot reach him. The dog, confused by circumstances, is frantic.

Kingsolver's happy ending (nobody is injured, nobody drowns) seems almost anti-climactic given the pages of tension she has earlier created. In this story, the characters do not talk enough.

Kingsolver's longest mother–child story is a narrative of a mother and her mature daughter, both of whom are pregnant at the same time. "Islands on the Moon" opens with some humorous descriptions of the artistic (and usually unpredictable) mother character, Magda. Annamarie, her daughter, has a nine-year-old son Leon, and still lives in the trailer park she has been trying to leave for a decade. When Magda asks Annamarie to go with her for the amniocentesis her gynecologist insists she have, since Magda is so far past childbearing age, the women share this medical experience. And they also share the car accident that occurs on their return home. Distant from each other for years, mother and daughter realize when they see that the boy Leon is safe, thrown far from the crashed car, and that they in their pregnant conditions are also safe, "Annamarie can't stop sobbing in the back of the ambulance. She knows that what she's feeling would sound foolish put into words; that there's no point in living once you understand that at any moment you could die" (Homeland 141).

A clear experiment in dialogue that avoids direct expression, "Islands on the Moon" winds through backstories for all the characters (even Leon), suggesting only that flawed communication is more effective than silence. Toward the end of the story, Magda finally says, "I never knew what you expected from me, Annamarie. I never could be the mother you wanted." To which apology Annamarie replies in her usual fault-finding voice, "I guess I didn't expect anything, and you kept giving it to me anyway. When I was a teenager you were always making me drink barley fiber so I wouldn't have colon cancer when I was fifty. All I wanted was Cokes and Twinkies like the other kids'" (Homeland 144).

An equally long, expressed by speakers equally undistinguished, "Bereaved Apartments" conveys the partial story of a gable-ended house and a ramshackle duplex (the source of the title, since each half has lost something essential). The lead character, who is the occupant of the house, filled with the debris of life, is Nola Rainey, sometimes said to be crazy. Mrs. Rainey claims she is being stolen from—hundreds of times, whether the theft be of her tea or her valuable furniture. The two occupants of the duplex ("a 1929 Meredeth bungalow with a Deco fireplace") are more ordinary characters, Sulie, on parole from Women's Correctional Prison, who does odd jobs and finds herself called on frequently to help Mrs. Rainey; and Gilbert McClure, the ex-husband of an antiques dealer who is himself a collector. When Gilbert begins courting Sulie, it is only because he wants to gain entry to Mrs. Rainey's household. His plan succeeds. Soon Sulie needs his help there: he sees the treasure now collected in the attic of the house. "In the furniture alone he recognizes five decades of perfection, and only a small part of it is visible. Cabriole legs turn out like demure ankles under dust skirts; glimpses of ivory-inlaid dresser tops gleam under pyramids of japanned boxes; and Gilbert's heart is struck with the deepest envy he's ever known" (Homeland 161).

Much of the plot hangs on Gilbert's physical handsomeness. He reminds Nola of a movie star. She shows him the cream-colored man's felt hat with a dark purple band ("Vallon and Argod, World Exposition"), the hat her husband wore for their wedding. Later that day, Gilbert steals the hat, which would bring him $1,500 in resale value. Sulie sees the theft. She cannot accuse him but she has no heart for his visits any longer. The story ends with Nola's having a heart attack, then waiting for her son from out of state, reconciled to giving up the house and being cared for. Similarly, Sulie is packing up as well, moving out of the duplex and away from the Gilbert who wanted only to spy and to possess.

Another lengthy story is based on Kingsolver's months in the Canary Islands. "Jump-Up Day" takes the reader into the convent where adolescent

Jericha lives, after the death of her mother and her father's return to England for convalescence from bilharzia. Even though Sister Armande cares for her, and St. Lucia is filled with interesting customs, Jericha fears being so alone. Frightened by the dancer dressed as "Jump Up," "his body, hair, eyelids all cracked and seamed with the thickness of whitewash," she realizes that she has not even known this was a holiday—she is so overwhelmed by the cultural differences that translate as sheer fear. Dreaming of the spirits of St. Lucia, Jericha becomes a friend of The Obeah Man and her adventures with him as they cast spells together bespeak the impossibility of the child's attaining any real knowledge, so long as she is so terrifyingly alone.

The two strongest stories in Kingsolver's collection are the prize-winning "Rose-Johnny" and the original story, "Homeland," which Kingsolver often chooses to open a reading—the story on which she labored for a decade, once she had discovered the fiction of Bobbie Ann Mason and had learned, accordingly, to trust her own intimate and local knowledge. Kingsolver has often spoken about her discovery of Mason: "I suddenly understood that what moved me about those stories was not so much the style or the execution: it was the respect that she has for her people—her characters who are her people—and the simple fact that she deemed them worthy of serious literature. My jaw sort of dropped open, and I just walked around for weeks thinking, 'I almost threw that away.' I have this wonderful thing, this place I come from, this life of mine, that I've been trying to ignore. Not just ignore, that I've been trying to pretend never existed." She continued, "What moves me most…is that when her characters speak, I hear them exactly. I'm hearing exact inflections, and it makes me homesick. I would say, for me, that's not what I'm trying to do as a writer. What I'm trying to do is…[convey] that burden of truth, of people who have had their voices stolen from them" (Beattie 157–8).

A decade later, Kingsolver added a comment about the way she is affected by her home country: "It's the only place on earth where the birds sound right, and people do too… The natural history and culture of Southern Appalachia were the most appealing and defining elements of my childhood" (Listen 330–1). And yet, to avoid speaking in every piece of fiction through the voice and language of Taylor Greer, Kingsolver chose a number of different kinds of women characters.

"Rose-Johnny" appeared in *The Virginia Quarterly Review*, and Kingsolver received a check for $300—at which point she wrote in her diary, on an otherwise blank page, "I am a writer." She also spent most of the check outfitting herself with supplies for the task ahead.

In one of her most complex stories, Kingsolver meshed the language of the unsophisticated speakers with their geography. In this tale of cruelty based on racial and sexual differences, and a small town's abhorrence of those differences, the ten-year-old observer character, Georgeann, watches what becomes of the admittedly low-born but unvanquished Rose-Johnny.

Georgeann speaks one recognizable language; Rose-Johnny, another. They are secret friends, even though Georgeann's school teacher aunt has warned her about the title character, said to be "Lebanese" (rather than "lesbian") in the view of the proper women of the town. In Georgeann's musing, "I was coming to understand that I would not hear the truth about Rose-Johnny from Aunt Minnie or anyone else. I knew, in a manner that went beyond the meanings of words I could not understand, that she was no more masculine than my mother or my aunt, and no more lesbian than Lebanese. Rose-Johnny was simply herself, and alone" (Homeland 218).

In the saga of the town's vendetta against the ethnically mixed Rose-Johnny, Kingsolver at first gives the reader some false comfort in thinking that Georgeann can befriend Rose-Johnny. In the story's denouement, however, the town wins. Mary Etta, Georgeann's older sister, is nearly raped by town boys because they think *she* is the sister who has become friends with Rose-Johnny. And Rose-Johnny and her grandfather quietly disappear, as does their store.

The story of Southern convention leading to enmity convinces not merely because of its narrative, but because of the intersection of specific idioms within the conflict. Kingsolver's method here differs from the effects she created in "Homeland," when Great Mam's infrequent bouts of language were in keeping with the ritualized tone of a native culture. When Great Mam, of Cherokee blood, says to her granddaughter, "If it's important, your heart remembers," the sonority is a piece with the rest of the text (Homeland 6).

Not dissimilar from "Rose-Johnny" in some ways, "Homeland" opens with a carefully paced description (on which Kingsolver had worked for years, by her own admission). "My great-grandmother belonged to the Bird Clan. Hers was one of the fugitive bands of Cherokee who resisted capture in the year that General Winfield Scott was in charge of prodding the forest people from their beds and removing them westward. Those few who escaped his notice moved like wildcat families through the Carolina mountains, leaving the ferns unbroken where they passed, eating wild grapes and chestnuts, drinking when they found streams. The ones who could not travel, the aged and the infirm and the very young, were hidden in deep cane thickets where they would remain undiscovered until they were bones. When the people's hearts could not bear any more, they laid their deerskin packs on the ground and settled again" (Homeland 1).

Poemlike, Kingsolver's paean to the refugees of the "Trail of Tears" strikes a chord of impassioned warmth. (Differently phrased than Annawake's description of this long horror in *Pigs in Heaven*, the third person narrator here seems to be one with what she calls "the forest people.") Kingsolver relates that she read Cherokee legends "from morning to night, and got a rhythm and a tone of voice in my mind" (Backtalk 158). She had also given up making Great Mam a personal, family-oriented character: she wanted this language to be suitable for the narrative, and for the strong woman who so seldom spoke.

The effective rhythms continue unabated: "They called their refugee years The Time When We Were Not, and they were forgiven, because they had carried the truth of themselves in a sheltered place inside the flesh, exactly the way a fruit that has gone soft still carries inside itself the clean, hard stone of its future" (Homeland 1–2).

Once the preamble has been voiced/spoken, the narration turns to Gloria St. Clair (nee Murray). She is the great-great-granddaughter of Great Mam, the woman who had lived with her family in Morning Glory, a coal town, for the last two years of her life. Calling Gloria "Waterbug," she told stories filled with essential wisdom: "Great Mam says the way to remember something you forgot is to turn your back on it. Say, 'The small people came dancing. They ran through the woods today.' Talk about what they did, and then whatever it was you forgot, they'll bring it back to you" (Homeland 16).

> Gloria brought Great Mam morning glories: "Surprise," I announced. "These are for you." The flowers were already wilting in my hand.
>
> "You shouldn't have picked those," she said.
>
> "They were a present." I sat down, feeling stung.
>
> "Those are not mine to have and not yours to pick," she said, looking at me, not with anger but with intensity. Her brown pupils were as dark as two pits in the earth. "A flower is alive, just as much as you are. A flower is your cousin. Didn't you know that?"
>
> I said, No ma'am, that I didn't.
>
> "Well, I'm telling you now, so you will know. Sometimes a person has got to take a life, like a chicken's or a hog's when you need it. If you're hungry, then they're happy to give their flesh up to you because they're your relatives. But nobody is so hungry they need to kill a flower ... "

Later in the conversation Great Mam holds with the child, the old woman tells her to throw the flowers over the porch fence. "I threw the flowers over the railing in a clump, and came back, trying to rub the purple and green juices off my hands onto my dress. In my mother's eyes, this would have been the first sin of my afternoon. I understood the difference between Great Mam's rules and the Sunday-school variety, and that you could read Mother's

Bible forward and backward and never find where it said it's a sin to pick flowers because they are our cousins."

"I'll try to remember," I said.

"I want you to," said Great Mam. "I want you to tell your children."

"I'm not going to have any children," I said. "No boy's going to marry me. I'm too tall. I've got knob knees."

"Don't ever say you hate what you are." She tucked a loose sheaf of black hair behind my ear. "It's an unkindness to those that made you. That's like a red flower saying it's too red, do you see what I mean?"

"I guess," I said.

"You will have children. And you'll remember about the flowers," she said, and I felt the weight of these promises fall like a deerskin pack between my shoulder blades. (Homeland 11–12)

Kingsolver's "Homeland" is a long story, but passages like this scene punctuate it and leave the reader immersed in the quiet voice of the old woman who acknowledges the world's wisdom—and her own, without any sense of false modesty. The irony that Gloria's family drives Great Mam (and all the family) to the town they think was her homeplace—only for her to tell them she has never been in this part of the state—adds no humor, only pathos. Returned home to Morning Glory, Gloria and Great Mam once again spend late nights outside on the porch, sometimes not talking, sometimes listening to her parents talking inside the house. Great Mam said at one point, "In the old days . . . whoever spoke the quietest would win the argument" (Homeland 21).

Thinking back to the pride she felt in the final version of "Homeland," Kingsolver acknowledged that "'Homeland' expresses my reason for being a writer. I hope that story tells about the burden and the joy and the responsibility of holding on to the voices that are getting lost . . . That's what I want to do as a writer . . . That's the reason I live" (Backtalk 158).

"Homeland" closes with a brief account of Great Mam's funeral, to which Gloria's mother carried a jar holding water and six white gladioli. And Gloria meditated, "As soon as we turned our backs, the small people would come dancing and pick up the flowers. They would kick over the jar and run through the forest, swinging the hollow stems above their heads, scattering them like bones" (Homeland 22).

In the power of this title story, and in echoes of it in "Rose-Johnny" and a few other stories, critics saw the stylist that Kingsolver had already become. For those who considered *The Bean Trees* something of an accidental success, page after page of *Homeland and Other Stories* gave them more information about the writer's incipient strengths. As Russell Banks commented in his *New York Times* review of this collection, Kingsolver might be something like Grace Paley in that her work shows "a determination to find value and meaning in a world where value and meaning have all but disappeared...Like Paley, Ms. Kingsolver mixes argot with aphorism, sexual frankness with delicate high-mindedness, the purely personal with class consciousness" (Banks 16). Few readers forgot the majestic rhythms of Kingsolver's "Homeland" and the way it sounded in their ears with unquestionable, idiomatic authority.

As Kingsolver comments when she reviewed Lee Smith's story collection, *Me and My Baby View the Eclipse*, "Getting a short story off the ground and safely landed again in its few allotted pages is a risk. In a collection of stories, the risk is multiplied, like an airplane flight that includes many stops: There are just that many more chances for failure...It's a rare collection that delivers its passenger smoothly from first page to last without a few hard landings" (Los Angeles Times 2).

6

Kingsolver as Essayist—A Different Expertise

*What keeps me awake at the wheel is the thrill of trying something
completely new with each book. I'm not a risk-taker in life ... but
as a writer I definitely choose the fast car, the impossible rock face,
the free fall.*

Web 2013

When Kingsolver was accumulating materials for books that HarperCollins
would be interested in publishing after the triumph of both *The Bean Trees*
and *Animal Dreams*, she agreed with her agent, Frances Goldin, that her
essays would make a strong collection. To those already published—at least
those of the published essays that she liked—she added seven more prose
pieces that covered unexplored topics. To everyone's surprise, including that
of the author, *High Tide in Tucson, Essays from Now or Never*, became another
best-seller.

Maureen Meharg Kentoff summarized the response to this 1995 essay
collection by pointing out that the book showed the way Kingsolver worked:
"With a keen eye trained on the zeitgeist, Barbara Kingsolver stands out as
a popular author whose work has persistently questioned the paradigms
of moral certitude, material meritocracy, and cultural dominance that
constitute 'the American way.'" She does this in unexpected ways (as she does
in her fiction), writing prose that is "unconventional, thought-provoking,
and compellingly readable" (in Leder 47).

According to critic Sandra Ballard, these essays reach beyond being
merely instructive because they take on a larger purpose: "Writing about
meaningful subjects—or making them meaningful by writing about them—
is at the heart of the essay form, especially as she [Kingsolver] practices it"
(Ballard 19).

Most reviewers at the time of the book's publication responded to
the writer's inclusion of the personal, so that the essays were never dull
compendiums of information. For instance, in "Reprise," one of the newly
written essays (which interests readers because it begins with a description of

the author's second marriage to Steven Hopp), the personal is folded in with
a succinct, poetic description of the importance of human belief:

> What to believe in, exactly, may never turn out to be half as important as
> the daring act of belief. A willingness to participate in sunlight, and the
> color red. An agreement to enter into a conspiracy with life, on behalf of
> both frog and snake, the predator and the prey, in order to come away
> changed. (High Tide 268)

Again, Kentoff praises *High Tide* as being "a collection of personal narratives
in which she balances social criticism—one that refuses to settle for blind
optimism or misdirected nostalgia—with her hopeful determination that
social progress is, in fact, achievable" (in Leder 48). Comparing Kingsolver
as essayist with such feminist writers as Donna Haraway and Rita Felski,
Kentoff places the art of today's essay into a rarefied intellectual category.

Kingsolver herself said that she saw the essay collection as unified (as if it
were a complete and intentional "book"). She opens the title essay (and gives
a gloss to the title itself) by telling the story of Buster, the hermit crab who
came from the Bahamas hidden in some sea shells for Kingsolver's daughter.
Cared for diligently, given water, food, and impeccable shelter, the hermit
crab who should never have lived in the Arizona desert survived and became
a part of Kingsolver's small family. Placed at the start of both the collection
and its title essay, the story of Buster takes on that resonant metaphoric image
that will link seemingly disparate essays, one to another.

"High Tide in Tucson" is one of Kingsolver's incremental essays.
Unusually long, it juxtaposes segments of Buster's story with thematically
related pieces from the author's life and philosophy: her having to chase
three thieves from her kitchen (they had entered while she was busily
writing), her backpacking in the Eagle Tail Mountains, her resolution to
carry on with raising her daughter no matter what kind of shambles her
marriage was in. As she wrote toward the end of the essay, "Every one of
us is called upon, probably many times, to start a new life. A frightening
diagnosis, a marriage, a move, loss of a job or a limb or a loved one,
a graduation, bringing a new baby home: it's impossible to think at first
how this all will be … In my own worst seasons I've come back from the
colorless world of despair by forcing myself to look hard, for a long time,
at a single glorious thing: a flame of red geranium outside my bedroom
window. And then another: my daughter in a yellow dress … Like a stroke
victim retraining new parts of the brain to grasp lost skills, I have taught
myself joy, over and over again" (High Tide 15). Positioning her agenda of
abstracted emotions so that it rides close by the "progress" Buster, the crab,

makes in the weirdly new Arizona desert, the author leaves her readers, once again, with the sense of forward motion.

Even when Kingsolver admits to being at a low point, during the failure of her first marriage, she finds ways to write about the process of divorce without invading the privacy of the two people involved. She chooses instead to write about how rare monogamy is among animals. In "Semper Fi," she charts the existence of infidelity (without linking the animal world to her own). Her coined term is "situational loyalty," and she points out that couples show more of it when the parenting demand is highest (as with newborn birds, voles, mice, and pigs). Otherwise, she admits "biologists are discovering that monogamy is rarer than unicorns in the animal world. Many species touted as mating for life—swans, bluebirds, Australian fairy wrens–are turning out to be hard-core sneaks. The tools of molecular genetics, similar to the tests used in human paternity suits, have shown that in the nest of the average fairy wren, one egg in five is sired by another wren's mate" (High Tide 68, 70).

One of her most interesting, and comic, essays is connected with the topic of painful divorce. "Confessions of a Reluctant Rock Goddess" describes the author's joining the Rock Bottom Remainders band, a group formed to play at the 1992 American Booksellers convention. The group then did a two-week tour during May of 1993, traveling from Boston to Miami. With Stephen King, Ridley Pearson, Ted Bartimus, Amy Tan, Dave Barry, and others, with Kingsolver on keyboard, the group played "These Boots Are Made for Walkin'," "Louie, Louie," "Nadine," "Money," and other crowd pleasers. The experience was about both getting back to some music and, primarily, about belonging. As she wrote in the *High Tide* essay, "Book tours are as lonely as a prison term … [W]hat they don't offer is the chance to belong to a group." In contrast, this was camaraderie—"I must have sought it out in the middle of my dark winter, like a pale seedling straining for sun, because somewhere in the basement of my boarded-up heart I knew it was what I needed" (High Tide 203).

The second essay in the collection helps to convey the sense of hopefulness. "Creation Stories" opens with Kingsolver's memory of the first drenching summer rain she experienced in the hot Arizona summer (the summer she describes as being so hot the tarmac at the airport may liquefy). Her point, however, is that between her present house and the town center, she travels 12 miles that cross through many different villages— each with its own set of beliefs and customs. The Yaqui village where she spends Easter. The Santa Cruz river with its Mexican residents. And the leading last paragraph which takes her readers to the essay built around her adventures with the javelinas ("woolly pigs," "peccaries," "pigs"). "Making Peace" recounts her fight for her garden produce, as well as her hollyhocks.

Kingsolver was waging a nightly battle: "Pioneering takes patience," she told herself in reassurance. Nothing worked. The pigs would eat every plant she managed to grow. Until ... until she built a fenced-in courtyard, and began feeding the pigs table scraps. They preferred the scraps; they no longer broke down barriers to reach her plants.

If this essay about human and animal territoriality seems a charming read, which it does, the praise should lay with the Kingsolver method, which is telling stories. As she recently wrote, "I'm a storyteller. Everything I write is a story. My novels are long stories or bunches of stories all kind of bound together at the center with twine. My short stories are stories. My poems are little true stories, sort of emotionally intense stories. My non-fiction is always stories. Even when I do some travel writing for the New York Times, what I find is I can't write a regular, straight travel article ... I have to write a story" (Kentucky Writers).

High Tide in Tucson is a substantial book, filled with essays on various topics. It is also a palpable, comfortable book. Many of Kingsolver's essays (i.e., stories) are autobiographical; some are about writing; others about Kingsolver's travels to Africa, Hawaii, and the Bahamas, but more are about the ecological concerns relevant to both Kingsolver's home states of Kentucky and Arizona—as well as the global home place. Incipient in this 1995 collection, these themes will become the centers of her novels—especially *Prodigal Summer* and *Flight Behavior*—as well as of the essays in her second collection, *Small Wonder* and of both her prose material in *Last Stand* and her food ecology testament, *Animal, Vegetable, Miracle: A Year of Food Life*. In 1995, reading through *High Tide*, readers knew only that they were inordinately moved by such essays as "The Memory Place," "In Case You Ever Want to Go Home Again," and "The Forest in the Seeds." Several of these come toward the close of the book; as she had noted in her preface, there should be a sense of progression: more than a few of the essays "connect with and depend on their predecessors" (High Tide x).

Some of these essays, too, are styled to be comic. While Kingsolver may not want the world of readers to laugh at her somewhat idiosyncratic taste in clothes, she is not above admitting the years she anguished over her lack of style. "Life Without Go-Go Boots" describes her ugly-duckling status during high school, just as "How Mr. Dewey Decimal Saved My Life" rhapsodizes the joys the shy (and very tall) young woman felt when the province of the school library was entrusted to her care. "The Muscle Mystique" recounts the sorrows of having very little upper-body strength, and the hours spent cultivating that strength in a commercial (and very visible) gym. In "The Household Zen," she describes—and defends—her style of "lick and a promise" housekeeping.

Although there is comedy in nearly all of these essays, many would not be labeled "comic." The essays about living in the Canary Islands, for instance— "Somebody's Baby," "Jabberwocky," and "Paradise Lost"—focus on the fact that "People there like kids" so her identity as the mother of a winsome child was pleasant (High Tide 99). She describes the difficulty of building self-esteem in a child, and uses as an illustration of her own lack of that, the story of her remorse at 16 when she failed her driving test. But she also segues into the warmth toward children that her family evinced: "My grandfathers on both sides lived in households that were called upon, after tragedy struck close to home, to take in orphaned children and raise them without a thought" (High Tide 101). These pieces are like "The Vibrations of Djoogbe" and "Infernal Paradise" in that they are more personal than most travel essays.

As if writing an abbreviated autobiography, Kingsolver sometimes interjects her personal life, often unexpectedly. "In my life I've had frightening losses and unfathomable gifts: A knife in my stomach. The death of an unborn child. Sunrise in a rain forest. A stupendous column of blue butterflies rising from a Greek monastery. A car that spontaneously caught fire while I was driving it. The end of a marriage, followed by a year in which I could barely understand how to keep living … " (High Tide 7). When she writes about driving her old yellow Renault from Kentucky toward Arizona, she notes, "I never cease to long in my bones for what I left behind" (High Tide 6). "I've never gotten over high school, to the extent that I'm still a little surprised that my friends want to hang out with me … I gained things from my rocky school years: A fierce wish to look inside of people. An aptitude for listening. The habit of my own company … From the vantage point of invisibility I explored the psychology of the underdog, the one who can't be what others desire but who might still learn to chart her own hopes" (High Tide 42). "On the day we met, my mate and I, he invited me to take a walk in the wooded hills of his farm … I told him I loved the woods, and he took my word for that, and headed lickety-split up the mountainside. I ran after, tearing through blackberry briars with the options of getting hopelessly lost or keeping up. He did remember, after all, that I was behind him. When he reached the top of the mountain he waited, and we sat down together on a rock, listening to the stillness in the leaves" (High Tide 268–9).

This evolution of an essay form that includes the highly personal—a kind of seeming transparency—may have stemmed from the fact that in Kingsolver's fiction, she seldom, if ever, used real people as models for characters. There is no "Barbara Kingsolver" in her fiction, but there is such a figure throughout her non-fiction works and her essays. One of the reasons readers made best-sellers out of those essay collections (both *High Tide in Tucson* and *Small Wonder*) was that they could FIND *Kingsolver* in those pages.

Sometimes, the insertions are less autobiographical, but they ring true as the author's opinion—in contrast to the more objective view of Kingsolver as essayist. In "The Spaces Between," for example, an essay largely about the Heard Museum and Native American culture, the author notes, "[L]ately we've been besieged with a new, bizarre form of racism that sets apart all things Native American as object of either worship or commerce...What began as anthropology has escalated to fad, and it strikes me that assigning magical power to a culture's every belief and by-product is simply another way of setting those people apart" (High Tide 148).

One of Kingsolver's best essays combines these techniques to create its impact. "The Memory Place" is about her Kentucky homeland, but it is also about herself as mother (and daughter and granddaughter) and about the pristine imagination of her young child. It is one of the earliest of her ecological essays, focusing in detail on the "jigsaw puzzle of public and private property" that is the Kentucky watershed she describes in an opening that is itself near poetry:

> This is the kind of April morning no other month can touch: a world tinted in watercolor pastels of redbud, dogtooth violet, and gentle rain. The trees are beginning to shrug off winter; the dark, leggy maple woods are shot through with gleaming constellations of soft white dogwood blossoms. The road winds through deep forest near Cumberland Falls, Kentucky, carrying us across the Cumberland Plateau toward Horse Lick Creek. Camille is quiet beside me in the front seat, until at last she sighs and says, with a child's poetic logic, "This reminds me of the place I always like to think about." (High Tide 170)

Setting the scene that blends the imaginary with the real, Kingsolver offers her reader a clearly detailed description of what should be preserved in this Kentucky locale:

> Deep in the woods at the bottom of a hollow we find Cool Springs, a spot where the rocky ground yawns open to reveal a rushing underground stream. The freshet merely surfaces and then runs away again, noisily, under a deeply undercut limestone cliff. I walk back into the cave as far as I can, to where the water roars down and away, steep and fast. I can feel the cold slabs of stone through the soles of my shoes ... Farther down the road we find the 'swirl hole'—a hidden place in a rhododendron slick where the underground stream bubbles up again from the deep. The water is nearly icy and incredibly blue as it gushes up from the bedrock. We sit and watch, surrounded by dark rhododendrons and hemlocks,

and mesmerized by the repetitious swirling of the water. Camille tosses in tiny hemlock cones; they follow one another in single file along a spiral path, around and around the swirl hole and finally away, downstream, to where this clear water joins the opaque stream of Horse Lick Creek itself. (High Tide 176)

Kingsolver continues, directly, with no evasion, "The pollution here is noticeable."

It is this mix of poetic and personal involvement with the scientific detail—what critic Christine Cusick calls Kingsolver's writing about "the poetry of science"—that makes essays such as this memorable, no matter where they are published. Cusick continues, "Through her narrative engagement with memory, story, and place, Kingsolver offers an environmental ethic of bioregionalism, ultimately suggesting that when humans begin to understand their place within an evolving biological context, their actions will move toward the sustenance of and care for their human and non-human communities" (in Leder 213–14). Although the essay in question appeared in the 1995 collection, Cusick moves it into the twenty-first century, saying that today's immediate "environmental crisis … calls us to honor our origins, to remember our stories, and to become reacquainted with our biological communities."

Given Kingsolver's training in the sciences, Cusick also notes that the author's forte is describing the "human relationship to nonhuman nature," descriptions enhanced by "her empirical skills of perception as a trained evolutionary biologist" (in Leder 214). She states that the author uses her "biologist's acuity" to bridge the human narrative with "the ecological explication."

Enthusiastic about "The Memory Place" as well as "The Not-So-Deadly Sin," "The Spaces Between," and "The Forest in the Seeds," Cusick joins with *New York Times* critic Casey King to praise the nonargumentative stance Kingsolver usually adopts. King points to the fact that Kingsolver does not try to upset her readers; he admired her "language rich with music and replete with good sense" (King 1995). Paul Trachtman also compliments the author on tackling such tough subjects as the lack of educational opportunities in Kentucky, and still keeping her poised and relaxed stance: "There is nothing artless about it, and the literary mind at work becomes visible now and then in the sudden splash of a figure of speech" (Trachtman 24). The pervasive thread of enthusiasm throughout reviews of *High Tide in Tucson* is that Kingsolver writes essays as if they were significant works of art, and that her repeated insistence on the beauties of the natural world connects many of her separable pieces.

It is Cusick who respects the uses Kingsolver makes of the personal, stating that "Our imaginative spaces begin with our own places of origin, our own locale, however these places might change with time and need ... Kingsolver's essays simultaneously articulate the biology, the animal nature of human beings that exceeds the capacity for rational thought, which we so often privilege as our salvation" (in Leder 221, 23).

In another often-praised essay, "The Forest in the Seeds," Kingsolver prefaces her essay with a meditation on Henry David Thoreau's last two years of his notebooks, excerpted and summarized by Bradley P. Dean (*Faith in a Seed*). Admittedly respectful of the life Thoreau had lived—and had attempted to live during a century when the natural world was likely to be accepted instead of revered, Kingsolver adopts a somewhat more scientific tone for her musings. From the pages of previously unpublished writings, she chooses Thoreau's last important manuscript, "The Dispersion of Seeds," which describes in meticulous detail "methods of seed ripening and dispersal, germination, and growth of a great many species: pines, willows, cherries, milkweeds, eight kinds of tick clover, and virtually every other plant known to the neighborhood of Concord, Massachusetts" (High Tide 237). She praises his thoroughness, compares his accomplishments to those of Charles Darwin, and realizes that it is the *way* Thoreau *expresses* his discoveries that transcends most other kinds of science writing. In the midst of this essay, Kingsolver abruptly stops, reminding her readers that the natural world is *slow*: to learn to see these unmistakable miracles requires patience—in contrast to what she terms "an unforeseeable glut of hurry" that dominates today's living. Speaking directly to her readers, the author writes, "I also long for all of us to rescue ourselves from the tyranny of impatience ... we seem to be running full tilt through the air beyond the edge of the cliff with our minds on something else." What our attitudes mean, in short, is that "As a nation we will never defer to the endangered spotted owl (let alone declare a National Squirrel Holiday, as Thoreau suggested) until we are much more widely educated. But the things we will have to know—concepts of food chain, habitat, selection pressure and adaptation and the ways all species depend on others—are complex ideas that just won't fit into a thirty-second spot" (High Tide 240–1).

Similarly, in the essay titled "Semper Fi," the author critiques Edward O. Wilson's "incendiary book, *On Human Nature*, in which he asserted that there are biological bases for a large number (he implies, all) of the characteristics that are general enough to be called our 'nature'" (High Tide 72). Although Kingsolver had as a prospective doctoral student applied to the program at Harvard, where Wilson taught, she decided that this ground-breaking book may have gone too far—insisting that nobody can catalogue all the possible human motives. She is particularly defensive about his belief that gender is a learned attitude. Set against Wilson are Stephen Jay Gould's *The Mismeasure of Man* and Richard Herrnstein and Charles Murray's *The Bell Curve*, other treatises within several hundred years of history that suggest the superiority of the Caucasian race.

Representative of several other essays in *High Tide*, "Semper Fi" allows Kingsolver to state her beliefs in an essay that seems to be partly historical review; in an essay titled "In the Belly of the Beast," she takes the same tactic to comment on the political stances of the US government. Here, her subject is the defunct Titan missile program based near Tucson, Arizona—in the era of nuclear missiles, submarines, and warheads, as well as Star Wars weapons research system. Billions of dollars went into the development and the testing of these, from the early 1980s until close to the twenty-first century. She concludes this essay with an account of her trip to Hiroshima, touring another bomb museum—this one representative of complete annihilation. As she closes her meditation, Kingsolver points out directly, "In 1994, half a century after the bombing of Hiroshima, we spent $150 billion on the business and technology of war—nearly a tenth of it specifically on nuclear-weapons systems" (High Tide 219). In this essay, she allows readers to draw sorrowful conclusions of their own.

In the essay titled "Jabberwocky," Kingsolver describes the reasons she moved for a year to the Canary Islands (i.e., southern Spain), angered about the US involvement in the first Gulf War. As she does in several other essays about that year, she tries to approach the concept that a writer—*any* writer, or, more generally, any *person*—might have objections to the on-going attitudes of her home country. In this essay, she tries to describe her antagonism to the dismissive use of the word "political." Even as she explains that "Good art is political, whether it means to be or not, insofar as it provides the chance to understand points of view alien to our own" (High Tide 234). In short, "a thing runs counter to prevailing assumptions"—and that makes it "political." "If 60% of us support the war, then the expressions of the other 40% are *political*—and can be disallowed in some contexts for that reason alone ... Cultural workers in the US are prone to be bound and gagged by a dread of being called political, for that word implies that art is not quite pure. Real art, the story goes, does not endorse a point of view. This is utter nonsense, of course ... and also the most thorough and invisible form of censorship I've ever encountered" (High Tide 229).

But Kingsolver did return, and does a riff about the way one cannot love and leave, one must stay loving and return. She points out that most of the international writers who have won the Nobel Prize for Literature did so taking on the politics of their times, and she points out in defense that literature can be about "environmental ruin, child abuse, or the hypocrisy of US immigration policy." Except for US readers, the rest of the world recognizes that it is legitimate to mix "art with conscience" (High Tide 229). There is a comic postscript to her defense in this essay, as she notes that "Barry Lopez is called political, and he writes about dying ecosystems and great blue herons and wolves" (High Tide 228).

Broadening the themes of some of these essays to include such matters as Kingsolver's defense of the political brings at least a few of her essays into the camp Christine Cusick describes as "*intellectual* scientific explorations" as well as biologic ones. In summary, "Human beings' evolutionary connection to the land is not exclusively biological; what we learn from a truly integrated understanding of natural history is that it is simultaneously connected to cultural histories" (in Leder 225).

7

Kingsolver as Poet

*When a poem does arrive, I gasp as if an apple had fallen into my hand,
and give thanks for the luck involved. Poems are everywhere, but easy to
miss.*

Small Wonder 229

Self-conscious about trying to straddle some imaginary line between art
that was or was not political, Kingsolver surveyed the poems she had already
written. The year was 1991 and both *The Bean Trees* and *Animal Dreams* had
won prizes. She was also asked regularly to write essays and opinion pieces
for newspapers and journals, the essays that would eventually be published
as *High Tide in Tucson*. But here too was an invitation from Seattle's Seal
Press to submit to them a book of her poems. Chomping against the bit
of what a *woman writer's* poem collection might suggest, Kingsolver knew
that the many formal verses she had written in college would not appear in
any book of poetry: rather, as she commented later, her current poems were
"little steam vents on the pressure cooker." Later she further explained that
"poems are deeply felt moments that don't necessarily have a beginning or
an end" (Backtalk 161–2). "On the Morning I Discovered My Phone Was
Tapped" opens the poem of that title; "Maura, there were people who said
you should not/be born" begins the third stanza of "Your Mother's Eyes"; "I
am the dirt that feels the boot./I have starved until my hair fell out" opens
Part 3 of "The Loss of My Arms and Legs."

The reviewers for this collection of poems were not going to talk about its
author's *moderate* voice. Everything about the book was designed to disabuse
readers of either Kingsolver's complacency or her pacifism. If those were
qualities that smart writers tried to show, in this collection the author aimed
to talk plainly, simply, metaphorically, and angrily.

Kingsolver began by choosing a title that allowed her a visible degree of
disenfranchisement. *Another America/Otra America* was the book's title,
and that signal of alienation was combined with the fact that every poem
included appeared in both Kingsolver's English and Rebeca Cartes' Spanish
translation. Cartes, herself a Spanish-speaking poet and musician from

Chile, had relocated to Tucson, where she lives as a musician and a writer, and runs a translation service.

Never dismissive of the fact that the rich and prosperous America often hid a dark underbelly of poverty, violence, and want, Kingsolver's poems were themselves strengthened by the book's division into five parts. (These comments refer to the first edition, that published in 1992; the 1998 second edition included six new poems and two important prefaces—one by Margaret Randall, the other by Kingsolver.) Grouping the poems into thematic units was a service to readers and, as a further aide, Kingsolver chose as epigraphs, section by section, excerpts from other poets' works—writing by Carolyn Forché, for example, and Walt Whitman, and Sharon Olds.

Part I, "The House Divided," is introduced with Adrienne Rich's "These are the things that we have learned to do/Who live in troubled regions." Juxtaposed with a maxim from David Byrne ("If this is paradise/I wish I had a lawn mower."), the Rich lines are balanced so that the reader is prepared for some variety, or at least some emotional scope, in the poems that follow. "Deadline" opens the 1992 version of the collection. A call to arms, the poem describes the peace vigils that marked much of the 1990s (the poem is dated January 15, 1991); this often-anthologized poem recalls the sentiments in pre-Gulf War America. The speaker with her three-year-old daughter walks in a quiet march, "a breathless cold/ocean of candles." The poet remembers, "It has taken your whole self to bring her [the child] undamaged to this moment … " Stanza three begins,

> The polls have sung their opera of assent: the land
> wants war. But there is another America,
> candle-throated, sure as tide.
> Whoever you are, you are also this granite anger …

Perfectly illustrative of both the section title, "The House Divided," and the book's name, *Another America*, the "Deadline" to which the poet refers as she attempts to separate the pro-war faction from the peace faction, comes and goes, and leaves between the two groups only an indistinguishable scribble of words.

The five other poems gathered in Part I trace the "otherness" of US lives—the rich condescending to the poor in "What the Janitor Heard in the Elevator" the women's bodies so distorted in "Reveille" that the hostile speaker is described as

> the nippleless,
> the bloodless, sweatless woman … ;

and the three-part "Street Scenes" where two women speakers together are suspect, no matter what their circumstances.

Both "Waiting for the Invasion" and "Justicia" close the section with the recounting of sheer physical dread. In the first, the poet remembers the Russian threat in her tiny Kentucky town, its twin water towers painted black, "hoping to save us." The town *was* saved, as was the America of her childhood—but the child's capacity to fear remains.

Kingsolver opens Part II, "The Visitors," with Walt Whitman's lines about the country that "prepares with composure and good will" for its awaited visitors. Apparently ironic, the group of poems here dissect appearances from the reality of human beings and their often evil designs. "Refuge" is dedicated to Juana, an immigrant woman raped by the immigration officer who "welcomes" her, and then deports her. Kingsolver's long-lined paean "For Sacco and Vanzetti" recounts the 1927 execution, another travesty of justice that the Boston courts administered to the Italian immigrants, more guilty of unionizing than of robbery and murder. Kingsolver makes her readers remember as well "the Rosenbergs,/Ethel, her two babies torn/like knots from the cloth, screaming." As the poet mourns for the country that kills, often without proof, she laments,

> We have been dying all our lives.
> My tears are just for morning, washed up again
> on a shore of pounded bones ...

United States' injustice becomes global injustice in the remaining poems: "The Monster's Belly," dedicated to Ernesto Cardenal; "In Exile," for Rebeca; and "Escape" with its mention of Palestine and its theme of the poet's leaving a place (the United States) where sins still stain its altars.

For the poignantly despairing "The Lost," the third section of poems, Kingsolver chooses lines written by a California school pupil, Angelo Logan. In "American Biographies" the poet describes a mélange of fear and death. In "This House I Cannot Leave" Kingsolver uses the metaphor of the house—broken into and robbed—to create the despair of her own rape. "Ten Forty-Four" pictures the stridently impersonal police response to her call about that acquaintance rape. "Family Secrets" strikes a fearful portrait of the poet's sister-in-law's killer, "a man/who carried the skill of murder/in the muscles of his hands." Death is the constant theme throughout Part III.

"For Richard After all" limns a friend's suicide while the poet tried to lift him out of his dismaying sorrow. Instead, she remains

looking for the word that happened while I
didn't hear. A stone fallen in
deep water among so many other stones.

The tercet that closes this poem is Kingsolver as poet at her best, relying on a metaphor that is couched in the natural spoken language of a bereaved friend:

Richard left me with every other friend in my life:
to read them with care, to the end, like
borrowed books.

One of Kingsolver's best and widest-reaching poems closes this section about loss. "The Loss of My Arms and Legs" operates like a montage of film, one sacrifice joined to another: dismembered human beings, immolated Buddhist monks, women raped and murdered throughout the world, and finally, the poet who feels this amalgam of pain:

I'm told I cannot allow the wounds
of all the world to bleed
through my own body,
that I will have nothing left for my own...

Less sentimental than this image in the fourth segment of the poem might suggest, the fifth section opens,

I am the only animal
that can die a hundred times
and still fear death inside...

The poem closes with a couplet that stands as a clear directive: "As long as I continue to be cut,/ let me still bleed."

The disclaimer to all these poems of dread, loss, and grief is Kingsolver's Part IV. Entitled "The Believers," Part IV has as an epigraph a short excerpt from Sharon Olds, "somewhere in me too is the path/down to the creek gleaming in the dark, a/way out of there." Effortlessly lighter, this section in the 1992 edition is varied: "Bridges" uses a musically defined line arrangement; "Naming Myself" is a coming-to-identity work filled with inspiring history; "Apotheosis" is a quaint poem addressed to the poet's chickens; "Orang-outang" draws from Lamarck's scientific study of this animal, and the brief poem "Possession" speaks of the passion that connects two human beings:

The things I wish for are:
A color. A forest.
The devil and ice in my mouth.
Everything
that can't be owned ...

A rhythmically determined poem, this rare composition of sparse words shows Kingsolver's yen to experiment. In the 1998 edition, this section contains many more poems, and more of them speak of contentment.

The fifth section reverts to what is the dominant tone of the collection: "The Patriots" opens with an epigraph from Carolyn Forché's second book, her testament to her experiences in war-torn Central America. "It is either the beginning or the end/of the world, and the choice is ourselves/or nothing." This section opens with a memorial to the Nicaraguans "killed by the Contras, 1980–1990." Titled "Our Father Who Drowns the Birds," this is one of Kingsolver's strongest poems, and in some respects it is particularly well suited to its expression in Spanish. The varied line lengths create an essential speech rhythm format. It opens,

There is a season when all wars end:
when the rains come.
When the landscape opens its own eyes
and laughs at your talk of dying ...

(In the Cartes' translation, "Hay una epoca en que terminan las guerras/es la estacion de las lluvias/Cuando el paisaje abre sus ojos/y se rie de tu hablar de muerte.") Speaking through a long second stanza about the relinquishment of "ancient anger," the poet concludes her memorial with a reminder that the role of the poet is to give the children hope, saying that

On the eighth day God made justice.
On the eighth day God sent the rains
to the other America,
to drown the birds, and give us a fighting chance ...

The next two poems are equally powerful: "On the Morning I discovered My Phone Was Tapped" makes use of the legalese inherent in the warnings of officialdom ("If you have nothing to hide, they say") while "The Middle Daughter" brings rebellion to a more personal application: "This middle daughter believes/she will make history." "In the City Ringed with Giants" extends the imagery Kingsolver chose for her essay about the decommissioning of the Titan missiles, and it is followed by her expert chronicle of persecution: "The Blood Returns." In cadence reminiscent of Forché's longer-lined poems from *The Country Between Us,* Kingsolver balances the matter-of-fact terror of the tortured woman ("telling me how they pushed needles/under her fingernails") with the description of the "olive green camp/in the secret pines of Georgia" where the United States trains the military from that Central American country: "mutilate a body in six ways,/each one deadly." Emotionally, the poem collection ends here but characteristic of Kingsolver's eternally hopeful spirit, she adds two of her strongest "hope" poems as conclusion: "Remember the Moon Survives" and the gently rebuking "Your Mother's Eyes," dedicated to both the woman who was raped and then the child born of that rape. The resonance of some interior lines from the latter poem remains,

> ... Your mother said
> the seed is the least of a tree
> that has lived through several seasons.
> Even before the first bud opens, the seed
> is not what it was ...

In 1992, *Another America/Otra America* was an important, definitive (read *feminist* and *angry*) poem collection. As Priscilla Leder stated in her introduction to her collection of essays about Kingsolver's work, this poem collection was meant "to reveal the 'other' America of poverty and exploitation hidden from non-Americans by cultural exports such as *Dallas* ... In addition, the visual presence of Spanish embodies the cultural presence so inextricably a part of Kingsolver's adopted Southwest" (Leder 11).

Several years later Seal Press as publisher decided the book needed wider distribution and so they asked Margaret Randall to write a preface. Kingsolver too wrote an essay that served as an introduction; both prose pieces prefaced the 1998 publication of what was called the "second edition" of the book, to which were added six new poems.

In her "Introduction," Kingsolver explains that the Margaret Randall commentary was especially significant to her because—in the late 1980s—it was Randall to whom she sent the first poetry manuscript. (Randall had written a laudatory review of *The Bean Trees* for *Women's Review of Books,* but she was known throughout the world for her own activism, and her own poetry in defense of her political positions.) As Kingsolver said, Randall did "encourage me toward publication" after she had read that first poem manuscript years before. And, in keeping with the history Kingsolver provides in the latter part of her introduction, she felt in need of that encouragement.

She noted that she had come to Arizona for adventure, beautiful scenery, and new ways of living. But instead, and much more importantly, she found "another whole America. This was not picture postcards, or anything resembling what I had previously supposed to be American culture…I'd stumbled upon a borderland where people perished of heat by day and cold hostility by night" (Another xviii).

"This is where poetry and adulthood commenced for me." Discussing the Sanctuary movement, the plight of Central American and Latin American refugees, and the complicity of the US government in supporting the oppressive conditions in these people's native lands, Kingsolver learned both words and their duplicity. She closes her introduction with the politics that she credits for giving her many of these poems, "I believe there are wars in every part of every continent, and a world of clamor and glory in every life. This is mine…We live in a place where north meets south and many people are running for their lives, while many others rest easy with the embarrassments of privilege. Others, still, are trying to find a place in between, a place of honest living, where they can abide themselves and each other without howling in the darkness. My way of finding a place in this world is to write one" (Another xix).

Once the 1992 poetry collection had been published, Kingsolver received numerous requests that she discuss writing poetry—requests she often ducked, or drew a comparison with the writing of novels. As she said in the Pence interview, "Writing [poems] felt like a release of the enormous emotional pressuring of those events. Poetry is not for me an intentional thing; I don't plan it, it just happens. It's very different from my fiction. I approach fiction pretty architecturally; I work out the foundations and I build it" (Pence 19). As she wrote in the 1998 introduction to the collection, "poetry remains a mystery." It "approaches, pauses, then skirts around us like a cat…It is…communicated from one soul to another" (Another xvi). That same year, in a now-famous essay entitled "How Poems Happen," Kingsolver writes, "Poetry is an elementary grace that reassures us of what we know and socks us in the gut with what we don't. It sings us awake. It's irresistible. It's congenital" (Snodgrass 9).

To the second edition of her book, Kingsolver added one of her now most famous poems, and placed it first. "Beating Time" was written in response to a statewide change in graduation requirements that occurred in August, 1997. Students in Arizona no longer had a poetry requirement for graduation, and, in the poet's words, "metaphor and rhyme take time/from science." As she lambasts the ignorant governor for his decision, Kingsolver uses the natural world to re-inscribe the importance of the poem—"while the rain beats time." Beset with strictures in all provinces of the humanities, American culture would, eventually, be handicapped by the attention to science, engineering, and the mechanics of the world of knowledge.

The other poems Kingsolver added to the second edition are more family based. She salvages one of those many sonnets from her days of learning about poetry, "Portrait," but otherwise the new poems are devoted to descriptions of her pregnancy with Lily or poems that use Steven's name as dedication; these four new poems are placed in Part IV, "The Believers" section. The impact of *Another America* is changed slightly, but its power remains.

By adding the poems about Lily and those mentioning, or dedicated to, Steven, Kingsolver softens a perhaps unplanned emphasis on women as the victims of rape. In the central section, "The Lost," Kingsolver had grouped "American Biographies" with "This House I Cannot Leave" and "Ten Forty-Four," to create the literal sense of breaking and entering—or, as she said in an interview, women face innumerable risks, especially since "the United States is a culture that regards its victims harshly" (Perry 163). Bringing Anita Hill into her reference system, she says in another discussion, "A lot of women do everything their mothers told them and they still get raped. Anita Hill did everything she was supposed to do and she was still sexually harassed. People don't believe her because they want to believe that if it happened she caused it in some way or another. We can only counter that myth by going public" (Pence 20). The last section of poems in *Another America* reifies this theme, and Kingsolver uses the rape of the innocent women and girls to chart the insensible, and intentional, brutality of the military (or, the ostensible winners) in conquered territory. The poems *about* rape in actuality combine with those about rape as *metaphor* to give the poem collection its haunting imbroglio of waste.

Long after the second edition appeared, Kingsolver published three new poems—in the Kingsolver Conference issue of *The Iron Mountain Review*, Spring, 2012. "How to Shear a Sheep" is a wry, single verse statement on the process of the title; "Snow Day" glimpses a family with a small child, fascinated by the transformation occurring outside; and "How to Be Hopeful," which Kingsolver used in her 2008 Duke University Commencement Address of the same title—although in that instance, the poem was divided into short stanzas. Each of these poems is fluid, exact and exacting, and of a piece with Kingsolver's later essays.

In Margaret Randall's essay for the 1998 edition of *Another America*, she writes succinctly about the impulses that Kingsolver had absorbed during the 1980s and the 1990s as she composed this original group of poems. Randall begins her commentary by describing *today*'s "times of almost total cynicism ... of terrible waiting and uncertain progress" and rehearses, in contrast, decades when poets could be political. She refers to the work of June

Jordan, Alice Walker, and Adrienne Rich (particularly Rich's *What is Found There: Notebooks on Poetry and Politics*), and compares Kingsolver's poetry to theirs. She argues that keeping one's belief in either the power of poetry or the quest for justice is difficult, especially "since the loss of Nicaragua and the very mediated victories in El Salvador, Guatemala, parts of Africa and Asia..." When Randall insists on making the reverence for poetry an international condition, one thinks of Kingsolver's essays already published in *High Tide in Tucson*, and the others to come in her 2002 collection, *Small Wonder*. Randall concludes her "Foreword," "In the poems I find beauty and power, and the answers to the questions that without these lines would be paralyzing indeed" (Another xi–xiii).

Deeply immersed in the writing of *The Poisonwood Bible*, Kingsolver remained encouraged by responses like these to her role in emerging US politics. When HarperCollins published Newt Gingrich's *To Renew America* in 1995, Kingsolver was inordinately troubled; it took negotiations over an extended period of time to bring her to terms with the only publisher she had ever had for her fiction and essays. Finally, using all the "clout" she had accumulated (and referring to the fact that her 1993 *Pigs in Heaven* had sold over a million copies), Harper offered her a million-dollar advance. With that funding, Kingsolver—"in conjunction with Gerald Freund, Rona Jaffe, and Lila Wallace, established the biennial Bellwether Prize, the nation's largest literary prize, to honor American writers engaged in writing a novel of social change" (Snodgrass 23). It was a significant, and on-going, way for Kingsolver as writer to encourage writers like herself to urge readers toward valuable social and moral change.

8

The Poisonwood Bible as Apex

I sit down at my desk every day and make novels happen: I design them, construct them, revise them. I tinker and bang away with the confidence of an experienced mechanic, knowing that my patience and effort will get this troubled engine overhauled, and this baby will hum.

Small Wonder 228–9

Ambition never clouded Barbara Kingsolver's aim—nor did it impact the effectiveness of her art. From the initial success of *The Bean Trees*, she knew her quintessential novel would in some way deal with South Africa: not only had her mother and father taken their three children there in the 1960s but the country had for decades been at the center of her own, mature political concerns. Just as she had worked conscientiously to make Nicaraguan politics an integral part of her 1990 novel *Animal Dreams*, so she had spent nearly a decade developing her knowledge of Patrice Lumumba's heroic attempts to bring order to the Congo. Further, from the perspective of a creator of literature, a writer fascinated with narrative ways to bring many threads of story into a comprehensive whole, Kingsolver's working with South Africa gave her both materiel and writerly opportunity.

She did not intend to write a book about South Africa *per se*. She had never intended that. Kingsolver knew her own strengths as a writer. From the start, she had envisioned using a cast of contemporary US characters and letting them observe real existence on the African continent, where day-to-day safety was capricious, and part of their own survival would be dependent on their intimacy with African people. She knew her American characters would not be politicians: they would not be aide workers as Hallie Noline had been in *Animal Dreams*. And unlike her father, who had worked in Africa as a medical professional—as he had in the Caribbean,[1] these American

---

[1] In her prefatory "Author's Note" to *The Poisonwood Bible*, Kingsolver wrote, "I thank Virginia and Wendell Kingsolver, especially, for being different in every way possible from the parents I created for the narrators of this tale. I was the fortunate child of medical and public-health workers, whose compassion and curiosity led them to the Congo. They brought me to a place of wonders, taught me to pay attention, and set me early on a path of exploring the great, shifting terrain between righteousness and what's right" (x).

characters would not have the protection of a powerful international oversight group. They would be on their own, and if the circumstances of their lives in South Africa grew dangerous, they would have to rely on their own perspicuity (and perhaps their ingenuity), as well as on some as-yet-undetermined kindness of the African people.

As Kingsolver would later explain on her Web site, she was not attempting to write a political novel. Much as she admired Chinua Achebe's *Things Fall Apart* (1959), she was not working in that somewhat nostalgic, sometimes hortatory, vein. In her novel there would be no lamenting the modern fate of Africa—partly because Kingsolver did not consider herself well versed in either the country's twentieth century circumstances or its politics, and partly because during her years of developing the ideas for this book, she was not allowed access to Africa (Americans were not given visas to visit Zaire/the Congo, although she made two trips to Western and Central Africa in both 1992 and 1993, living with African families there).[2] Kingsolver's aim, then, was to use the continent—and the condition—of Africa as a means of creating "a political allegory." She intended, she said, to use "the small incidents of characters' lives [to] shed light on larger events in our world. The Prices carry into Africa a whole collection of beliefs about religion, technology, health, politics, and agriculture, just as industrialized nations have often carried these beliefs into the developing world in an extremely arrogant way, very certain of being right (even to the point of destroying local ideas, religion and leadership), even when it turns out—as it does in this novel—that those attitudes are useless, offensive or inapplicable" (Web 2001).

More critically, the author several times stated her philosophy about all cultures that could be described as "postcolonial." "I live in a society that grew prosperous from exploiting others. England has a strong tradition of postcolonial literature but here in the U.S., we can hardly even say the word 'postcolonial.' We like to think we're the good guys. So we persist in our denial, and live with a legacy of exploitation and racial arrogance that continues to tear people apart, in a million large and small ways. As long as I've been a writer I've wanted to address this, to try to find a way to own our terrible history honestly and construct some kind of redemption..." (Dialogue).

---

[2]   Recalling the Kingsolvers' time in 1963, the author pointed out that most of the residents "had never experienced electricity or plumbing." Later, when she went to Western and Central Africa, she was hoping "to experience the sounds, smells, textures, tastes, and domestic trivia...I stayed with local residents, walked through village markets to bargain and bring home the ingredients of a meal...A university student in Cotonou suffered my curiosity for days on end, giving me his frank views on religion, history, and family life that would permanently alter my universe" (Web 2013).

In addition to this underlying thematic interest, then, *The Poisonwood Bible* was a personal goal in Kingsolver's writing career. As she explained, "Some three decades after I lived in a village on the Wamba River in central Africa, I began writing a novel set in that place." She then ties this effort to her own novel-writing practices: "For me, the genesis of fiction is tenuous and labyrinthine and inscrutable and deeply inefficient … fiction is nothing but a collection of details piled carefully one upon another until they resemble a universe. If you leave out the details, you have a black hole … " (Off the Beaten 16–17).

The Poisonwood Bible, finally, for all its information about Africa and its people and languages, is not separable from Kingsolver's first three novels; it is a part of her characteristically recognizable fictional *oeuvre*. The primary characters—Nathan and Orleanna Price and their four daughters—are Southerners who come from the state of Georgia and do not recognize the limitations being Southern Americans might carry in the eyes of the international community. They are common people with minds and hearts devoted to their definition of service, both public and religious. Not very well educated, particularly in matters African, they are bright and earnest people, even though the war-damaged Nathan has always been too proud a man to accept help willingly. His choice to become a minister signals his need for power (albeit occupying a humble place in the hierarchy of either education or autocracy); his dominance both in life and in the construction—and his implicit destruction—of his family provides the means for his eventual downfall. Most men of the cloth do not use learning Bible verses as a means of punishing their children.

I doubt that Barbara Kingsolver ever saw the profession of religious ministry as negatively as *The Poisonwood Bible* presents it. Her animus is less a critique of either religious belief or of a person's aptitude for ministering to human needs than it is a scrutiny of the character of Nathan Price. When readers questioned what they called her "attacks" on Nathan, she explained, "I'm only opposed to arrogant proselytizing. Nathan Price is, indeed, an arrogant proselytizer, but he's not the only agent of Christianity here. His wife and daughters take different paths toward more open-minded paths of spirituality, and I called in Brother Fowles specifically to represent Christian mission in a kinder voice … My favorite character is Brother Fowles, whose role in the novel is to redeem both Christianity and the notion of mission. I happen to think religion is a wonderful thing" (Web 2001).

As a writer, Kingsolver uses an important strategy to take power away from Nathan Price: she does this first of all by taking *language* away from him. There are five narrators in the novel who speak, describe, and assess, and they all are women: Orleanna Price, the close to powerless wife and mother, and her four daughters. The reader "hears" Nathan only as words filtered through the voices and language choices of these five female speakers. When Leah, for example, praises her father's achievements, they radiate with the glow that her admiration for him creates. In the hemiplegic Adah's more cynical words, however, Nathan is seen to be a sham from the day he sets foot on this strange and inimical continent. At times Kingsolver juxtaposes one daughter's words with those of another, so the reader— always without direction—is given a basis of comparison. As Anne Marie Austenfeld notes, "The fact that *The Poisonwood Bible* consists entirely of *what women say*, moreover, puts into perspective the social and political conditions under which the characters in the novel live, and does so in ways unprecedented in novels about Africa written by male authors" (in Austenfeld 252).

As Kingsolver had throughout *The Bean Trees, Animal Dreams*, and *Pigs in Heaven*, here also she very consciously forces her readers to both acknowledge and pay attention to *gender*. Such an emphasis might seem strange for a book about an exotic continent (as subject matter for an American writer), a text in which readers might be expecting geographical concerns, anthropological details, and politics. *The Poisonwood Bible* seems at moments to be less "about" Africa than it is "about" the lives of a somewhat lost colony of five women. A kind of multiple-character *Robinson Crusoe*, Kingsolver's fourth novel stems in part from its author's early fascination with both Charles Dickens' worlds of social injustice as defined, usually, by class, and the luminous and wide-ranging *Little Women*, Louisa May Alcott's powerful domestic novel.[3] Kingsolver adapts the basic narrative principles of the quest novel (setting her characters adrift in an atmosphere of harsh danger and self-inflicted sabotage), adds an overlay of political injustice in the guise of factual historical information, and then lets her four young female protagonists tell both their own stories and the enveloping story of their family.

Most effectively, by giving her readers a fifth voice—that of the girls' mother, Orleanna Price—Kingsolver complicates the family-oriented domestic novel so that it becomes an example of the more contemporary (and more feminist) wife-and-mother-searching-for-autonomy story. Of all Kingsolver's narrators in *The Poisonwood Bible*, it is Orleanna who grows the most, and finds the greatest, least questionable, stability. From her peaceful garden on quiet Sanderling Island off the coast of Georgia, Orleanna does

---

[3] In *High Tide in Tucson*, Kingsolver had written, "I, personally, am Jo March … A pen may or may not be mightier than the sword but it is brassier than the telephone" (44).

become a kind of tranquil Robinson Crusoe figure. Her "recovery" from a malaise both spiritual and familial, however, takes decades.

The Poisonwood Bible also bears the marks of Kingsolver's work as a student. She spent months absorbing the Kikongo language from a "two-volume Kikongo-French dictionary, compiled early in the century (by a missionary, of course). Slowly I began to grasp the music and subtlety of this amazing African language, and its infinite capacity for being misunderstood and mistranslated" (Dialogue). The title underscores this difficulty with the common language—"poisonwood" as negative rather than Biblical—and the irony that Nathan Price cannot ever learn to speak so that his African audience can understand him. The coupling of "poison" with "Bible" foreshadows Ruth May's being killed almost instantly by the poison of the mamba snake, even though she was never meant to be its target.

Kingsolver uses Nathan Price's language dilemma in an early cataclysmic scene, a moment Orleanna recalls as "the day we lost them both, Mama Tataba and the accursed parrot, both released by Nathan" (Poisonwood 90). The Prices have inherited Brother Fowles' parrot, Methuselah, whose explosive remarks both enliven and frustrate the household. The parrot, however, does understand the language, even though its most frequently used word ("Mbote") means both "Hello" and "Goodbye." At the opposite pole is the capable Mama Tataba. She finds food, cooks it, serves it; she cleans; she does all the family's washing—and she argues with Nathan. Whether or not he can understand what she says, on the day in question, he wanders in his carefully tended garden. Although he has used the African method of planting the seeds he has brought from the states in mounds of earth, the large blossoms growing rapidly never bear fruit. Frustrated at what seems to be his failure, he calls to Mama Tataba and she finally manages to explain that his plants have no pollinators (no African bugs or bees that recognize these strange plants). She also shouts at him that his constant urging that parishioners be baptized in the river angers everyone. She tells him that a year ago one of the families watched their small daughter be killed and eaten by crocodiles in that river, and that now all children are forbidden to go near it.

Mama Tataba quits and returns to her own village.

Nathan angrily opens the door of Methuselah's cage and throws the bird up into the forest while he complains that no one has previously told him of the tragedy in the river (Poisonwood 80–1).

Orleanna later remembers her solitary drudgery without Mama Tataba, "the efforts it took to push a husband and children alive and fed through each day in the Congo" (Poisonwood 90).

As this episode suggests, Kingsolver also spent months learning about the natural world of the Congo, as well as about the intricacies of politics there during the mid-twentieth century.[4] But the remarkably fluid and impassioned effect of the long book comes less from its author's applied learnedness than from her evolving commitment to showing power struggles within human relationships, and to providing contemporary readers with a complex prolegomenon on successful parenting. It is in Kingsolver's creation of the family dynamic—perhaps more visibly silhouetted because of the Prices' being isolated in Africa—that she here excels.

Of all dimensions of twentieth century family life, perhaps the question of "what constitutes morality" looms largest. From the eighteenth- and nineteenth-century concerns in US culture about the human position in life—concerns that are religious as well as moral, with religion often being the stepping stone toward intricate moral decisions—readers have never stopped looking for answers that tackle large philosophical questions. Critic John Lang places Kingsolver in a continuum with such nineteenth-century writers as Emerson, Thoreau, and Whitman because he sees her *oeuvre* as raising "crucial questions about our nation's attitudes and practices as they affect ordinary people both at home and abroad—and as they affect the health of the earth itself... [she is] committed to exploring and upholding the fundamental principles of our... democracy." He goes on to point out that although Kingsolver is "rooted in both the Appalachian South and the American Southwest, she has often painted her fiction on a global canvas" (Lang 2). Differing from the usual critiques of Kingsolver's books, which are geared to explain and discuss what a single publication achieves, Lang's commentary links this author with what he sees as her continuing seriousness of purpose to that moral strand still dominant in US literature.

By allowing readers to place *The Poisonwood Bible* in this historical progression, Lang suggests the difficulty in reviewing the novel. He could have gone on to note reviewers' praises that might have been expected—that the novel avoids stereotyped commentary on the United States' involvement with the Congolese struggle, or that the book's criticism of the American

---

[4] Any summary of those events is necessarily incomplete. There is, however, this set of facts: **May, 1960**, Patrice Lumumba and Joseph Kasavubu shared power for a week. Army units mutinied and nearly all Europeans and Americans left the country. **June 30, 1960**, the Congo declared its independence and then asked the United Nations for help. **July, 1960**, Katanga province, known for its production of diamonds, declared its independence. Moise Tshombe led this movement. **July 15, 1960**, United Nations troops came to Africa and stayed until June 30, 1964. **September 5, 1960**, President Kasavubu dismissed Lumumba. Joseph Mobutu, an army colonel, set up a provisional government at Leopoldville (now Kinshasa). Lumumba was imprisoned but his followers under Antoine Gizenga set up a rival government at Stanleyville (now Kisangani). **November, 1960**, four distinct and rival governments were set up in the Congo. **January 17, 1961**, Lumumba was assassinated in Katengo.

missionary effort to change the beliefs of the African people is too harsh. He instead allowed Kingsolver's works to maintain their own resonance, and to err on the side of appreciation.

After spending more than five years working on *The Poisonwood Bible*, and as long a period developing her ideas about its political condition, Kingsolver knew that what the book achieved fulfilled her intentions. Reviews were uniformly good, and, more important, accurate. For example, as Verlyn Klinkenborg wrote in his *New York Times Book Review* essay, although "The Congo permeates [the book, but] this is a novel that is just as much about America, a portrait, in absentia, of the nation that sent the Prices to save the souls of a people for whom it felt only contempt... The Congolese are not savages who need saving... and there is nothing passive in their tolerance of missionaries" (7). In the words of British critic Carol Birch, this "brilliantly realized epic [is] filled with convincing portraits" (*Independent* 1999). John Leonard's *Nation* review uses the term "matrohistorical" to stress that Orleanna is the primary character and that "the child lost" is the heart of the plot (28). Leonard's approach complements Gayle Greene's *Women's Review of Books* essay, in which she praises the book as "a complex, textured work, its imagery patterns resonating across levels of meaning. The idea of feeding, for example, plays out on ecological, biological, psychological, and political levels: ants eat their way across Africa, the forest eats itself yet lives forever, crocodiles devour children; there is famine, hunting, poison, a snake in the belly, a dog-eat-dog world, a consumer society, a stewpot we're all in together. It is multivocal and multiphonic, its meaning not in a single voice but in the play of voices against one another" (April 1999).

Besides feeling an immense satisfaction in *The Poisonwood Bible*, Kingsolver was also aware that some of the qualities of her earlier three novels that had garnered praise from critics had *not* been appropriate for this long and intricate work. Was a "successful novelist" allowed to change her own approach and style? Difficult as it was for the comparative novice to relinquish techniques she had worked hard to perfect, in *The Poisonwood Bible* Kingsolver created voices that were barely distinctive, one from the other. For instance, the voice she had given Codi Noline in *Animal Dreams* had been frequently praised. Among others, Sheryl Stevenson had shown the way that "[T]he opening chapter of Codi's narrative... reveals how the dialectic of trauma—the deadlocked impulses to remember and to repress—produces an indirect, impeded disclosure... Codi's narration is one of gaps, evasions, and sudden fissures of erupting emotions—an unstable discourse." (Stevenson 89–90). Such an analysis cannot easily be made of the speaking patterns among the five women narrators, because at the start of the book, except for Orleanna's prologues, they weave experiences into texts more similar than different. Beginning the book, the author intends that the reader absorb the particles of *story* necessary. It takes until near the midpoint of the novel for the daughters' voices to become more than cosmetically differentiated.

The sonority of the novel initially stems from the "prologue" sections which Orleanna Price speaks: these occur in retrospect, datelined from the Sanderling Island location where she has gone to live once returned from Africa. In each early section of the novel, Orleanna's monologue occurs first and becomes something other than a part of the four-section "story" readers learn to identify. This is a small glimpse from Orleanna's first such prologue: "In the year of our Lord 1960 a monkey barreled through space in an American rocket; a Kennedy boy took the chair out from under a fatherly general named Ike; and the whole world turned on an axis called the Congo. The monkey sailed right overhead, and on a more earthly plane men in locked rooms bargained for the Congo's treasure" (Poisonwood 8).

With regular alternation, Kingsolver then creates the pieces of the novel's story, spoken through the four daughters' voices: the beginning order, for example, being "Leah," "Ruth May," "Rachel," and "Adah." Most alternations begin with the words of Leah, who is the intellectual leader of the sisters, twinned with the less-communicative (or more privately communicative) Adah. Both are in gifted programs in their schools. But as the chapters progress, order diminishes: eventually Rachel begins the progression and by the time of the middle of the book, the monologues are given in rapid succession, each sometimes taking only a page or two to complete. The dynamic of the entire novel changes with the pace of the daughters' alternating monologues.

Initially, it appears as if their personalities *do* show in their language choices. Rachel, the oldest, is given to slang and to malapropisms, as well as to superficial commentary about customs. The child Ruth May speaks in a voice that has some qualities of childhood, although she also seems prescient. Adah, for all her brilliance, is plagued with a number of palindrome fixations that include rhyming patterns; she seldom speaks aloud. Only Leah appears to be conversationally acute, and her speech rhythms are patterned after those of her mother. Kingsolver provided clues in the openings of each daughter's monologues to these characteristic deliveries.

In the first chapter, titled "Genesis," Leah's monologue opens with a comic, quasi-Biblical tone: "We came from Bethlehem, Georgia, bearing Betty Crocker cake mixes into the jungle. My sisters and I were all counting on having one birthday apiece during our twelve-month mission" (Poisonwood 13).

Ruth May's voice is second: "God says the Africans are the Tribes of Ham. Ham was the worst one of Noah's three boys: Shem, Ham, and Japheth.

Everybody comes down on their family tree from just those three, because God made a big flood and drowneded out the sinners. But Shem, Ham, and Japheth got on the boat so they were A-okay" (Poisonwood 20). Reminiscent of Bible class recitations, Ruth May's speech is that of the literally good student; sometimes she goes beyond the rote, but no reader can forget how young she is.

In the words of Rachel, the third speaker, Kingsolver uses whatever slang—and whatever strange grammatical phrasing—she can incorporate: "Man oh man, are we in for it now, was my thinking about the Congo from the instant we first set foot. We are supposed to be calling the shots here, but it doesn't look to me like we're in charge of a thing, not even our own selves. Father had planned a big old prayer meeting as a welcome ceremony, to prove that God had ensued us here and aimed to settle in. But when we stepped off the airplane and staggered out into the field with our bags, the Congolese people surrounded us—*Lordy!*—in a chanting broil. Charmed, I'm sure" (Poisonwood 22).

Adah in these opening sections is most distinctive because readers will have to decipher the way her mind works, guided entirely by what words appear: "Sunrise tantalize, evil eyes hypnotize: that is the morning, Congo pink. Any morning, every morning. Blossomy rose-color birdsong air streaked sour with breakfast cookfires. A wide red plank of dirt—the so-called road—flat-out in front of us, continuous in theory from here to somewhere distant. But the way I see it through my Adah eyes it is a flat plank clipped into pieces, rectangles and trapezoids, by the skinny black-line shadows of tall palm trunks. Through Adah eyes, oh the world is a-boggle with colors and shapes competing for a half-brain's attention … Congo sprawls on the middle of the world. Sun rises, sun sets, six o'clock exactly." Amid the sense that Adah speaks (despite her cumbersome and defensive phrasing, "Adah eyes"), the rhyming of the grasping mind in search of language gradually diminishes and later sentences in Adah's monologues resemble Leah's. For instance, from this same monologue, Adah speaks normally: "The church building, scene of our recent feast, resides at one end of the village. At the other end, our own house" (Poisonwood 31).

Similarly, midway through Rachel's opening monologue: "Finally we were allowed to sit down about as close together as humanly possible at a table, on an oily bench made out of rough logs" (Poisonwood 23). Even Ruth May's young voice contributes to the details that will create the African village: she describes "Reverent and Misrus Underdown, who started the African children on going to church way back years ago" (Poisonwood 21). And in Leah's locutions, the sensible if terse descriptions that will carry much of the narrative of *The Poisonwood Bible*: "Just then a married couple of Baptists in tortoiseshell sunglasses came out of the crowd and shook our hands. They had the peculiar name of Underdown—Reverend and Mrs Underdown. They'd come down to shepherd us through customs and speak French to the men in uniforms. Father made it clear we were completely self-reliant but appreciated their kindness all the same. He was so polite about it that the Underdowns didn't realize he was peeved" (Poisonwood 17). The reader is asked implicitly to juxtapose the power of "Price," with the Biblical phrase "pearl of great price," against "Underdown," which names the couple that briefly appears but lingers in the vocabulary of the novel for pages.

Much diligent care goes into the structure of the novel. It consists of seven chapters, of varying lengths. Within each chapter, there may be two or three sets of the daughters' monologues, placed after Orleanna's prologue. The beginning sections are not only titled with the name of a book of the Bible; they also open with a verse or several from that book. "Genesis," "The Revelation," "The Judges," and then the turn—the climactic section, "Bel and the Serpent," the shortest section, and in it Ruth May dies. From then on, the voices of only three daughters carry the story. It is the "Bel" chapter that provokes a new kind of formatting for the narrative. Rapid fire, the voices of Leah and—surprisingly—Rachel alternate, and Rachel's opening section begins, "Maybe I shouldn't say so but it's true: Leah is the cause of all our problems" (Poisonwood 335).

Of the dozen monologues in this section, Adah contributes only three and her prose poem based on Emily Dickinson's "Because I could not stop for death" marks the emotional center of the book. Strangely personal, considering that it opens with the first lines from Dickinson's poem, Adah can be seen here voicing a meaningful lament. It is the first sign of real feeling that Kingsolver attributes to this daughter. Adah describes her sister's dying as her becoming "impossibly small … she moved away to where none of us wanted to follow. Ruth May shrank back through the narrow passage between this brief fabric of light and all the rest of what there is for us: the long waiting … " (Poisonwood 365).

"Bel and the Serpent" is followed by "Exodus," "Song of the Three Children," and "The Eyes in the Trees," a change in source that suggests the primacy of the supposedly "corrupt" books of religious faith, the Apochrypha, instead of the Christian Bible.

Orleanna's prologue sections had all been written well after the basic narrative of the Price family—first arriving in the Congo and then fleeing for their lives—but with the death and funeral of Ruth May, the family has broken apart. Later sections of *The Poisonwood Bible* give the reader continuations of only the existences of Leah, who remained, married to Anatole, in the Congo;

Rachel, who became prosperous as the wife of several African businessmen; and Adah, who took a medical degree in Atlanta and managed her physical disabilities so that the world did not see her as impaired.

The book as a whole benefits from another organizing principle Kingsolver devised. She divided the seven chapters under three other large headings (they do not appear in the Table of Contents). After Orleanna's first prologue in chapter one comes the first larger title, "The Things We Carried, Kilanga, 1959." The chapters then describe the family's packing— we have seen the inclusion of cake mixes—as well as their reception, Nathan Price's sermons, as well as his orchestration of the major event he sees communal baptism to be, and his complete lack of understanding of his captive parishioners. Various skirmishes with the Africans and their long-established culture—as well as respect for that culture—dot the monologues of particularly Leah, who finally sees her father for the irreligious tyrant he is becoming.

The second larger division title again follows Orleanna's prologue, this time to the fourth chapter, "Bel and the Serpent." That larger title is expressed cryptically—"What We Lost, Kilanga, January 17, 1961." Orleanna's words summarize the actual death of Ruth May, which occurs on the day of Lumumba's assassination; they also describe the cavernous vacuum that living in the Congo has created for the Price women.

Fifteen years after it all happened, I sat by my radio in Atlanta listening to Senator Church and the special committee hearings on the Congo. I dug my nails into my palms till I'd pierced my own flesh. Where had I been? Somewhere else entirely? Of the coup, in August, I'm sure we'd understood nothing. From the next five months of Lumumba's imprisonment, escape, and recapture, I recall—what? The hardships of washing and cooking in a drought. A humiliating event in the church, and rising contentions in the village. Ruth May's illness, of course. And a shocking scrap with Leah, who wanted to go hunting with the men. I was occupied so entirely by each day, I felt detached from anything so large as a month or a year. History didn't cross my mind. Now it does. Now I know, whatever your burdens, to hold yourself apart from the lot of more powerful men is an illusion. On that awful day in January 1961, Lumumba paid with a life and so did I. On the wings of an owl the fallen Congo came to haunt even our little family, we messengers of goodwill adrift on a sea of mistaken intentions.

Strange to say, when it came I felt as if I'd been waiting for it my whole married life. Waiting for that ax to fall so I could walk away with no forgiveness in my heart ... (Poisonwood 323)

The turn in the novel, for the three Price daughters as for Orleanna, is that the loss of Ruth May allows them to leave the artificial family structure. As a patriarchal unit, that grouping has been as unsafe as the snake-infested forest. Nathan Price barely knows that Ruth May has died. In fact and with the bitterest of ironies, he hardly notices that his youngest child has been lost to death without ever having been baptized.

The rapid changes in the monologues of Rachel, Leah, and Adah after Ruth May's death suggest that each daughter is now free to become herself—or the woman she is to become. Each woman's language choices bespeak an independence that was previously either lacking or disguised. And each monologue makes clear that Nathan has lost all power to guide—or, more likely, to *mis*guide—them.

The third larger title appears after Orleanna's monologue in the fifth chapter—"Exodus"—and it bears a different location line: "What We Carried Out" has no dateline, but Leah's section, appearing first, is sourced "Bulungu, Late Rainy Season, 1961." The second section is Rachel's and Kingsolver uses her full name, "Rachel Price Axelroot" even though Axelroot, the counterrevolutionary pilot who flies her out of danger in exchange for sex, never marries her. Her location is "Johannesburg, South Africa, 1962." The place designation for Adah's monologue, the third, is "Emory University, Atlanta, 1962." Adah again quotes Dickinson, "Tell all the truth but tell it slant," as she declares her intention to speak, walk straight, and accomplish, even though she may physically remain "a crooked little person, obsessed with balance" (Poisonwood 407).

Kingsolver's maintaining the three daughters' voices but changing their locations creates a new dynamic for the novel. As she had recognized in finishing *Animal Dreams*, bringing various plots into alignment—or even simply concluding them—was often difficult. For the fourth monologue, Leah's, the place line reads "Mission Notre Dame de Douleur, 1963" and in it Leah explains that she has entered the convent to avoid being imprisoned—as her fiancé Anatole, a Lumumba sympathizer, has been.

"Rachel Axelroot" continues her life in Johannesburg (1964) with an opening cynicism, "If I'd known what marriage was going to be like, well, heck, I probably would have tied all those hope-chest linens together into a rope and hung myself from a tree!" (Poisonwood 424). In this fifth section, she announces that she plans to marry not Eeben Axelroot but the Attache to the Ambassador.

By the sixth segment, Leah has married Anatole (she is now "Leah Price Ngemba") and she writes from Bikori Station, January 17, 1965—the anniversary of Ruth May's death as well as Lumumba's. Persecuted by Motutu sympathizers, she and Anatole live in secrecy. She cannot write to her mother or to Adah. She mourns, "*I'm losing my family* piece by piece. Father is lost, wherever he is. Rachel I would only despise more if I knew for sure which way to direct my ire … " (Poisonwood 436).

Adah opens the seventh segment (still in Atlanta at Emory Hospital, Christmas 1968) with an echo of the above. "*I am losing my slant*." Reminding the reader that she and Leah are twins, this positive repetition describes the changes to her body, changes which she has both invoked and practiced (Poisonwood 439).

Successive monologues carry the narrative through the 1984 reunion of Orleanna with her three daughters. Leah's segments relate the horrors of living in the Congo once she and Anatole have been identified as Lumumba supporters, but she also describes her joy as Anatole's wife and the mother of his four sons. Rachel's segments—one titled "Rachel Axelroot Du Pree Fairley" (Poisonwood 460)—speak of her prosperous luxury hotel, aimed at international travelers: she seems as ignorant of African politics in the 1980s as she had been 20 years earlier. Adah continues on at Emory Hospital. Chapter Five, "Exodus," has merged with Chapter Six, "Song of the Three Children," and the narrative moves through the individualized voices of Leah, Rachel, and Adah. The distinctive markers of the three daughters' language choices have once again fallen away, and they sound much more uniform.

The missing element as *The Poisonwood Bible* concludes is Orleanna's voice. The reader learns of her and her life through Adah's worrying reminiscence: would her mother have left her to die during their flight out of Africa? Obsessive in its repetition, Adah's need for reassurance charts the force of the maternal, finally set positively here, in opposition to the *failed* paternal. To have only silence from Orleanna, however, reverses the chronological progression of the narrative. The reader is forced to reassess what appeared at the beginning of Orleanna's opening monologues. Instead, they become conclusions. After the prologue to Chapter Five, Orleanna does not speak again. As she had said in her first prologue, describing her entry to life in Africa,

> I had washed up there on the riptide of my husband's confidence and the undertow of my children's needs. That's my excuse, yet none of them really needed me all that much. My firstborn and my baby both tried to shed me like a husk from the start and the twins came with a fine interior sight with which they could simply look past me at everything more interesting. And my husband, why, hell hath no fury like a Baptist preacher. I married a man who could never love me, probably. It would have trespassed on his devotion to all mankind. I remained his wife

because it was one thing I was able to do each day. My daughters would say: You see, Mother, you had no life of your own.

They have no idea. One has *only* a life of one's own … (Poisonwood 8)

The spirit of Orleanna appears in the last chapter, however, but as the spirit of ruin in a country she never understood—no longer an isolato, no longer simply a bereaved mother.

In the forcefully titled "The Eyes in the Trees," Kingsolver brings the Price family of Orleanna and her three daughters (and by implication Leah and Anatole's four sons and from those men three more children, for whom the now great-grandmother—Orleanna—buys small carved ebony elephants) into the still struggling Africa. That section recounts the continuing national strife and the death of Mobutu; it also insists on the disappearance of any village beyond Bulungu (so that the Price family's experiences in Kilanga are, in effect, erased). It returns the noisome whites to the status of alienated outsiders, and marks their 17 months trying to convert the Africans in whatever ways as only interference. The disembodied voice here represents the natural denizens of the country—the wild crops, the animals, and most powerfully the snakes, all surrounded by and embedded in forests—that remain. In the figure of the female wood carver, who makes a gift to Orleanna of the delicate okapi, which she calls "a small miracle," some sense of human life endures.

Kingsolver figuratively wipes the story of the holier-than-thou Price family from the annals of both country and time. Lost is the bravado of the congregation's voting *not* to accept Jesus as their savior, with that election held within the walls of Nathan's own church. Gone too is the memory of Leah's success on the animal hunt (which began with the destructive fire surround and ended with Ruth May's death from the warning snake, placed in their shed to kill either Anthony or Nelson); the relinquishment of all possessions in her funeral rites: and the conclusion of both the Lumumba government and the Price "occupation." As the figure of what the author calls "shopkeeper a mother a lover a wilderness" insists to the family which had returned to Africa to mark Ruth May's grave, "There has never been any village on the road past Bulungu" (Poisonwood 542).

The novel does not, however, end with what could be considered resignation. From the now-lost grave spirals a "vine that curls from the small square plot that was once my heart." Ruth May's grave already carries the only marker it requires. And the closing voice of the consciousness of both Africa and some representation of Christian effort soothes Orleanna, who walks away with the okapi in her pocket and the assurance that once she has recognized her own complicity in the debacle of US power mongering, she will be forgiven. Kingsolver's last seven words are those of the unseen spirit directing her to "Move on ... Walk forward into the light" (Poisonwood 543).

Without regard for the interlacing history that the 1960s provided for the Congo—and its implications for both that country and the world, even if Kingsolver attempted later to downplay how much *The Poisonwood Bible* was "about" Africa—her closing chapter brings together the impact of deaths— unchosen, only partially acknowledged, and heretofore unforgiven—on a culture that remains only tangentially dominated by human beings. The unacknowledged elements of the Kikongo culture, which Rachel like her father succeeded in ignoring, flourish in the final section; whereas the puny efforts of such then-powerful Africans as Chief Ndu and his elders have also come to nothing. That the author incorporates into this closing the fact that Ruth May, even in her innocence, cavalierly killed a small spider, and that Orleanna and her four children, equally innocent, frightened the young okapi away from the stream, implicates the *distaff* side of the Price family in the same kind of evil that readers had long recognized in Nathan's behavior, and in his heart. The human condition may be one of supercilious and imperious behavior, untouched by the eternal maxims that nature— regardless of geography—provides.

When Orleanna speaks, in the monologue quoted earlier, of "Fifteen years after it all happened," Kingsolver herself might well have appropriated those words. As she recently toured England and France to celebrate the publication of the foreign editions of her 2012 novel, *Flight Behavior*, many of the audience questions still focused on *The Poisonwood Bible*. Fifteen years, and the resonance of that book was still tangible: in the spring and summer of 2013, the author was asked repeatedly and insistently to discuss her 1998 novel.

In a discussion sponsored by *The Guardian*, for example, Kingsolver told the decade-long history of "the Damned Africa Book," an idea which began when she read (and reviewed) Jonathan Kwitny's *Endless Enemies*, a study of "the business of governments making enemies by overruling the autonomy of developing nations." Using as an analogy the way parental arrogance might stifle a child's development, Kingsolver found that her wide-ranging studies of the Congo in the 1960s kept suggesting the microcosm of Nathan Price's dictatorship, "a gaggle of sisters under the dominance of a fierce patriarch."

She admits that the evolution of *The Poisonwood Bible* was very slow. "I read and read, for years. Political history, African religion, the King James Bible, self-published missionary memoirs" (Guardian Book Club 2013). As she adds in her 2013 Web discussion, "I'm keen to look at history, and study truth in all its facets. I think this is one of the ways novelists can earn our keep, morally speaking. So I decided to dive into the heart of darkness and write about paths to redemption. It's a large ambition. I waited many years to begin ... "

Never reductive, in either a moral or a political sense, Kingsolver explained further—about the need for answers to the moral dilemmas found in the novel—"I don't believe there is one single answer to that question; there are many. In the four Price daughters and their mother, I personified attitudes crossing the spectrum from Orleanna's paralyzing guilt to Rachel's blithe 'What, me worry?' I wanted to create a moral conversation. That's what literature can do" (Web 2013).

9

The Prodigality of *Prodigal Summer*

Even wilderness is seen as having value only as it enhances and serves our human lives, our human world. While most of us agree that wilderness is necessary to our spiritual and psychological well-being, it is a container of far more, of mystery, of a life apart from ours... It is something beyond us, something that does not need our hand in it.

Linda Hogan, *Dwellings* 45

Kingsolver's fifth novel was published in 2000, close on the heels of *The Poisonwood Bible*. It seems clear that *Prodigal Summer* benefited from the international acclaim for her African work,[1] although reviewers seemed puzzled by the scarcity of overlapping themes. If there is more than a chronological connection, it might be said (wryly) that *Prodigal Summer* attempts to correct the failure of Nathan Price's efforts in gardening in the Congo. In contrast, Kingsolver's novel supplies fruits and forests aplenty as she creates a tripartite narrative of characters who mine the beauties of their natural surroundings—the mountainsides and valleys of Southern Virginia, terrain marked by a mountain that connects Kentucky with Virginia. The author herself saw *Prodigal Summer* as a return to her own deepest interests. She recently wrote,

> I've been trained as a biologist, more or less from the beginning. I grew up chasing butterflies, went to graduate school in Ecology and Evolutionary Biology, and still look at the world through the eyes of a scientist... Leaving the halls of science for the world of literature and the humanities was like jumping across the Grand Canyon: I can plainly

---

[1] Tracking all the awards that *The Poisonwood Bible* accumulated is difficult; Snodgrass lists nominations for the Pulitzer Prize in Fiction, the Orange Prize, the Edward Abbey Award for Ecofiction, and the PEN/Faulkner award. It garnered the National Book Prize of South Africa, American Booksellers Book of the Year, *Los Angeles Times* Best Book, *New York Times* "Ten Best Books of 1998," *Village Voice* Best Book, New York Public Library "25 Books to Remember," The Poetry Center's Patterson Prize, Canada's North Forty-Nine Books Most Valuable Picks, and an invitation from Oprah Winfrey that the book become the selection of the Oprah Book Club (Snodgrass 24).

see a great divide that exists between two kinds of thinking. I wanted to write a novel to bridge that gulf somehow. Specifically, I wished I could explain a handful of important ecological principles: speciation and natural selection, the keystone predator, genetic diversity and resilience, and the Volterra principle, which (for instance) shows mathematically why spraying a field with pesticides actually will increase the number of pests in the next generation. These principles profoundly shape the world around us, in which we hope to survive ... So I took my leap across the canyon, and *Prodigal Summer* is its name. Translating scientific ideas from clean, elegant mathematics into vernacular English was a huge challenge. It's easy to oversimplify or alter meaning. (Web 2013)

Prodigal Summer is set within the complex environments that are representative of natural habitats. The novel's three story lines all center on Zebulon Mountain—the first on the Zebulon National Forest (the forest preserve)—but the stories initially appear to be separable. Kingsolver has explained that *Prodigal Summer* was about "a county and three months" (Adams interview).

Part I, "Predators," gives the reader Deanna Wolfe, a woman who has spent two years alone in this forest province, working as a kind of ranger, maintaining the trails, drinking in the wilds that surround her. Although the red wolves are gone, Deanna watches for the coyotes, "small golden ghosts of the vanished red wolf, returning" (Prodigal 14). Living in a small cabin, with food and supplies brought up to her at intervals, Deanna begins a tryst with a young would-be hunter, Eddie Bondo, who tries to understand the way she preserves the forest and its animals—and eventually his participation in her life. Coming from a Wyoming ranch, Eddie is a hunter. He puts those traits aside, however, in order to learn what he can from Deanna. And although she knows that he has probably come to the area for the Mountain Empire Bounty Hunt, she forgives him and takes him in, and for a time, into her heart—though no words of love are ever spoken. The biology of their relationship exists without language.

What Deanna searches for during her daily life and work is a den of elusive coyotes, keeping their presence secret from Eddie Bondo. This is the way Kingsolver shows the reader Deanna's forest self: "She jumped up, shuddered from the cold and nonsense, and went inside to get dressed and find her day" (Prodigal 56). Never wearing a watch, she knows from the movements of the sun and the light when the day progresses. Following the Bitter Creek Trail down the mountain, she looks for a site on which to build the blind she has planned; every morning she will come and observe the coyotes' den. As she tracks the male coyote, she thinks of her father's words:

"You learn what he is by knowing what he isn't." She understands that her father's words refer to a host of male pronoun referents, but in this case she reminds herself, "This is not a gray fox, and not a red fox. Coyote. A big one, probably male" (Prodigal 60).

The second strand of Kingsolver's narrative is the story of Lusa Maluf Landowski and the farmer-land owner she has married, Cole Widener. The couple now lives on the Widener family farm. A scientist who specializes in moths, Lusa has moved to that farm, leaving behind her lab mates, her research work, and her grants—which she misses. Lusa has found that she is not skilled at doing the farm work that Cole expects her to handle. When Cole had come to University of Kentucky for a workshop in integrated pest management, he and Lusa, one of the instructors, had fallen in love. But Lusa discovered that the lives of Cole's five sisters and their families, who lived nearby, each on a one-acre plot divided off from the main acerage, were far different from theirs.' Sensitive to being an outsider to the culture, Lusa felt that each of the five sisters begrudged her both Cole and the large farm: she could not read past their behaviors to find the hearts of these people.

When Cole is killed and Lusa is left to run the farm, her loneliness grows greater. What she remembers is the story of Cole's brother-in-law, Herb, killing a den of coyotes the week before their wedding—and her dismay at the waste of the lives of those animals. What she finds to adopt as *her* work is the care of Cole's sister Jewel's two children, Crystal and Lowell, who may be orphaned if Jewel's cancer cannot be arrested: these family ties keep Lusa from leaving the farm and returning to her university position.

The third narrative focuses on an older man who is expert in grafting chestnut trees. Garnett Walker, widowed now for eight years, wages whatever battles he can take on against his nearest neighbor, Nannie Land Rawley. Miss Rawley, as an organic gardener, does *not* spray. Mr. Walker *does* spray. But mostly what Walker does is to graft his American chestnut trees with Chinese chestnuts: "he would produce a tree with all the genetic properties of the original American chestnut, except one: it would retain from its Chinese parentage the ability to stand tall before the blight. It would be called the Walker American Chestnut" (Prodigal 130). Garnett loves his husbandry of the trees: "It wasn't so much the work; he loved messing with his chestnut trees. People presumed it was awfully tedious to bag all the flowers in the spring, do the careful cross-pollinating, collect the seeds, and plant the new seedlings, but every inch of that was exciting to Garnett because any of those seeds might grow up to be his blight-resistant chestnut tree. Every white bag slipped over a branch tip, every shake of pollen, each step carried the hope of something wondrous in the making. A piece of the old, lost world returning, right before his eyes" (Prodigal 204).

What Kingsolver has given her reader in this book is a trio of hard-bitten scientists, regardless of their formal credentials. Deep into the natural lore of the mountain and its forests, Deanna, Lusa, and Garnett try to lead lives that do not harm. In each case, however, they slight some of the human elements that would enrich their living. They believe that being immersed in the Blue Ridge and its environs suffices. Their love for that place stirs their jealousy: Deanna does not want to share either her coyotes or her hollow tree; Lusa does not want to share her moths or Cole's farm; Garnett does not want to take advice from Miss Nannie, or to share the evolution of the Walker chestnut he is developing. As each narrative progresses, however, they begin to sense the value in community, and eventually they take on roles that allow them to apply their human energy toward a wider good.

In the canon of criticism of Barbara Kingsolver's fiction, up to and including *Prodigal Summer*, there has been a great deal of attention to *place* as she chooses locations for her narratives. Sometimes considered a Southwestern author; again considered a Southern or Appalachian or Blue Ridge writer, the Kingsolver persona and her affinity for one place or another is only part of the typology. The author herself makes candid remarks about her comfort levels when she draws characters that are Southern: beginning with Taylor Greer, Kingsolver often chooses to draw the Southerner, and often that Southerner is female. *The Poisonwood Bible*, then, played the role of a monkey wrench tossed into the narrative mix. It is hard to reconcile the seventeen months the Price family spent in the Congo (and for Leah and Rachel, the seventeen months grew into much more than 17 years) with any rubric that says the novel *is*, somehow, "Southern."

An overlay of critical and theoretical attention has fallen on Kingsolver's creation of location. Vexed by the fact that *The Poisonwood Bible* was set in the Congo, more and more attention fell on the author's own interest in place. Part of this attention stemmed from Kingsolver's personal emphasis (in her various denials that she wrote "autobiographical" fiction). As she said in her 1992 speech to the American Booksellers Association, "I set my novels in geographic and psychic territory that I know" (Web 2013). Her detailed enumerations of the steps in her learning to know a *place* contributed to readers' accepting that location was truly significant to her and to her fiction.

A second part of the critical attention to her use of place stemmed from a newly identified set of theories about locations. At base for these emerging concepts about *place* is anthropologist James Clifford's definition of the "translocal," the idea that any place contains a culture that becomes "a complex articulation of 'local *and* global' processes in relational, non-teleological ways"—rather than being considered as place *per se*, based largely on geography (in McDowell 210).

A spin-off of this broad notion is that some places must, then, be "invented" in order to be able to contain such inclusiveness. For example, when Kristin Jacobson writes about Kingsolver's turn to Africa as setting for *The Poisonwood Bible*, she describes the author's having structured the book so as to illustrate these "translocal domestic politics." Jacobson here follows some of the reviewers at the time of the novel's publication in 1998, who suggested that the book's being set in the Congo did not lessen the author's scrutiny of the United States: "[Here Kingsolver] engages the 'translocal' home and redefines conventional American domesticity's boundaries by explicitly and self-consciously locating home within national and global political contexts. These domestic sites also often highlight hybridity and mobility and serve as points of cultural negotiation and translation" (in Leder 180).

Jacobson also supports the views of several other observers who have commented that—in most of Kingsolver's fictions—the author uses "invented locations." She refers to critics Kimberly Koza and Krista Comer, who object to this method: Comer calls Grace, Arizona, a "fantasy topography" and says that "*Animal Dreams* could happen anywhere in the United States." For that reason, Comer finds that "Kingsolver's progressive politics implode" (Comer 142, 149).

In Jacobson's readings, however, she finds that Kingsolver "plots the real global alongside the fictional local domestic story as a means to situate the narratives politically and historically" (in Leder 178). When race comes under consideration, Jacobson finds that Kingsolver's use of white characters becomes an important part of her complicated background. "Kingsolver's decision to set so much of her fiction in invented locations emphasizes her aim to engage reality while imagining a place's potential. Kingsolver's focus on Anglo protagonists, furthermore, simultaneously centers white experience and works—through her uncanny translocal settings—to decenter white privilege" (in Leder 182). When this latter point is applied to the three strong women characters—all white—of *Prodigal Summer*, it creates a different level of questions about the suitability of power within the various strands of the novel.

As she often does, Kingsolver gives her readers more than plotlines. She creates a world as well through her stylistic effects. In this novel, she makes these practitioners of science conscious of the tactile. Here, Deanna in her nightgown watches a moth's careful attempt at procreation by leaving a "double row of tiny eggs, as neat as a double-stitched seam" on the window glass. "It made Deanna sad to see such a last, desperate stab at survival. She'd read that some female moths could mate with many different males, save up all their sperm packets, and then, by some incomprehensible mechanism, choose among them after the boys were long gone—actually deciding whose sperm would fertilize the eggs as she laid them ... 'You poor thing,' she said quietly, 'quit bashing your brains out, you've earned your freedom.'" Catching the moth within a plastic cup, Deanna opens the door and releases it into the gorgeous day. "This was summer, surely. These morning chills would soon be gone for good, dissolved into the heat of breeding season. She inhaled: even the air smelled like sexual ecstasy. Mosses and ferns were releasing their spores into the air. Birds were pressing the unfeathered brood patches on their breasts against fertile eggs; coyote pups, wherever on earth they lived, were emerging for their first lessons in life ... " (Prodigal 183–4).

Known quickly as Kingsolver's most important ecological novel, as if *Animal Dreams* had somehow disappeared from sight in only a decade, *Prodigal Summer* surrounds and almost swamps the reader with these accurate yet romantic descriptions. The author here combines the sensible with the sensory—keeping our eyes firmly on the powerful effects that all kinds of natural aphrodisiacs can create. In the case of Lusa's watching Cole signal her from the field where he drives the tractor, for example, she breathes in the smell of honeysuckle as he leans "out from the tractor seat, breaking off a branch of honeysuckle that had climbed into the cedary fencerow high enough to overhang the edge of the field. Maybe the plume of honeysuckle was just in his way. Or maybe he was breaking it off to bring back to Lusa." This scene follows her memory of their harsh argument at breakfast, when she could not get enough distance to assess her own unhappiness—and her conclusion that follows his gesture.

> Here was what she'd forgotten about, the full, straight truth of their attachment. Her heart emptied of words, for once, and filled with a new species of feeling. Even if he never reached the house, if his trip across the field was disastrously interrupted by the kind of tractor accident that felled farmers in this steep country, she would still have had a burst of fragrance reaching across a distance to explain Cole's position in the simplest terms conceivable.
>
> Lusa sat still and marveled: This is how moths speak to each other. They tell their love across the fields by scent. There is no mouth, the wrong words are impossible, either a mate is there or he's not, and if so the pair will find each other in the dark. (Prodigal 46–7)

Cole does return home, bearing the honeysuckle; his death occurs soon, however, while he drives his truck. But what shimmers throughout the remainder of Lusa's section is the sexual bond that she here recreates and, remembering, values.

Critic Priscilla Leder points out that what Kingsolver creates in this novel is not just a narrative trilogy but, more important, "a narrative ecosystems by describing levels of distinct organisms and demonstrating how those organisms interact within and among those levels. She details the biology of a range of species, from producers such as chestnut trees to primary consumers such as Luna moths and keystone predators such as coyotes" (Leder Slovic 303). Leder refers to Kingsolver's admonition on the HarperCollins Web page, that readers will need to absorb this novel slowly because "this is the most challenging book I've ever given my readers ... My agenda is to lure you into thinking about whole systems, not just individual parts."

In Leder's important essay, she urges readers to see the patterns of deft sexual scenes throughout the book as a strategy for emphasizing that people, too, are parts of ecosystem. Such an emphasis on sex is unusual for Kingsolver, notes Leder, but it is an effective way to reveal "the interaction between biology and human agency" (Leder Slovic 305). Amanda Cockrell puts it more stridently, noting that this novel "is about sex: people sex, bug sex, coyote sex; about pheromones and full moons, and the drive to pass on your genes. Lacewings, newly hatched, are 'everywhere suddenly, dancing on the sunbeams in the upper story, trembling with the brief, grave duty of their adulthood: to live for a day on sunlight and coitus.'" Hawks mate in midair, "coupling on the wing, grappling and clutching each other and tumbling curve-winged through the air in hundred-foot death drives" (in Austenfeld 188). As she chooses quotes from *Prodigal Summer* itself, discerning which are Kingsolver's words and which are the critic's becomes difficult. The humor that underlies this paragraph makes Cockrell's point, that there is nothing indiscreet in people who mate—it is no more scandalous than the mating that occurs everywhere in the natural world. In Cockrell's summation, "Sex is urgent and dangerous, to the human heart as well as the lace-wing" (in Austenfeld 188).

In the novel's third narrative strand, however, there is not going to be sex. Garnett Walker at 80 thinks of himself as only a widower; Nannie Rawley has already borne Rachel, a child the community calls illegitimate, a child who lives for a time with a heart defect and Down syndrome; Nannie is ready to become a grandmother, not a mother. At 75 she is smart enough to know that Garnett Walker would make a better friend than the enemy he is now, and when she takes him a fresh-baked berry pie, it is a calculated move. Although Nannie does not know that Walker is hoarding the shingles *she* needs to have her roof repaired, she knows that in her woodlot she has some Chinese chestnut trees that he doesn't yet know exist.

One of Walker's maladies is a dizziness that strikes unannounced. He finds such attacks not only unpleasant but frightening. When Nannie is able to show him how to stop the spiraling nystagmus—and in effect, give him a cure in the Epley maneuver—he begins to warm toward her. While the physicality of her touch during his distress is never intended to be sexual, the lonely man at least understands the comfort of touch. More important than helping Walker learn to care for the health of his body is Nannie's insistent teaching about the use of pesticides and other poisons common to farms. Although she implies that his wife's death from lung cancer may have resulted from his spraying, she does not say this directly. Eventually she shares the chestnut flowers from her woodlot so that he will be able to incorporate new lines into his chestnut experiments.

Garnett's work with the chestnuts reminds him and his community of the importance of family branches. Garnett and Ellen's only child, Garnett Sheldon Walker IV, has married young: he is no longer a part of his father's life. Married to Jewel Widener, Shel is the father of the children Lusa plans to adopt—Crystal and Lowell. When Lusa phones Garnett to ask about raising goats, because as a widow she needs to find income to supplement the earnings of the Widener farm, the reader sees how the various family branches begin to shape the community. Garnett Walker is Jewel's father-in-law; he is her children's grandfather, though they do not know him.

The last piece of the community assemblage is Deanna's return "home" to Nannie, her foster mother, once she has discovered that she is pregnant from her lovemaking with Eddie. Living her customary isolated life in the ranger station is no longer a viable option. The structure of the novel in itself, then, emphasizes that "Every world is a world made new for the chosen" (Prodigal 444).

Another theme *Prodigal Summer* insists upon is the permanence of family customs. Family traditions are not just tied to livelihoods—how the land is farmed, what the planting and harvesting customs are. Such traditions also have to do with the simpler domestic practices of child rearing, cooking, keeping house, the very selection of foods. Much of Lusa's hostility to Cole's sisters accrues because she gets offended at their response to her cooking as well as her other domestic practices; she also dislikes the way the four women treat (and, essentially, mistreat) Crystal, who had never wanted to be considered "ladylike." Lusa herself, in fact, had originally thought the girl was masculine and in her own misidentification, she finds pity for the independence the child has created through her choices in dress and behavior.

Kingsolver does not miss a chance to emphasize gender roles in all parts of her ecosystem. In the lovemaking scenes between Eddie Bondo and Deanna, as well as between Cole and Lusa, both women are self-conscious about their bodies. But their lovers find those bodies beautiful and their appreciation for the physical makes both Deanna and Lusa fall in love with their lovers. Kingsolver wrote on her Web site at the time of *Prodigal Summer*'s publication, "Sex in our strange culture is both an utter taboo and the currency of jaded commerce" (Web 2000). Surrounded by the natural world, where procreation is the *only* primary need, the characters here easily reflect the natural sexual world. There is no irony in sexual satisfaction as Kingsolver depicts it, and as Nannie explains to Deanna in "the nearest thing to a birds-and-bees lecture she's ever gotten from Nannie," "That was the world, honey. That's what we live in. That is God Almighty. There's nothing so important as having variety. That's how life can still go on when the world changes. But variety means strong and not so strong, and that's just how it is. You throw the dice. There's Deannas and there's Rachels, that's what comes of sex, that's the miracle of it. It's the greatest invention life ever made" (Prodigal 390).

A brief consideration of these several themes from Kingsolver's *Prodigal Summer*, then, shows its clear relationship to parts of *The Poisonwood Bible*. When the author referred to herself as a cultural anthropologist, she confessed to being interested in these very customs that mark domestic life. As she scoured writings about the African Congo, she also looked for details about the way things were done—seeds planted in mounds of earth, manioc as the basis for nearly every meal, men as community leaders (and "medicine men") and women as their followers, their helpers. Part of what she is able to achieve in *Prodigal Summer* is that all three of the women protagonists in the triad of stories assume leadership positions for themselves. The community does not miss the audacity of Lusa's raising goats (and selling them in the city for holiday fare at excellent prices); no one from Nannie's area tries to dissuade her from gardening organically, just as no one has urged Deanna to come back down the mountain so as to live more safely. The stern yet comfortable independence that Orleanna Price finally achieves, after years of difficult work both in Africa and Atlanta, comes much more easily—even naturally—to Lusa, Nannie, and Deanna. It is less a generational aim than it is one that grows from the strength, and the privacy, of knowledge responding to reasonable demands.

Prodigal Summer also continues the emphasis on nourishment—eating, and growing or scavenging food—that appeared frequently in *The Poisonwood Bible*. As Leder had suggested, throughout her books, Kingsolver is driven by a kind of "food ethic." The critic describes such a notion by suggesting that Kingsolver writes often about "the wasteful process of producing food that's been seeded, fertilized, harvested, processed, and packaged in grossly energy-expensive ways and then shipped, often refrigerated for so many miles it might as well be green cheese from the moon" (Leder Slovic 312–14).

Underlying what seems to be a very specific concern is the more general belief that proper nourishment—with carefully grown foods—is a way of attaining and protecting personal health. Ruth May's second monologue opens "If somebody was hungry, why would they have a big fat belly? I don't know" (Poisonwood 50). Besides the mass of African residents living on the brink of starvation, Kingsolver draws a Nathan Price who slowly loses control of his emotions and his behavior—whether or not that deterioration can be attributed to poor nutrition. As the novel builds to the catastrophe of Ruth May's death, there is a period of some weeks when both Orleanna and Ruth May are seriously ill with malaria. Nathan does nothing to help them and, in fact, when the other three daughters try to cook meals, he finds their food disgusting and beats them for their efforts. Surely such behavior plays a role in the concept of "food ethic."

Despite the ravaged, raving Nathan, and the struggling Orleanna and her remaining three daughters, readers found some triumph in *The Poisonwood Bible*: after all, four of the novel's five narrating voices still exist at the book's end. They found even more triumph, however, in *Prodigal Summer*, a book that drew evocative responses from a range of readers. As Christine M. Battiste wrote, "Kingsolver illustrates how we can and must give voice to those who have been 'disproportionately' harmed—namely, women and ecology" (in Austenfeld 54). Comments such as these may refer equally to *Poisonwood Bible* and this 2000 novel, but Battiste continues that here in *Prodigal Summer*, the author has a much more local, and perhaps a more imperative, message. Her essay parallels the early Suzanne Jones' essay that emphasizes Kingsolver's "abiding concern for community and family, and her intimate knowledge of a particular place." Jones claims that the author has created "a blueprint for saving the small family farm and for restoring the ecological balance in a southern Appalachian bioregion that is struggling to survive" (in Austenfeld 157). Battiste, too, echoes Jones by writing that "Kingsolver's focus on the rehabilitation of a southern Appalachian region attests to her own dedication as a committed biologist, environmentalist, artistic activist, and ecofeminist author...her aim is more sustainability," and what remains important in life, as *Prodigal Summer* shows, is "the living environment and all its harmonious living components" (in Austenfeld 54). Amanda Cockrell adds a coda, "We are all linked, to other humans, to other mammals, to birds and blacksnakes and moths" (in Austenfeld 189).

By focusing on only the human characters of *Prodigal Summer*, as readers and critics have tended to do, they ignore Kingsolver's own directive that the novel is "not exclusively—or even mainly—about humans" (Web site 2000). The people she has drawn as characters exist, but their primary purpose is to "function as part of the same ecosystem...organisms and human artifacts circulate together" (Leder Slovic 303). To create the effects of entire ecosystems, Kingsolver writes a second kind of text—one based on a consciousness that pauses, observes, and records as if in a scientist's notebook—and the lushness, the prodigality of the novel, resides in those often-overlooked passages.

Kingsolver includes a great amount of description of the mountains and the land, and insects and animals, in the first part of her novel. This kind of inclusion seems appropriate since Deanna was a graduate student in ecobiology, specializing in the study of coyotes: she, like Kingsolver, has a remarkable eye for detail. In one memorable scene, for example, the author shows the wealth of information Deanna finds in the scat of the male coyote—who appears to have been lurking around her cabin, judging from the pieces of birdseed that likely came from her birdfeeder as well as the unseasonable apple remains, again, from her storage area.

> She spent the afternoon in an edgy distraction, curled into the dilapidated green brocade armchair that sat on her porch against the outside wall, sheltered under the eave. With her field notebook on her knee she cataloged the contents of the scat and the size and location of the tracks... What she had here on this mountain was a chance that would never come again, for anybody: the return of a significant canid predator [the coyote] and the reordering of species it might bring about. Especially significant if the coyote turned out to be what R. T. Paine called a keystone predator. She'd carefully read and reread Paine's famous experiments from the 1960s... (Prodigal 62)

Kingsolver's weaving of important scientific information about the process of extinction (here, with mussels who had become the main food source of the starfish—once the wolves and coyotes were gone) makes her novel a compendium of science. In Deanna's words, "There was no telling how the return of a large, hungry dog might work to restore stability, even after an absence of two hundred years. Rare things, endangered things, not just river life but overgrazed plants and their insect pollinators, might begin to recover."

Providing good scientific information, Deanna also muses about the process that explains that the coyote, "a scent hunter that could track in the dead of night," may have been rejoining life by "insinuating" himself "into the ragged hole in this land that needed them to fill it—taking the place of the red wolf." She continues, Kingsolver making good use of Deanna's impassioned voice, "The ghost of a creature long extinct was coming in on silent footprints, returning to the place it had once held in the complex anatomy of this forest like a beating heart returned to its body. This was what she believed she would see if she watched, at this magical juncture: a restoration" (Prodigal 63–4).

The last four paragraphs of this chapter give the reader less than a glimpse of the coyote, although Deanna, sleeping outdoors, doesn't hear so much as

> the crackle of a step...It wasn't anything, really. She sat up in bed hugging herself under the blanket, holding her braid in her mouth to keep herself still. It was nothing, but *nothing* isn't an absence, it's a presence. A quieting of the insect noise, a change in the quality of night that means something is there, or someone...
>
> Out in the darkness beyond the end of the porch where she scattered the seed—that was where he was. She could actually see movement...suddenly two small lights appeared, bright retinal glints— not the fierce red of a human eye, but greenish gold. Not human, not raccoon. Coyote. (Prodigal 66–7)

Kingsolver uses the Widener difference of opinion about the possible coyotes—when Cole's brother-in-law claims he has shot them—to stress the interrelationship of the Widener land with the mountain above it. But it is not until Garnett Walker, seemingly at peace with himself and his environs, drives out from town that the coyote makes its appearance. "There it stood in broad daylight...a dog but not a dog. Garnett had never seen the like of it. It was a wild, fawn-colored thing with its golden tail arched high and its hackles standing up and its eyes directly on Garnett." The male is joined by a second one, more tentative, and Garnett thinks to himself that "what he'd witnessed was just that kind of magic. This was no pair of stray dogs dumped off bewildered beside the road and now trying to find their way back to the world of men. They were wildness, and this was where they lived" (Prodigal 392–3). Lusa sees at least one of the coyotes too, just as she hears their call following the frightening storm, a call she describes as "amazing, like singing. Dog singing" (Prodigal 407). Deanna, too, hears their call following the massive storm that fells trees and makes her realize that the mountain forest is no place for her child. Kingsolver concludes Deanna's strand of story with that sound:

> When the rain and thunder died and the wind had gone quiet, coyotes began to howl from the ridge top. With voices that rose and broke and trembled with clean, astonished joy, they raised up their long blue harmony against the dark sky. Not a single voice in the darkness, but two: a mated pair in the new world, having the last laugh. (Prodigal 435)

As she had in *The Poisonwood Bible*, here too Kingsolver appends a final chapter that draws from nothing in the novel proper. Here, as a coda to *Prodigal Summer*, the "she" who speaks in chapter 31 is one of the female coyotes that has lived with her sister, the mother coyote, and her cubs from the late spring nesting. *She* speaks of the arrival from the north of another coyote family, one that she and her sister have heard singing. The coyote's poem-like monologue is filled with the smells of the forest and the land, "a nutty-scented clearing where years of acorns and hickory nuts had been left buried under the soil by the squirrels that particularly favored this place." But Kingsolver emphasizes more directly the *sounds* the coyote guides by: "Nothing. It was a still, good night full of customary things. Flying squirrels in every oak within hearing distance; a skunk halfway down the mountainside; a group of turkeys roosting closer by, in the tangled branches of a huge oak that had fallen in the storm; and up ahead somewhere, one of the little owls that barked when the moon was half dark. She trotted quickly on up the ridge, leaving behind the delicate, sinuous trail of her footprints and her own particular scent" (Prodigal 443). Avoiding the didactic, Kingsolver leaves the reader—and the rare, evanescent coyotes—to create personal imaginative existences in this "sweet, damp night at the beginning of the world."

In conjoining the human and the natural worlds, Kingsolver makes use of repeated phrases. Several reviewers commented on the fact that the imagery from the opening paragraph of *Prodigal Summer* is echoed in the last paragraph, moving the reader from page 1 to page 444 and back. That comment is not quite accurate, however, because the passage in question occurs on page 1 in connection with Deanna, and on page 444 in connection with the female coyote. Following are the passages in question:

> **From page 1,** "But solitude is only a human presumption. Every quiet step is thunder to beetle life underfoot; every choice is a world made new for the chosen. All secrets are witnessed."

> **From page 444,** "Solitude is a human presumption. Every quiet step is thunder to beetle life underfoot, a tug of impalpable thread on the web pulling mate to mate and predator to prey, a beginning or an end. Every choice is a world made new for the chosen."

The way this description resonates for the female coyote is more complicated than the meaning it carries in its initial appearance. Yes, both Deanna and the coyote are threatened by the perhaps undisclosed presence of the unnamed "man with a gun, for instance, hiding inside a copse of leafy beech trees"

(Prodigal 1, 444). Deanna neutralizes the threat posed by the willful hunter, Eddie Bondo; she uses his strident masculine force to create a child, *her* child. Given this pattern, the reader imposes a similarly kindly presence for the independent coyote. In short, the archetypal danger from a man with a gun is, in *Prodigal Summer*, modified if not erased. The women, like the female animals, procreate rather than die.

As she has in her other novels, Kingsolver here uses all parts of her text to underscore a turn toward optimism if not hope. When she chooses Aaron Kramer's poem "Prothalamium" as epigraph for the novel, his song for the marriage bed ("a bower for love") creates the joyful tone of procreation. Tying together not only the tripartite plots of Kingsolver's novel, this sonnet turns the loneliness of the single human character into

> a splendid marriage-bed
> fragrant with flowers aquiver for the Spring.

Prodigal Summer privileges the domesticity of homemaking and mothering— whether the site be the coyote's home or Deanna's returning to live with Nanny (the return home fitting into what Murrey called a "matriarchal community," contrasting with the male character's return home—which would be more isolated and aggressive) (Murrey 162).

There is also a particularly feminist strand of geographical critique, building on the work of James Clifford and others. Kerstin W. Shands, in *Embracing Space*, describes what she considers two kinds of locations, "resisting space" and "embracing space." She describes the latter (which she prefers) as "an open 'parabolic' space that is not only politically but also spiritually empowering."

Linking women's writing with these concepts, Shands speculates that contemporary women's writing is filled with "a proliferation of movable borderlands, sandbars in motion, pavilions of desire, half-open labia" and other images she categorizes as suggesting "a desire for openness and fluidity...and for a dismissal of traditional dichotomies and misogynistic hierarchies" (Shands 2–3).

Later in her book, Shands describes a feminist ideal of "personal space...As [being] invisible as glass" (Shands 42). While these descriptors do not apply directly to Kingsolver's aims in *Prodigal Summer*, the bewilderment that some reviewers felt—especially as they considered this novel in tandem with *The Poisonwood Bible*—might have been clarified by aligning *Prodigal Summer* with mature feminist (or a kind of post-feminist) thinking.

She achieves a sense of feminist concerns by adding to the coyote narrative a parallel story of the fragile worlds of the Luna and Io moths. With this ecological strand, the author emphasizes the tenuous hold on life that this species confronts. For instance, when Deanna helps the trapped moth escape—in the scene referenced above—it is only seconds later that she sees the moth snapped up by a predator bird, a phoebe that "darted out from the eaves" and "was gone again … in a vivid brown dash" (Prodigal 184).

Because Kingsolver uses "Moth Love" as a continuing title for the novel's Lusa–Cole narrative, the reader has no opportunity to forget that Lusa *is* a well-trained scientist, whose work *is* the study of moths, particularly the Luna moth and the Io. Even as Deanna's forest habitat is filled with the moths and birds natural to a quasi-rain forest, the unspoken narratives of moth life resume whenever the Lusa–Cole story appears.

What the author creates as she builds the story of the recently married Ph.D. and the sensitive farmer is a fabric of scientific information that works metaphorically as well as literally. "*In many species of moths,* Darwin had observed, *the males prefer to inhabit more open territory, while the females cling under cover*" (Prodigal 35). Here Kingsolver uses an actual quotation to set up one of the frequent quarrels that run between Cole and Lusa—he is farm while she is city; he is uneducated while she has studied for 20 years; he is rural in outlook while she is global.

For the first year of her marriage, Lusa had talked frequently with her former lab partners Arlie and Hal, but recently they only advised her to cut her losses and return to the university and her fellowship. As she recalls one of those last somewhat abrupt conversations, she sends her mind back to an ancient litany,

> *Actias luna, hyalophora cecropia, Automeris io,* luna, cecropio, Io, the
> giant saturniid moths, silken creatures that bore the name of gods
> into Zebulon's deep hollows and mountain slopes. (Prodigal 36)

Lusa's frame of reference for nearly all her life has been the scientific—her father and mother each left their family farms and became scientists whose lifework occurred inside laboratories. The arguments between Lusa and Cole, then, pitted one family identity against another, and the resolution of such a duel—both figurative and factual—would never be quick: layers of custom, as well as family lore, had to be combined and, hopefully, compromised.

In one of the last "scientific" excerpts in the "Moth Love" sections, Kingsolver chooses a lengthy passage that dovetails with the sharply etched honeysuckle scene mentioned earlier: "*The spiraling flights of moths appear haphazard only because the mechanisms of olfactory tracking are so different from our own. Using binocular vision, we judge the location of an object by comparing the images from two eyes and tracking directly toward the stimulus.*

But for species relying on the sense of smell, the organism compares points in space, moves in the direction of the greater concentration, then compares two more points successively, moving in zigzags toward the source. Using olfactory navigation the moth detects currents of scent in the air and, by small increments, discovers how to move upstream." (Prodigal 68).

As the turn in Lusa's story becomes her willingness to remain on the Widener farm, relinquishing forever her academic title and life, Kingsolver appends one last quote to the opening of the final "Moth Love" narrative. The insistence here is on the brevity of the male moth's existence: *"The males of the giant Saturniid moths have imperfect closed mouths and cannot feed. Their adult lives, poignantly brief, are devoted fully to the pursuits of locating and coupling with a mate"* (Prodigal 436). Startling in the detail that has not been previously given—that the male moth cannot feed—the author's choice of describing the male of the species, which occurs in a section that has been designed to be a food fantasy of the August harvest and Lusa's herculean efforts to preserve those rich foodstuffs, emphasizes the irony of Cole's own short life. Lusa tells Jewel that she is, for the first time, taking on the Widener name. She will become "Miz Widener" and she will make a success of the farm in all its components. If Jewel's cancer takes her life, Lusa will also adopt Crystal and Lowell, and give them the Widener name, and then she will give the family farm to the two of them.

Moreso than the other two narrative strands that comprise *Prodigal Summer*, the Lusa–Cole story takes on the always freighted subject of Family—its origins, its existences, its proliferation, or its demise—and creates a kind of ecological/ecofamilial text that resonates with a wealth, and a welter, of meanings. Christine Battista uses the term "bioregional" when she summarizes, "Ecofeminist theory is a productive way to interrogate how we think about land and what kinds of discourses…are embedded within Western, male-centered narratives of domination" (in Austenfeld 53). But as readers familiar with more literature than the contemporary know, the greatest books in the canon of novels in English have long been concerned with those same paired themes—*family* and *land*. As Judith Bryant Wittenberg wrote long before the prefix "-eco" was in vogue, William Faulkner's 1942 novel, *Go Down, Moses*, seemed to stem directly from the consciousness evoked by the writings of John Muir (1938) and by Aldo Leopold's later *Sand County Almanac*, men representing the greatest of our "environmental ethicists."

Wittenberg terms *Go Down, Moses* "a protoecological work of fiction," and says further that Faulkner created "the complicated interracial dramas— the negative effects of the 'colonizing white settlers taking the lands from the Chickasaw and Choctaw Indians'" (Wittenberg 51). He also made his readers consider "the interrelationship of the human problems with basic questions concerning not only land ownership—most vividly apparent in Isaac McCaslin's radical gesture of repudiation—but also the very essence of the connections between human beings and the natural environment" (Wittenberg 49). Multicultural, multivalent, coming along quickly after the tragedies of the Dust Bowl, Faulkner's novel illustrates firm ecological beliefs, "that all elements on earth are interconnected, that any organism is simply a 'knot' in the biospherical field." She emphasizes "the conceptual scope" of the book (Wittenberg 53). She also discusses the uses made of the wilderness as a figure in itself, and the role of the bear in that existence.

With an obvious link to John Steinbeck's *The Grapes of Wrath*, for its focus on making the land a kind of character, though the figures of the human in that book are almost exclusively white, Faulkner's *Go Down, Moses* appeared at nearly the same time. Few literary critics have acknowledged the effects of any kind of ecological movement on these novels—partly because the hiatus between the American Depression and the onset of World War II leaves little room for any other considerations, and partly because the vocabulary of Aldo and others would have seemed obscure. (It will be 1973 before the enactment of the Endangered Species Act.) But the prescient commentary about Faulkner as a writer who understood the natural world makes clear that he held a "reverential regard for the wilderness and its enriching effects on those who respect it and respond to it … [serving] finally as elegiac witness[es] to the ways in which it is being destructively altered, moving gradually and perhaps irrevocably beyond the point of reclamation" (Wittenberg 67).

Kingsolver herself has frequently written about these giants of the ecocritical (or, earlier, the environmentalism) movement. As she had said in *Last Stand* about Leopold, for example, grouping him with those conservationists who valued wilderness preservation, he was "gifted with a longer vision." The wilderness itself, she writes in a section tinged with sadness, represents "history's small acts of grace" (Last Stand 17–18).

10

Traveling to *Animal, Vegetable, Miracle: A Year of Food Life*

Eggplant Papoutzakia

2 pounds eggplant
Olive oil (slice eggplant lengthwise and sauté lightly in olive oil. Remove from skillet and arrange in baking dish).
2 medium onions, garlic to taste
2 large tomatoes, diced
2 teaspoons nutmeg, salt and pepper to taste
6 ounces grated or sliced mozzarella
Chop onions and garlic and sauté in olive oil. Add tomato and spices; mix. Spread mixture over eggplant and sprinkle an even layer of cheese over top. Bake at 350 degrees for 20 minutes. (Animal 145)

The wide variety in the kinds of writing Barbara Kingsolver attempts has often prompted her reviewers and critics to comment on that versatility. She seems less inclined to be self-conscious about whether what she writes is non-fiction or fiction (or story or essay or recipe or poem) than she is about the themes of her work. She also concentrates in the several books that follow *Prodigal Summer* on the state of the natural world, and particularly on what critics had seen as her interest in the family farm (maintaining it, growing food on it, helping it become a contributor to the health of the natural world).

In her introduction to Norman Wirzba's *Essential Agrarian Reader*, for example, she states, "Sometime around my fortieth birthday, I began an earnest study of agriculture. I worked quietly on this project, speaking of my new interest to almost no one, because of what they might think. Specifically, they might think I was out of my mind. Why? Because at this moment in history it's considered smart to get out of agriculture ... " (Intro ix).

As the characters in *Prodigal Summer* had believed, using the natural world for the good of all was one means of saving this existing world. When Kingsolver speaks about her having developed "a good agrarian state of mind," she saw that mindset as inclusive. She was interested not only in preserving the wild and the wilderness; her vision spread to include helping people see that safe, life-sustaining food was a crucial dimension of preservation.

In addition to essays, the two books that Kingsolver published immediately after *Prodigal Summer* explored the themes of both food and the preservation of the natural world. Her prose text for the latter was published as part of the collection of the photographs of Annie Griffiths Belt in the book *Last Stand, America's Virgin Lands*, which National Geographic brought out in 2002. Stunningly poetic, Kingsolver's essays—the large, encapsulating ones that preface each of the five divisions of the photos; and the shorter pieces interwoven in sections to highlight specific emphases— are a testimony to the importance of the natural world. They are as well a testament to Kingsolver's own beliefs about that world.

Last Stand is a kind of illustrated, informal history of the pioneers who worked to educate the public about the values of uncorrupted lands. Kingsolver begins her introductory essay with references to, and a biography of, William Bartram, whose *Travels* set a high standard for all readers interested in the descriptions of the natural in America. In addition to William Bartram, Kingsolver names—and sometimes quotes from the writing of—Henry David Thoreau, John Muir, Edward Abbey, Aldo Leopold, and Rachel Carson along with such contemporaries as Barry Lopez, Terry Tempest Williams, and Louise Erdrich.

Kingsolver begins her initial essay by describing what she considered her own idyllic childhood among the fields and rivers of the family's Kentucky farm—"Most of all I remember lying on my back in summertime, staring skyward through the leaves with my head resting on woody roots that were the bunioned feet of a particular old maple ... It felt like flying, or better yet, a breathless suspension in a living world that had bigger things on its mind than gravity" (Last Stand 13–14). Amid a number of such poignant recollections, the reader believes in the centrality that the author ascribes to the natural world. The author continues,

In the wild places that call me out, I know I'll recover my wordless childhood trust in the largeness of life and its willingness to take me in ... It will come to me as I sit watching ravens, my favorite bird, the only animals I know that will routinely go out of their way for the heck of it, looking for fun. I've seen ravens perform barrel rolls in the air or dive suddenly toward the ground, purely for thrills. (Last Stand 14)

Asserting her opinions as she understands that her reader is comfortable with the world she has worked hard to create, Kingsolver talks then about "the folly of what we're doing on the face of this world, behaving as if it were ours, utterly. And I wonder at the arrogance of the agenda we've inherited from our forebears…" She praises the authors she is drawing from throughout the book because of the fact that they—Muir, Leopold, Abbey, and others—created "wilderness conservation." She continues, "wildness deserves to persist, not because of what it can give *us* but simply because of what it is. Because it was here first. Because life, by definition, is its own reason for being…" (Last Stand 15, 19).

As critic Sandra Ballard has pointed out, the organization chosen for *Last Stand* adds to its unusual effectiveness: the book is "strikingly arranged to highlight the fact that California's Mojave Desert has more in common with Arizona deserts than with other parts of California, for instance." Instead of placing the photographs and texts into geographic areas, or segmented divisions of the United States, Kingsolver arranged the collection by "habitat type" (Ballard 19). The book begins with wetlands (complete with many photos of various sites in Yellowstone National Park), and Kingsolver writes, "The capacity of wetlands to store surface water is key to flood control and moderates seasonal stream flow between rainy-dry spells. Where nature is inconstant, wetlands provide stability" (Last Stand 29). This kernel of information no doubt drives her imaginative re-creation of the flooding in the Tennessee hills that she draws so vividly, and so tragically, in *Flight Behavior*. Further, meditating on the function of the rushing water in streams as well as rivers, she writes, "Still waters may run shallow or deep, but they hold the roots of floating marsh plants in undulating, upside-down forests that create the complex filtering system of a swamp. A river contains the chemical vocabularies that drive the intricate plot… that is the life story of a salmon. Water is ancient and endless: The immortality of molecules, the originality of a tadpole, a history of the world in the eye of an alligator. Beneath all else, water is the thing we cannot live without" (Last Stand 28).

There is less hyperbole in the "Woodlands" section, though the author points out that "virgin forests are now just as endangered as elephants and rhinos" (Last Stand 63). She also pares down her commentary in the discussion of "Grasslands." But in the segment on "Coasts," she notes the biological importance of the *fusion* of waters: "In the lagoons where rivers meet the sea, the mingling of freshwater and saltwater performs alchemies of nutrient-enriched productivity. This special estuary habitat produces more food per acre than the richest farms in Iowa" (Last Stand 92).

Kingsolver's partiality to the fifth division, "Deserts," is evident in her tenacious insistence on the value of such fragile spaces. She quotes from

Edward Abbey: "How strange and wonderful is our home, our earth ... We are none of us good enough for the world we have," lines positioned across from Belt's photo of cholla and saguaro cacti. Some of Kingsolver's prose here echoes phrases that had been incorporated in both *The Bean Trees* pairing and *Animal Dreams*. Throughout, however, Kingsolver gives the reader the voice of a scientist:

> Drylands are a permanent consequence of Earth's immense exhalations. Moist air warmed by the sun at the Equator continually rises, cools, and then descends in great cascades of air falling toward the north and south, sucking up every molecule of water to be had, while tumbling earthward. These strange, reverse waterfalls of atmosphere descend from a high-pressure belt at the north latitudes into the flow of tropical trade winds and touch down on broad arid belts that circle the planet between 15 degrees and thirty degrees north—the Sahara, Libyan, Arabian, Lut, Thor, Sonoran, Chihuahuan, Mojave, and Great Basin Deserts—and the equivalent latitudes in the Southern Hemisphere ... (Last Stand 154, 157)

Besides providing good, clear information, Kingsolver's prose in this volume follows through what she describes in the Signatures film as her underlying aim throughout her writing: "I want people to be hopeful, to think they can change the world." She returns to that idea in a 2011 interview, when she notes,

> "I would say that I'm a hopeful person, although not necessarily optimistic. Here's how I would describe it. The pessimist would say, 'It's going to be a terrible winter; we're all going to die.' The optimist would say, 'Oh, it'll be all right; I don't think it'll be that bad.' The hopeful person would say, 'Maybe someone will still be alive in February, so I'm going to put some potatoes in the root cellar just in case.' And that's where I lodge myself on this spectrum. Hope is a mode of survival. I think hope is a mode of resistance. Hope is how parents get through the most difficult parts of their kids' teenaged years. Hope is how a cancer patient endures painful treatments. Hope is how people on a picket line keep showing up. If you look at hope that way, it's not a state of mind but something we actually do with our hearts and our hands, to navigate ourselves through the difficult passages. I think that as a fiction writer—or as any kind of writer—hope is a gift I can try to cultivate. It's one of the great community builders. One of the great things we can do for one another is get together and help each other cultivate hope." (in Fisher 28)

Speaking from her already well-known position as an environmentalist, with definite roots in the ecology of both conservation and literature, Kingsolver moved from this set of statements about preserving our natural lands to creating a very different kind of non-fiction work. To a great many people's surprise, her 2007 book about farming—*Animal, Vegetable, Miracle: A Year of Food Life*—became yet another best-seller. Written with her older daughter Camille and her ornithologist/ecologist husband Steven Hopp, the book (accompanied by a recipe-laden Web site) sold to her usual readers but also to thousands of people who were coming to consciousness about nutrition in relation to personal health. The "Foodies" of America saw Kingsolver's highly personal and readable book as a new kind of taxonomy about nutrition.

In the years after Kingsolver and Hopp had married, they alternated between living in Arizona and Virginia. Her base remained Tucson, and her daughters had grown up there (and in the case of Lily, were growing up there). But before meeting Kingsolver, Steven Hopp was reclaiming his family's farm in the southern Blue Ridge. During summers, beginning in the mid-1990s, the combined family moved to the Southern Virginia farm. As Kingsolver wrote in "Lily's Chickens," during the school year in Arizona they grew "the cool weather crops that can take a little frost: broccoli, peas, spinach, lettuce, Chinese vegetables, garlic, artichokes" and in the Appalachian summers, "everything else: corn, peppers, green beans, tomatoes, eggplants, too much zucchini, and never enough of the staples (potatoes, dried beans)" (Small Wonder 116). As she explained with calm interest, "By turns we work two very different farms."

Kingsolver's essay also discussed such elements of food production as meal planning, reminding her readers that most Americans live with a bevy of "fortunate" choices. "I find both security and humility in feeding myself as best I can, and learning to live within the constraints of my climate and seasons. I like the challenge of organizing our meals as my grandmothers did, starting with the question of season and which cup is at the moment running over" (Small Wonder 117).

In her turn to writing that made use of both her childhood and adolescence on the Kentucky farms of her parents and one set of grandparents, Kingsolver augmented that wealth of knowledge with this newer set of dual-season gardening experiences. She emphasized in an interview with Noah Adams, reifying the value for any writer of truly knowing a place, "When researching a setting, you have to know a lot more about a place than you can learn from looking at a picture. You have to know what it smells like after a rain. You have to know the quality of the air, how it feels on your face. You have to know what's blooming in May and how that has changed by July. And you have to know how people are, how they talk... You can't just visit a place and write about it, in my opinion, not a whole novel" (Adams 18). It seems clear that Kingsolver's convictions as a writer merged with the days and weeks that she and her family spent farming all kinds of foods, and after the family had moved to the Hopp farm in Virginia, the surroundings of the natural world—sometimes in conflict with the commercial—thrust Kingsolver into an international conversation about farming, economics, and the various issues related to food and its production. Less famously, Kingsolver was becoming a kind of Michael Pollan, whose interview in the *Oprah Magazine* for April 2013 was titled "The Man Who Changed the Way We Think about Food." Along with his well-known book, *The Omnivore's Dilemma*, Pollan often brings world economics as well as food preparation into his discussions. As he said recently, "Cooking is how we transform nature into culture. It's a really profound thing—a spiritual thing" (Pollan 178).

In *Animal, Vegetable, Miracle*, it was evident that Kingsolver was about to attempt a Michael Pollan kind of book. She devised a sortie that would exist both in the family's real life, and then in written form. As she says in the introduction, she intended the year in question to benefit all four members of the Kingsolver–Hopp family. "We had come to the farmland to eat deliberately. We'd discussed for several years what that would actually mean. We only knew, somewhat abstractly, we were going to spend a year integrating our food choices with our family values, which include both 'love your neighbor' and 'try not to wreck every blooming thing on the planet while you're here'" (Animal 23).

The project was quite a different scenario from the details of growing and preserving food that Kingsolver had created for the kitchens of her 2000 novel, *Prodigal Summer*. There, Deanna was a thoroughly disinterested eater, adept at cooking meals (like a thick Navy bean soup) that would last for days. Lusa did cook and she delighted in cooking for Cole; she also canned vegetables: she knew how to use the produce the farming culture gave her. Nanny knew that people should avoid pesticides, but Kingsolver does not show any joyful mealtimes in that household. None of the women characters in this novel was doing anything more than existing in a normally contemporary fashion. In contrast to the scenes of food deprivation that Kingsolver had presented in *The Poisonwood Bible*, what happened in *Prodigal Summer* was unexpectedly dull. (*Animal Dreams* had, in fact, paid much more attention to the ways food supported the necessary ceremonies of life—and especially the ways it contributed to Doc Homero's existence. When Codi looked into her father's refrigerator and found all the evidence of his neighbors' gifts of food to him, she was struck with such ample generosity.)

Animal, Vegetable, Miracle: A Year of Food Life had a very different purpose. It was to educate. It was to *test* the possibility of making good choices about food, and then to *test* that possibility over an entire year—in times of both plenty and scarcity. The proposed undertaking at first seemed overwhelming, and the family had many supper table discussions about the plan. In fact, as Kingsolver said in the early pages of the book, the family had moved away from Tucson "in order to live in a place where rain falls, crops grow, and drinking water bubbles right up from the ground" (Animal 3). The looming artificiality of the Arizona desert cast its shadow on people who had lived on, and loved, the small southern farms of Kentucky and Virginia: their personal experiences left them little choice but to uproot their lives in a continuing search for basic sustenance.

Throughout Kingsolver's writings, whether or not the focus was on food and eating, many of her descriptions of past experiences had to do with the joyful gathering and eating of food. In *Last Stand*, for example, she recalled being a child and eating the "wild pawpaw, a fruit that few people have tasted because it can't be transported, only pulled from the branch and licked from the fingers like a handful of rich, banana-scented custard." In another section, she described the fact that she and her siblings "picked blackberries that stained our tongues and colored our insides, we imagined, with the juiciness of July's heat. We ate cattail roots and wild onions" (Last Stand 12–13). Such memory nourishment seemed almost fantasy, underscoring as it did the actual plight of Tucson, Arizona, a town that "might as well be a space station where human sustenance is concerned. Virtually every unit of food consumed there moves into town in a refrigerated module from somewhere far away. Every ounce of the city's drinking, washing, and goldfish-bowl-filling water is pumped from a nonrenewable source—a fossil aquifer that is dropping so fast, sometimes the ground crumbles" (Animal 3). In short, speaking for the four of them, Kingsolver says, "We wanted to live in a place that could feed us."

The Kingsolver–Hopp family settled in, and that process took much of a year. Then the question was raised, WHEN to officially begin the year of food *living*—planting and harvesting, cooking and preserving, and, compatible with the emphasis on producing as much of their own food as possible, the alternating discipline of avoiding foods from afar, foods with no nutrient value, foods that were more commercial than nourishing. While the family made decision after decision, it became clear that besides the rare, exotic, and well-traveled foods, most of the foodstuffs that were sugar based would also be on the list to avoid. Camille was not happy about the fact that honey would become the family's substitute for sugar; Lily, who yearned to raise animals, could barely content herself with the promise that she could continue to raise chickens. Avoiding what the Cherokee called "Hungry Month"—February—their project began with March, and with the delicacy of asparagus.

Animal, Vegetable, Miracle, in fact, includes a long section on asparagus—its history, various growing methods, varieties, cooking directions—as if to sweeten the catastrophic opening of the year: "Like so many big ideas, this one was easier to present to the board of directors than the stockholders." Kingsolver describes the six eyes scrutinizing her, as she "crossed the exotics off our shopping list, one by one. All other pastures suddenly looked a whole lot greener than ours. All snack foods came from the land of Oz, it seems, even the healthy ones. Cucumbers, in April? Nope. Those would need passports to reach us right now, or at least a California license. Ditto for those make-believe baby carrots that are actually adult carrots whittled down with a lathe ... " (Animal 33).

Thinking of each fruit or vegetable in terms of its cost to transport, Kingsolver labeled bananas and pineapples "the Humvees of the food world." The many ingredients that comprise most salad dressings added to their basic cost, in terms of transporting spices or flavors: therefore, oil and vinegar became the family's dressing of choice. With the daughters' quest for fresh fruit, in all months of the year, Kingsolver saw stretching before her and her plan a kind of war-damaged Rubicon. As a compromise, the family decided that each member would be allowed one extravagance: Steven chose coffee; Camille, dried fruit; Lily, chocolate (Animal 35). Even with compromise, prevarication, and sometimes ribald justifications, it was clear that the family was going to go through long weeks of withdrawal. Normal food purchases (as for nearly any family in the United States) were fraught with heavy transportation costs, as well as the temptation to indulge in purchases regardless of expense.

Kingsolver has recently written a kind of correction:

> "This was not an experiment in deprivation. We just wanted to stop pushing pampered fruits and vegetables around the globe on our behalf, so we changed our thinking. Instead of starting every food sentence with 'I want,' we began with 'right now we have ... ' Each season brought a new menu. We tried to celebrate asparagus in April and apples in September, rather than whining about not having apples in spring or asparagus in the fall ... Our farmers here grow salad greens under row cover even in the snowy months, and in January we loved the pears we'd canned in cider last summer. It's not as if we were chewing on acorns." (Web 2013)

The strategy of presenting the readers such a book—a strange composite of rhapsodic commentary about asparagus, of supper table scenes of arguments replacing eating, and of simple chronologies of growing food on a farm—was also up for discussion. How could Barbara Kingsolver, author, create a readable and interesting "book" from this slim "plot"? The answer was, obviously, that *Animal, Vegetable, Miracle* had no plot. It did, however, have the energy of a multipart narrative, a kind of daily journal that—as all journals do—encompassed every detail of each day in the Kingsolver–Hopp family life. In the words of Sandra Ballard, it was "a family collaboration" (Ballard 18).

To order and manage this narrative, the book is voiced by three storytellers (with the fourth, the young Lily, enacting her narrative as she goes about raising the baby chickens and gathering the hens' eggs). Carrying the primary responsibility for writing the book, as well as for both devising the year's narrative and overseeing its implementation and activities, is the established "author," Barbara Kingsolver. But the title page and book jacket share credit for the authorship, necessarily, with both Steven L. Hopp and Camile Kingsolver. The boxed commentaries by Hopp reflect his training in biology/ornithology/economics as he gives readers a somewhat cryptic commentary on the facts of food transportation, of the cost of oil production, and of many other topics that need to be covered—but would be disruptive coming in the journal-style commentary of the primary text. For Camille, whose expertise is a series of subjective essays on various topics important to her life and her energetic preparation of foods, the italicized essays that interrupt the mainstream flow of information (the journal sections) add a condensed poetry; Camille provides menu planning (usually by the week) and references to the Web site that houses many of the family recipes.

The somewhat busy mainstream sections—depending on how many fruits have been harvested, how many tomatoes ripened—are divided into the months of the food's production, a mechanical but effective arrangement that gives the reader a way to keep the place even as these sections are being interrupted by Hopp's factual commentaries or by Camille's excited descriptions of a new recipe for cold soup.

Perhaps the most important decision the writers of the book made was to use the phrase "food life." The subtitle of the book is, simply but interestingly, "A Year of Food Life." For most readers, that compound noun is unusual. Enigmatic in its phrasing, "food life" means a number of things: (1) the year as marked by the availability of this product or that (and the book's organization which supports that "meaning"); (2) the resonance of the positive noun "life" coupled in this dynamic with "food." (How does the adjective modifying the noun "life" work in this construction? What other modifier might replace "food"—"literary" life? "musical" life? "athletic/sports" life? "professional" life? It remains a distinctive coupling.)

Difficult as it may be to replace "food" in the construction, the reader could also phrase one possible meaning as "a year demarcated by the growth of foods." It is, in factual truth, a charting of the production of plant life, plant life that produces food.

It seems to me that Kingsolver intends to create a new kind of phrase, to endow the production of food with a reverence for the life that that food embodies and, in turn, can itself create. The sonority in the tone of "food life"—enigmatic as the coupling of those words seems to be—expresses succinctly the aura of the author, herself a "character" in this work, enamored of the bevy of life processes she knows intimately from her careful, considered immersion within the calendar of growth she describes so lovingly.

The primary title is also provocative. The reader expects the sequence to read "Animal, Vegetable, Mineral," since that is the usual compound, useful for analysis, for games, for locutions the world around. Changing the third term from "mineral" to "miracle" not only calls attention to the word choice; it also creates a puzzle. Here again Kingsolver is using expected language tropes and then adding a twist: the reader anticipates "animal, vegetable, mineral" because those are the usual categories. To end with "miracle" is the surprise, the deft quirk that makes the reader pay attention—and leads to the descriptor, "A Year of Food Life," discussed earlier.

Because Kingsolver followed *The Poisonwood Bible* with *Prodigal Summer*—as if she were beginning to give a more ecologically based narrative arc to her writing, the logical connection—between Nathan Price as a man of God and the word "miracle"—cannot be made. Any such forced connection would be only ironic since Nathan Price in his Congo ministry never achieved anything remotely resembling a miracle. He could not even get the Congolese children (or his own youngest child) baptized. Yet as she has said and as we have intuited, Kingsolver lives, and writes, with echoes of hope running through her consciousness. And in the beauty, and the life-giving production, of the contemporary natural world rests the basis for much of her personal hope. It was the character of Adah Price that turned regularly to the poems of Emily Dickinson for language that was difficult for her to achieve in the real world: *Hope is a thing with feathers*, wrote Dickinson. For Kingsolver, perhaps the phrase would be turned to read "Hope is a thing with *tendrils*." Growth, the immersion and re-entry from the earth, the shooting green spurts of all kinds of hope—Kingsolver created that green world in *Prodigal Summer*, though she emphasized the actual growth of plants less visibly there than she did the growth of human beings' understanding of themselves and of themselves in communities. It is as if *Animal, Vegetable, Miracle* must conjoin with *Prodigal Summer*—which in one real sense it does because the calendar of the summer of growth in the former is so extravagantly prolific—in order to impress upon the reader a true meaning of both the words *prodigality* and *miracle*.

When Kingsolver published *Small Wonder*, her second essay collection, in 2002, she chose as epigraph a sentence from a writer long beloved to her, Wendell Berry, the Kentucky environmentalist poet, novelist, and essayist. That sentence is "To treat life as less than a miracle is to give up on it." (Small Wonder no page). More inclusive, perhaps, than the "miracle" connected with food production, Berry's use of the encompassing noun provides one gloss on the word's importance for Kingsolver.

John Lang uses the word with the same inclusive properties when he speaks about the author's skills. He describes Kingsolver as "an author unafraid of the term 'miracle,' though she generally uses that term not to denote supernatural events but rather the daily wonders and mysteries of life in *this* world" (Iron 2).

As if somewhat unsatisfied with what *Animal, Vegetable, Miracle* succeeds in conveying, Kingsolver wrote an essay in 2007 which appeared in the *Washington Post*: "The Blessings of Dirty Work" restates a number of points from the book itself, and eventually is published as a "coda" to that book. As we have seen, Kingsolver often uses her essays and comments to undergird, or to introduce, or to summarize positions she has taken less explicitly in her fiction. Here her approach is similar, although the essay's content is more the kind of writing that Steven Hopp had done throughout the book. The essay completes that quasi-religious tenor, taking us from "miracle" to "blessings," and leaving the quasi-religious posturing of *Poisonwood Bible*'s Nathan Price far behind. It includes the personal, as Kingsolver's essays often do.

Primarily, however, the essay is a substantial commentary on the misuse of land in India (applied in a corollary fashion to implications about the future of United States farming). After her opening (in which "dirty" farming and gardening is set against the more respectable kinds of housework, and labor of all types—illustrating the continuing denigration of those who work with their hands), Kingsolver segues into an informed discussion of the considerable work of Vandana Shiva, who is the director of the Research Foundation for Science, Technology and Natural Resources Policy. Trained as a physicist, she has long been an advocate for farmers' rights, and is an expert on the soil of India. Kingsolver explains, "Traditional farming retains soil structure, but intensive modern agriculture does not: Since the 1970s, while global grain production has tripled, an estimated thirty percent of the world's farmland has become too damaged to use" (Dirty 8). In Navdanya, Shiva's farm-based institute in Dehradun, she studies the rebuilding of the soil, as well as the extinction of traditional seed varieties—another catastrophic result of contemporary farming. Indian farmers come to learn her methods, and because the suicide rate among the farmers in India is so high, whatever ideas they can find to continue their occupations is useful in many ways.

Navdanya also hosts "the Grandmothers' University, a series of cooking festivals to help connect the conservation of traditional crops with the practical skills of cooking and eating them. Clearly, traditional farming and time-honored food customs are mutually dependent" (Dirty 10). Part of the rationale, then, for the inclusion of recipes—as well as food preparation sections—within *Animal, Vegetable, Miracle* no doubt stems from Kingsolver's visit to Navdanya and her respect for the ongoing work there.

Another essay that foreshadowed the project described in *Animal, Vegetable, Miracle* is the deft description of Lily's raising chickens. Obsessed as a five-year-old with the process of being in charge of the rooster and his hens, Lily was a careful observer of the brood and its practices; she was by natural instinct a good caregiver.

Titled "Lily's Chickens," Kingsolver's description makes the essay one of the high points of her second collection, *Small Wonder*. Humorous and focused primarily on the small child's role, "Lily's Chickens" gives the reader the small bantam rooster, "Mr. Doodle," learning how to coerce his hens into sharing both grasshoppers and bodies.

Kingsolver writes comically about the flock's becoming acclimated to their new surroundings: "it is hard to put much stock in the emotional life of a creature with the I.Q. of an eggplant. Seems to me you put a chicken in a box, and she looks around and says, 'Gee, life is a box.' You take her out, she looks around and says, 'Gee, it's sunny here'" (Small Wonder 112). But by the time that Lily's occupation of raising chickens appears in *Animal, Vegetable, Miracle*, such use of obvious humor is gone: what is left is the seriousness of the child—no longer five—seeing what she does as a meaningful contribution to her family's existence.

Kingsolver includes data about the facts of farming, quantities of food growing, and the waste in long-distance transporting. She also foreshadows their lifestyle as it will be explained more clearly in the book: "We don't go to the grocery very often; our garden produces a good deal of what we eat, and in some seasons nearly all of it. This is not exactly a hobby. It's more along the lines of religion, something we believe in the way families believe in patriotism and loving thy neighbor as thyself. If our food ethic seems an unusual orthodoxy to set alongside those other two, it probably shouldn't. We consider them to be connected" (Small Wonder 112–13).

Given this statement written in the very early years of the twenty-first century, the fact that the Kingsolver–Hopp family chose to both experiment and write about their year of "food life" five years later seems less idiosyncratic, and more an integral part of the ethos of a growing family: *what the children will learn* justifies a number of seemingly experimental procedures, not all of them connected so precisely with daily existence. As Kingsolver has recently described the pragmatics of the project, "Food is inspiring. It's that simple. Eating is the most important human activity, and a consumer choice we make every day. Suddenly, a three-ring food crises: we have unprecedented health and obesity problems, due to poor diets. We're putting almost as much fossil fuels into our refrigerators as our cars. And our farmers and rural communities are struggling to survive. All these problems have one cause; we're buying so much of our food from far away. We rarely look at our plates and ask, 'Where has this stuff *been?*'" (Web 2013).

Animal, Vegetable, Miracle for the most part avoids such direct "lecturing." There is reason that Sandra Ballard, as she points out that the book won the *James Beard Award*, comments that the text "spurred a revolution that calls us back to what people used to know about food when America was more rural than urban" (Ballard 19). Adopting some of the narrative strategies that she had perfected in *The Poisonwood Bible*, Kingsolver relied on the alternation of Hopp's scientific and economic segments, set again Camille's very subjective and natural-seeming essays, replete with recipes and weekly meal plans, set against the dominant narrative voice—that of Barbara Kingsolver, mother and chief cook and planter and harvester—to create useful diversity, as well as humor.

Sampling the varied flavors of these three voices, each expressing a different part of the complicated food text, shows the way a simply defined prose conveys more than a literal meaning. In the "August" segments of the book, for instance, Kingsolver writes about having kept a journal for many years, so that she would remember which seeds and plants bore best. Titling this larger section, "Life in a Red State," she focuses on the production of tomatoes: "The first tomato of the season brings me to my knees." Any reader familiar with the truly "seasonal" exuberance of the tomato knows that this section will eventually show readers that kind of hyperbolic plenty. But at the start, the author gains a smile by using this analogy: "Its vital stats are recorded in my journal with the care of a birth announcement: It's an Early Girl! Four ounces! June 16! Blessed event, we've waited so long. Over the next few weeks I note the number, size, and quality of the different varieties as they begin to come in: two Green Zebras, four gorgeous Jaune Flammes, one single half-pound Russian Black … "

"As supply rises, value depreciates," the author states. Eventually the tomatoes are weighed, not counted, and by mid-August 302 pounds are harvested, as compared to only 50 pounds in July (Animal 196–7). True to her character as the loving mother, and planter, and harvester, Kingsolver adds that the family still loves this bounty of tomatoes, and compares their reaction to the fact that parents take an incredible number of pictures of a child's first smile, first bath, first steps...but then the photos diminish radically. The author's prose stays in the tenor of an earlier sentence: "however jaded I may have become, winter knocks down the hollow stem of my worldliness and I'll start each summer again with expectations as simple as a child's."

The Steven Hopp essay that is grouped with the plenty of August is an economic one, titled "Sustaining the Unsustainable." Here he describes what federal support is available to the small farmer, showing that the "Federal Farm Bill" that people may remember existing—since just after the Depression—has been whittled away by the lobbies of corporate farming, the agribusiness concerns. Ironically, since the small farmers are more likely to use practices that build soil rather than deplete it, there is almost no federal aid available, although Congress has included "a tiny allotment for local foods in the most recent Farm Bill" (2002). He supplies the address of a useful Web site, and suggests that readers weigh in with their local representatives (Animal 207).

Hopp similarly performs this somewhat cryptic but useful service throughout the book—beginning with "Oily Food," where he discusses the cost of lengthy transportation that should be figured into the costs of supplies such as tropical fruits and out-of-season vegetables, and scattered throughout the book. "The Price of Life," for example, discusses the dominance of Concentrated Animal Feeding Operatives (CAFO) dilemma, just as "Losing the Bug Arms Race" presents useful information about pesticides. "Home Grown" discusses the role of community supported agriculture (CSA). In each essay, Hopp provides Web sources or print references, and this kind of information appears at the back of the book as "References" along with a double listing of food-friendly organizations and global resources for interested readers.

Readers read for this variety. Hopp's information is both useful and concise. Camille's essays—which include weekly menu plans as well as recipes—are the softer side of food talk. "Getting over the Bananas" is an essay that focuses on her initial sense that she would feel deprived, hungry, less-than-healthy as the year went on: she did not easily give up her quotient of fresh fruits. But as a practice, her essays are grouped with the thematic divisions of *Animal, Vegetable, Miracle*, so in the "August" section, she writes about tomatoes—canning tomatoes—and their useful recipes. For a change of flavor, her bluntly titled essay "Canning Season" opens, "When I was a kid, summer was as long as a lifetime. A month could pass without me ever knowing what day of the week it was. Time seemed to stretch into one gigantic, lazy day of blackberry picking and crawdad hunting.

My friends and I would pretty much spend our lives together, migrating back and forth between the town swimming pool and the woods, where we would pretend to be orphans left to our own devices in the wilderness. School was not on our minds. Our world was green grass, sunshine, and imagination" (Animal 212).

Lyric, and reminiscent of some of Kingsolver's own essays about growing up in Kentucky, this opening does not prepare the reader for the clear and somewhat terse description of the advent of August, that month when "Pounds of them [tomatoes] will roll down from the garden each day, staining every one of our kitchen towels with their crimson juices." Whether the bounty is sliced to be dried or cooked into sauces, eventually those 302 pounds of tomatoes must be conquered. Most of this chapter's essay deals with the processes of canning. It does include the recipes for the family's tomato sauce and a mole.

However, Camille's essay that precedes this one, "The Spirit of Summer," is more typical in that it focuses on ways of taking care of an immense crop of zucchini. Two significant recipes from this essay are "Disappearing Zucchini Orzo" and "Zucchini Chocolate Chip Cookies," and these are appended to a "Squash-Season Meal Plan" that lists a possible menu for the week. As with her essays proper, Camille does not give the reader dry listings: for the "Disappearing Zucchini Orzo," she notes that the reader should choose a cheese grater to shred the vegetable, and then sauté it briefly with chopped onion and garlic until "lightly golden." To this, one adds the thyme and oregano, "stir thoroughly, and then remove mixture from heat" (Animal 194). Practical and useful, even these directions take on the voice of the essayist. (The corresponding chapter in the primary text is Kingsolver's "Zucchini Larceny," another humorous description of the role of seasonal plenty on the farm. "But there sat this pile on the kitchen counter, with its relatives jammed into a basket in the mudroom—afloat between garden and kitchen—just waiting for word so they could come in here too: the Boat Zucchinis.") (Animal 188).

The author does not mince words about the importance of this conception of useful food knowledge. "Cooking is good citizenship," she notes as she explains, "It's the only way to get serious about putting locally raised foods into your diet, which keeps farmlands healthy and grocery money in the neighborhood. Cooking and eating with children teaches them civility and practical skills they can use later on to save money and stay healthy, whatever may happen in their lifetimes to the gas-fueled food industry ... Households that have lost the soul of cooking from their routines may not know what they're missing" (Animal 150). On her current Web site, Kingsolver notes a kind of apologia,

We're a pretty ordinary family, in that we all have a thousand things to do including full-time jobs or school. Part of the point we wanted to make in *Animal, Vegetable, Miracle* is that regular, busy people can pay more attention to where our food comes from, and use healthier ingredients for the rituals of our lives. All over the world, people have food cultures, cooking special meals on various occasions (or even every day) because it's traditional, enjoyable, and considered to be worth the effort. In this country, the closest thing we have to a distinctive food culture might be feeding our kids burgers in a speeding car. Are we busier than families in Italy or Japan? (Web 2013)

One of the closing sections of the book lists the approximate costs for what Kingsolver calls "our locavore year." She computed that "Between April and November, the full cash value of the vegetables, chickens, and turkeys we'd raised and harvested was $4,410" (for the total year, a figure closer to $7,500) (Animal 130). While any computation would be somewhat inaccurate, this financial benefit might undergird a family's resolve to take on a similar, if modified, project. Kingsolver notes, "Our family took a somewhat formal pledge in order to push ourselves into doing something we knew would improve our lives. We had to do it together, or not at all. To be honest, it was much easier than we expected... Not everybody can walk away from the industrial food pipeline altogether, but all of us can take a few steps, and the benefits are immediate" (Web 2013).

She also has said repeatedly,

Thoughtful food life is not just about growing your own... Our intention was to explain why food is not strictly a product, but a process. That's the lesson our culture has lost, and why we're so dubious of the 'product.' An important step in anyone's food security is to recover an understanding of processes—for example, to learn the differences between feedlot meat operations and pasture grazing, why one requires universal use of antibiotics while the other eschews it. Why a pasture-rasied chicken lays eggs with crayon-orange yolks, full of healthy beta-carotenes. Why lettuce comes in early in the growing season, and watermelons arrive late... we provided a seasonal account of how foods grow—we thought readers might be interested in the natural history of what they eat... It's a very basic human urge, it seems, to plant a seed, watch it grow, provision ourselves first-hand. (Web 2013)

Most reviews of *Animal, Vegetable, Miracle* were descriptive, straightforward in their interest; a few showed some bewilderment.

Most quoted a great deal from Kingsolver's prose, and nearly each review summarized the roles that Steven Hopp and Camille Kingsolver had played. It remained for Janet Maslin in the *New York Times* to simultaneously praise and denigrate the book by calling it "a wonderfully neighborly account of *stunt eating*" (Maslin 2007). In Kingsolver's own words, she was surprised by "the overwhelming response of our readers." She adds, "As an ongoing commitment to our own local food economy, Steven founded the Meadowview Farmers Guild in our community, a project that includes a local-foods restaurant, The Harvest Table" (Web 2013).

As Kingsolver's note above suggests, another offshoot of the several years' involvement in the period of "food life" recorded in the book was the creation of the family's restaurant and crafts center in Meadowview, Virginia. Named "Harvest Table Restaurant," the place carries out the convictions described in *Animal, Vegetable, Miracle*: for as much of the cooking as possible, foods are locally grown. The old country store next door has become an area crafts shop, and the cobblestone streets in the quaint downtown courtyard location add to the sense of authenticity. The site—restaurant and store—employs between 30 and 40 people. Together, this development provides good illustration for what Cusick had termed an understanding of "bioregional living ... Attention to the person, to the local, is the first integral gesture toward a global social consciousness." Both the book and the Harvest Table establishment show "the consequences of a personal, biological and emotional investment in place origin" (Cusick in Leder 230).

11

Small Wonder: Staying Alive and the Bellwether Prizes

We are of the animal world. We are part of the cycles of growth and decay ... We are in relationship with the rest of the planet, and that connectedness tells us we must reconsider the way we see ourselves and the rest of nature.

Linda Hogan, *Dwellings* 114

The disastrous terrorist attacks on the World Trade Center, the Pentagon, and a crash in a Pennsylvania field impacted Barbara Kingsolver's life—and that of her family—as much as those attacks did the national consciousness. To the question of why Kingsolver did not immediately publish a new novel after the unchallenged (and some might say phenomenal) successes of both *The Poisonwood Bible* in 1998 and *Prodigal Summer* in 2000 might be explained with her involvement in the politics of combating terror.

Kingsolver's title essay in the 2002 collection, *Small Wonder*, speaks to her immense shock, and horror, as "9/11" played itself out over millions of television sets and radios, as well as in the lived experience of thousands of people in New York and Washington, in the United States and the world over. To erase the sheer wall of horror between that morning and the continuing human recognition of it, which was necessarily focused on the nearly 3,000 deaths—and many more casualties—that resulted: the world of Americans fearful of what might happen next became the extant circumstances. Millions felt the pangs of loss; millions more felt the trauma of the shocking physical invasion.

It was the *Los Angeles Times* that contacted Kingsolver immediately. Accordingly, on September 12, 2001, her essay appeared in its pages: her writing was, of course, filled with grief and horror, but Kingsolver never equivocated. Whether or not her equivocation here was an error, she still maintained her long-running commitment to truth. Faced with the deaths of innocent people, America as a culture—right then—wanted nothing to do with blame. For the honest-speaking Kingsolver, however, *not* taking some portion of that blame was inconceivable. "A Pure, High Note of Anguish" lamented the deaths of the innocents who had done nothing "to deserve it"— that dying. In a later section of the piece she wrote, "You bear this world and everything that's wrong with it by holding life still precious, each time, and starting over." Calling to those she named first-class patriots (all described as "Americans who read and think"), the author insisted that there would be ways around—and past—viewing 9/11 as simply, irrevocably, tragedy.

For her statement that "Some people believe our country needed to learn how to hurt in this new way," Ross Douthat, writing in *National Review*, criticized Kingsolver for what he called her pervasive view of America as dark, limping toward authoritarianism. He closed his essay with a snide comment at her very visible success as writer: "However healthy and wealthy and successful she may become, she can never truly enjoy it—because the jackboots are always sounding on the street, and the Gestapo is always at the door."

With a finesse equal to anything she had published in her *High Tide in Tucson* essay collection, "Small Wonder"—the title essay here, which draws from parts of some of the newspaper essays she had published within the first month after the attack—speaks of a lost 16-month-old boy who managed to toddle away from his babysitter and then disappeared for days. Found eventually, and to everyone's great surprise, in a mountain cave where he lay quietly beside a large bear, nursing from her, the story is the lynchpin for this long essay, the essay that reprises the terrifying experiences of "9/11" without ever specifically mentioning them.

The essay concludes "Political urgencies come and go, but it's a fair enough vocation to strike one match after another against the dark isolation, when spectacular arrogance rules the day and tries to force hope into hiding … I have stories of things I believe in: a persistent river, a forest on the edge of night, the religion inside a seed, the startle of wingbeats when a spark of red life flies against all reason out of the darkness. One child, one bear. I'd like to speak of small wonders, and the possibility of taking heart" (Small Wonder 21). Earlier in this essay she had commented, "I believe in parables. I navigate life using stories where I find them, and I hold tight to the ones that tell me new kinds of truth. This story of a bear who nursed a child is one to believe in. I believe that the things we dread most can sometimes save us. I am losing faith in such a simple thing as despising an enemy with unequivocal righteousness" (Small Wonder 6).

As Kingsolver rapidly assembled these essays (and others that she expanded, or made more relevant to the 2001 events) into the essay collection named for this long composite piece—*Small Wonder*, which appeared in 2002—she compressed much of the "9/11" history, and her part in creating a broadly dimensional response to "9/11" itself, into the book's

"Foreword." In this shorter statement, Kingsolver describes the way she personally faced down the demons of fear and anguish after the attack. She begins with a reference to Adrienne Rich's poem, "Diving into the Wreck," using the image of diving (going "deeper and deeper") to explain that immersing herself in what she terms "the process of grief" clarified what she had experienced. In her quasi-scientific mode, the author describes, "You look at all the parts of a terrible thing until you see that they're assemblies of smaller parts, all of which you can name, and some of which you can heal or alter, and finally the terror which seemed unbearable becomes manageable" (Small Wonder xiii).

By the time she had ordered and organized these 23 essays, she was ready to admit that her real, integrated purpose was less about terrorism striking the world's people than it was about "who we seem to be, what remains for us to live for, and what I believe we could make of ourselves" (in her words, "I have tried to address, ultimately, things that don't rapidly change") (Small Wonder xv). Accordingly, Kingsolver then dedicates the book to "every citizen of my country who has suffered bereavement with honor, trepidation without panic, and the insult of fundamentalist condemnation without succumbing to similar thinking in turn" (Small Wonder xvi).

Although critics consider the two essay collections to be separate, both best-selling books from the Kingsolver *oeuvre*, there is more reciprocity between *High Tide in Tucson* and *Small Wonder* than most reviewers acknowledge. In fact, some of the more ecological essays in the 2002 collection readily build on essays that had been published in the 1995 collection. As Kingsolver had written in that earlier title essay,

> It's starting to look as if the most shameful tradition of Western civilization is our need to deny we are animals. In just a few centuries of setting ourselves apart as landlords of the Garden of Eden, ... we have managed to behave like so-called animals anyway, and on top of it to wreck most of what took three billion years to assemble. Air, water, earth, and fire—so much of our own elements so vastly contaminated. We endanger our own future ... the mercury in the ocean, the pesticides on the soybean fields, all come home to our breast-fed babies. In the silent spring we are learning it's easier to escape from a chain gang than a food chain ... (High Tide 10)

In "Small Wonder," the title essay for the second book, she similarly notes that "We are all beasts in this kingdom, we have killed and been killed, and some new time has come to us in which we are called out, to find another way to divide the world. Good and evil cannot be all there is" (Small Wonder 6).

Critical as her tone is in each of these essays, Kingsolver's work reminds the reader that Christine Cusick had said repeatedly, "In all of her nonfiction, hope lies in the persistent human desire to find a connection to land" (in Leder 231).

Critic Mary Ellen Snodgrass includes a chronology of events in her *Barbara Kingsolver, A Literary Companion*, along with a detailed description of the 2001–2003 period, when the author continues to comment about her chagrin over US politics, as well as the organizations she joins and the track record of her political moves. Snodgrass notes that in later September and in October, 2001, Kingsolver warns that fanatic patriotism squelches free speech. In "No Glory in Unjust War on the Weak," an essay written for the *Los Angeles Times*, "Kingsolver pressed a pacifist agenda. While American bombers struck Afghanistan, she flinched at the thought of human misery" as she described "explosives raining from the sky on a place already ruled by terror, by all accounts as poor and war-scarred a populace as has ever crept to a doorway and looked out" (October 14, 2001, M1). Snodgrass comments in this description on Kingsolver's use of self-deprecating humor. Describing a November 22, 2001, essay in the *Washington Post*, Snodgrass says that the author's "distrust of President George W. Bush's philosophy derives from a love of First Amendment rights... Taking a parent's point of view, she mourned the endangerment of the world's children as fiercely as she warded off threats to her own two girls" (Snodgrass 27).

This critic mentions that Kingsolver was awarded the National Award, given to a Kentucky native who has achieved national acclaim, and that *Small Wonder*, when published in 2002, won the annual Nautilus Award, honoring a work that contributes significantly to conscious living and positive social change. She also listed Kingsolver's having been honored by President and Mrs. Clinton (in December, 2000), when she was awarded the National Humanities Medal for activism (along with Toni Morrison, Maya Angelou, Ernest Gaines, Mikhail Baryshnikov, Horton Foote, and others).

From that high point, Kingsolver worked diligently to express her personal displeasure at the United States going to war. A winter, 2002, article for the *Los Angeles Times* made her irritation with George W. Bush clear. She also appeared with Bruce Babbitt, Jimmy Carter, Stewart Udall, and others as signatories of a full-page ad supporting the work of Americans for Alaska (calling for "protection of the Arctic National Wildlife Refuge from oil drilling") (Snodgrass 28). She then "joined the controversial antiwar group *Not In Our Name*, which published a two-page statement of conscience in the *New York Times* attacking the Bush administration and calling on citizens to resist the policies and overall political drift toward right-wing extremism. The statement called for due process, a public forum on retaliation, defiance of the Patriot Act, and adherence to a global common cause" (Snodgrass 28).

In retrospect, Priscilla Leder speaks to the political trouble that visited Kingsolver after her publishing newspaper stories that expressed a more complicated attitude than "blame the terrorists." Some adversarial critics also pointed out the author's swipes at the policies of the Bush administration. Issues taken together, Kingsolver became one of the more prominent objects of attack by the ultra-conservatives.

> That grief and frustration shadows much of *Small Wonder*, which seems haunted by an implicit question: Why does our culture so often seem to lack respect for life—to view it as a commodity or to see violence as a solution? The struggle to confront this difficult question [says Leder] shapes form as well as content: the essays of *Small Wonder* are darker, longer, less often playful, and more stringently analytical than those of the earlier collection. Characteristically, though, Kingsolver seeks out and calls for solutions, documenting efforts to preserve the San Pedro River in Arizona, and a program that encourages people to grow native crops in an endangered forest in Yucatan, and advocating less violence on television, responsible eating, and communal actions of all kinds. The human drive for self-preservation can overcome our destructive tendencies. (Leder 15)

In Leder's summary, she sees the "9/11" commentaries as less frequent than the Kingsolver essays that speak of ecological themes, as well as "celebrating the wonder of the natural world and considering how humans might relate more responsibly to it" (Leder 14). Placed securely between the terror of "9/11" and the book that would eventually be published as *Animal, Vegetable, Miracle: A Year of Food Life*, *Small Wonder* anchors the beginning of this twenty-first century as if the decade of the 1990s were—for Kingsolver—little more than personal exploration.

As with *High Tide in Tucson*, Kingsolver again organizes her essay collection in a meaningful progression. Following the lengthy and wide-ranging title essay, *Small Wonder* begins with a group of seven essays that relate to the writer's natural surroundings: among those seven essays are the three which she cowrote with her husband for a natural history magazine ("The Patience of a Saint," "Seeing Scarlet," and "Called Out"). The collective impact of these writings about rivers, natural beauties seen from either their Virginia cabin or their Arizona house, and the strong bond between the human and the animal—a pervasive theme increasingly in Kingsolver's twenty-first century writing, is unified, moving, yet ultimately modest.

"Saying Grace" is a classic Kingsolver commentary that uses her family as starting point and then moves to descriptions of the natural world. Here, coming the fall of the terrorist attack, the Arizona family has decided not to return to Kentucky for Thanksgiving—flights being difficult or dangerous, or considered to be so in people's imaginations, the Kingsolver–Hopp family stays in Arizona and visits the Grand Canyon. Playing with the metaphor of the holiday feast, Kingsolver writes, "How greedy can one person be, to want more than the Grand Canyon: What feast could satisfy a mother more deeply than to walk along a creek through a particolored carpet of leaves, watching my children pick up the finetoothed gifts of this scarlet maple, that yellow aspen, piecing together the picture puzzle of a biological homeplace? We could listen for several days to the songs of living birds instead of making short work of one big dead one" (Small Wonder 23). The point of this essay, finally, becomes the great generosity that would be possible were the United States to share as much as it might—with both this country's poor as well as with the world's poor.

Similarly, "Knowing Our Place" works from the intimacy of those various views into the surrounding country—reminiscent of Kingsolver's essay from *High Tide*, "The Memory Place"—and stressing, again similarly, the values of wilderness:

> Oh, how can I say this: People *need* wild places. Whether or not we think we do, we *do*. We need to be able to taste grace and know once again that we desire it. We need to experience a landscape that is timeless, whose agenda moves at the pace of speciation and glaciers. To be surrounded by a singing, mating, howling commotion of other species, all of which love their lives as much as we do ours, and none of which could possibly care less about our economic status or our running day calendar. Wildness puts us in our place. It reminds us that our plans are small and somewhat absurd. It reminds us why, in those cases in which our plans might influence many future generations, we ought to choose carefully. (Small Wonder 40)

In the essays that Kingsolver cowrites with Steven Hopp, there is usually less emphasis on the family locale; otherwise, as would be expected, the careful descriptions of the natural world, the poetic touches, continue. "Seeing Scarlet" recounts their discovery of the thousand remaining scarlet macaws ("a fierce, full meter of royal red feathers head to tail, a soldier's rainbow colored epaulets") seen in the Corcovado National Park in the Osa Peninsula—the Costa Rican setting for not only the macaws but also for the 400 species of birds and 140 of mammals. Even though the macaw is globally endangered, the two observers saw the birds playing tag through the tall trees of the peninsula—just two days south of San Jose in the Talamanca Highlands (Small Wonder 59). "Called Out" describes the effusive annuals that on occasion grow in desert lands, in this case during the summer of 1998. These "desert ephemerals" survive, but seldom show such efflorence as they did that season—and the authors use the unusual season to discuss seed selection, seed variation, and life itself (Small Wonder 91). "The Patience of a Saint" draws a luminous map of rivers but includes children straddling the small width of the San Pedro to illustrate how difficult, how prized, rivers are in the Arizona desert.

Grouped with these essays are two others, "Setting Free the Crabs" (located on Sanibel Island in the Gulf) and "The Forest's Last Stand." In the first, as Kingsolver's daughter tries to disengage a crab from what she is sure is the prettiest shell on the beach, the writer is moved to mourn how seldom anything alive remains in its natural habitat. The author notes, "When humans decide to work our will, we are so tragically efficient. Now that we've used up all the prairie, we've taking to burning the rain forests to clear pasture for fast-food beef… In the meantime, and largely as a result, the rate of species extinctions has reached astounding new highs; many scientists predict we will lose about a quarter of the world's wildlife over the next two decades" (Small Wonder 64). Kingsolver's theme here is the child's relinquishment of the beautiful shell (which contains the tenacious crab) rather than taking what she most wants for her own.

"The Forest's Last Stand" recounts the couple's journey into Mayan (Guatemalan) lands, voraciously learning whatever comes their direction. Seeing the positive results of education by a Mexican conservation group, the author enumerated her and Steven's encounters with a troop of howler monkeys, the chachalacas, iguanas, trees whose outstretched branches "were lit like candles, aflame with birds," a pygmy owl, a jaguar, "keel-billed toucans," a woodpecker, agoutis, foxes, tapirs, opossums, "turkeys colored like peacocks" and "the dark embrace of trees… the pyramid of Mirador" (Small Wonder 78–80).

The group of seven essays leads to one of the most forceful, and perhaps the longest, in *Small Wonder*, "A Fist in the Eye of God." She is coalescing strands of her own observation of the natural world (at the start, the author washes her dishes and observes a nest being built in a tree outside the kitchen window) with significant principles from Darwin's ecology, as well as the plant studies of Nikolai Vavilon—and quotations from poet (farmer, philosopher, friend) Wendell Berry. The essay moves from "lesson" to "lesson" in the author's characteristic way. "We dilute and toss at our peril. Scientific illiteracy in our population is leaving too many of us unprepared to discuss or understand much of the damage we are wreaking on our atmosphere, our habitat, and even the food that enters our mouth ... " Biodiversity is crucial. (Small Wonder 96–7). With this essay, Kingsolver sets up an introduction for several much more personal pieces, beginning with "Lily's Chickens," and continuing through "Letter to a Daughter at Thirteen" and "Letter to My Mother." Strangely shortsighted as to the impact these very personal essays have on her readers, Kingsolver in her recent Web pages has written that she is "squeamish about autobiography. I've never written anything in that line" (Web 2013).

The reader has seen that the gist of "Lily's Chickens" appears in *Animal, Vegetable, Miracle: A Year of Food Life*—and elsewhere as well. And biographers have long mined the materials Kingsolver included in "Letter to My Mother," published in 1997 (five years earlier than its inclusion in this collection), a range of intimate re-creations that move from her sorrow at three that her parents have been happy on a vacation without her, to her vivid insights into being a teenager, comically described at 13 and at 15, "raging at you in my diary." When her parents drive her to college in Indiana, she is provoked at them—particularly at her mother—and says coldly, "*I won't need anything*, I tell you" (Small Wonder 166). But it is in this essay, too, that she describes her frighteningly lifeless reaction to the acquaintance rape she endured, as well as her natural fear at the threatening intruder with his knife some years later. The tone changes from anger to love as Kingsolver as writer admits that becoming a mother herself has made her understand how much her mother loves her, and she accordingly confesses her own love—for both her mother and her daughters. Especially poignant is her account of her second pregnancy (she is 40, and she is overdue—in the midst of finding out that late babies run in their family). In a subsequent paragraph about this ordeal, the true alliances between mother and daughter are finally spoken:

> A week past my due date you are calling every day. Steven answers the phone, holds it up, and mouths, "Your mother again." He thinks you may be bugging me. You aren't. I am a woman lost in the weary sea of waiting, and you are the only one who really knows where I am. Your voice is keeping me afloat. I grab the phone. (Small Wonder 174)

The connecting essay between "Lily's Chickens" and "Letter to My Mother" is the lengthy "Letter to a Daughter at Thirteen," written for Camille. Using the tactic of describing her older daughter with her memories of herself at those respective ages, Kingsolver breaks into the tandem sections by saying, "I stare, wondering. How did I wind up with this totally cool person for a daughter?"

(There is also material about Kingsolver's mother—Camille's grandmother—in this essay.) The author, however, seldom avoids her tendency to suggest a lesson, and in this essay, she points out vividly, "answers will work for you [her daughter] only when you've stitched them together yourself."

> People say it's because parents *love* their kids so much that they want to tell them how to live. But I'm afraid that's only half love, and the other half selfishness. Kids who turn out like their parents kind of validate their world. That was my first real lesson as a mother—realizing that you could be different from me, and it wouldn't make me less of a person. (Small Wonder 149)

The only nonbiographical essay in this grouping is the comic anti-television piece, "The One-Eyed Monster, and Why I Don't Let Him In." More in the tone of several of Kingsolver's comic essays in *High Tide*, particularly the effective "Stone Soup" where she writes about various definitions of family and community, this essay does not compare with the prose that focuses on either beloved figures in her life or the richness of the natural world.

Leaving the group of personal essays about Lily, Camille, and her mother—and herself, Kingsolver moves back to essays that were originally commissioned: "Going to Japan," written for the *New York Times*, several essays about writing, and "Flying," which gives the reader the first mention of the fears resulting from "9/11" since the beginning of the collection. There she continues her mode of commemoration, showing the reader her personal continuing grief as she grows "a long raft of Legion of Honor poppies." That essay concludes, with a promised return to the author's normally kindly spirit, "A few things I have always known for certain, and this is one: If I had to give up my life for anything, it would have to have the resilience of hope, the elation of new literacy, the brilliant life of a field of flowers, the elementary kindness of bread … something as sure as love" (Small Wonder 194).

This essay is followed by "Household Words," in which Kingsolver provokes readers into considering how we derive the complex meaning of "home" and contrasts that comfortable, reassuring word with the more alien word, "homelessness." Aggravated that homelessness now exists so visibly in the United States (as well as in Kosovo, Kenya, India), the author scolds her readers:

> This is a special country, don't we know it. There are things about the way we organize our society that make it unique on the planet. We believe in liberty, equality, and whatever it is that permits extravagant housing developments to be built around my hometown [Tucson] at

the rate of one new opening each week ('Model homes, 6 bedrooms, 3-car garages, starting from the low $180s!'), while fully 20% of children on my county's record books live below the poverty level. Nationwide, though the homeless are a difficult population to census, we can be sure they number more than one million. How does the rest of the world keep a straight face when we go riding into it on our latest white horse of Operation-this-or-that-kind-of Justice, and everyone can see perfectly well how we behave at home? Home is where all justice begins. (Small Wonder 200–01)

"Whatever else 'home' might be called, it must surely be a fundamental human license ... Homelessness is an aberration."

By implication, Kingsolver emphasizes the goodness of American life through her insistence that residents (whether or not they are citizens) are entitled to a plethora of givens—housing, a small parcel of land, the right to grow vegetables, fruit, and flowers (the result of her pervasive concern with healthful foods will be the 2007 *Animal, Vegetable, Miracle: A Year of Food Life*), as well as the less tangible freedoms—worship, speech, work, legal performance, and caring for others.

Because the author is unwavering in her conviction that people—regardless of class or caste—are entitled to this quantity of (truly) inalienable rights, her *oeuvre* consists of statement and repetition, metaphor; statement and repetition, metaphor. What changes within the body of Kingsolver's writing is not the theme but her careful approaches to stating that theme: here, as the title insists, people's rights and freedoms are so basic that the statement of them should be "household words." Drawing from Robert Frost's poem "Death of a Hired Man" (and its succinct definition of "home" as "the place where, when you have to go there, they have to take you in"), she closes this important essay with words of Martin Luther King, Jr., words that incorporate *home* but also expand on that word's impact: "True peace, he said, is not merely the absence of tension. It's the presence of justice" (Small Wonder 205).

Perhaps one of Kingsolver's other "9/11" essays is the true conclusion of this collection of essays. "And Our Flag Was Still There" draws from several of her 2001 newspaper pieces and repeats the positive insistence that America is a survivalist nation: it lasts, its people learn, no amount of destruction can truly damage either the country or its people. Early in the essay, the author describes bursting "into tears of simultaneous pride and grief" as she listened to school children play "Stars and Stripes Forever" on what she called "their earnest, vibrating strings" (Small Wonder 236). Moving within the boundaries of this longer essay (length helps clarify sentences that may, in a single unit, be misread), Kingsolver speaks plainly, as if to take away any hesitation, any ambivalence, from her committed citizenship: "I love what we will do for one another in the name of inclusion and kindness... I love my country dearly" (Small Wonder 235–6). When she had earlier referred to "9/11" as "that monstrous massacre," she gave life to the perpetrators; here, she focuses instead on the unerring symbol of America's greatness and its continuity.

Kingsolver admits in this essay that she is no pacifist: she also insists that "There are as many ways to love America as there are Americans, and our country needs us all." Listing such patriots as Medgar Evers, Malcolm X, Karen Silkwood, Addie Mae Collins, August Spies, Adolph Fisher, Joe Hill, and others, the author claims a kind of sainthood for "Dissidents innocent of any crime greater than a belief in fair treatment of our poorest and ill-treated citizens" (Small Wonder 241). More to the point of her own sometimes misread statements about the terrorist attacks, and the United States' quick move to war, Kingsolver claims, "Questioning our government's actions does not violate the principles of liberty, equality, and freedom of speech; it exercises them, and by exercise we grow stronger. I have read enough of Thomas Jefferson to feel sure he would back me up on this. Our founding fathers, those vocal critics of imperialism, were among the world's first leaders to understand that to a democratic people, freedom of speech and belief are not just nice luxuries, they're as necessary as breathing" (Small Wonder 242–3).

Her closing essay as well, titled "God's Wife's Measuring Spoons," repeats that pervasive theme, that writers who find coercion to remain conventional effectively abandon their true purpose as writers: "whether I stand alone or with many, I'm still bound by that heart of mine to stand where we vote 'none of the above' when presented with the equally odious choices of kill or be killed... I'm insulted by the shallowness of the public debate, especially in wartime, founded as it seems to be on news reports devoid of any historical context" (Small Wonder 254). In this closing essay, however, the author does not pretend to have answers. One of her concluding ideas is that she grieves already: "the end of nature and biodiversity, of safety and the privilege of travel... We may already be looking at the end of the world, in the form we least expect. It would be a pure, hellish irony of history if the same smallpox germ that was let loose on this continent two hundred years ago by the European arrivals, which quickly killed some 98% of the indigenous American population, were to revisit us again with the same results. It does not seem safe to assume we will ever know the moral of our story" (Small Wonder 262).

Some of her most impassioned essays included in this collection are about what she sees as her means of living in today's world—her writing, as well as the necessary world of readers, booksellers, and publishers. If the convictions in "And Our Flag Was Still There" and "Household Words" were permanent parts of the writer's philosophy, her means of joining the important conversations about all elements of philosophy was her control of, and contributions from, language. But she also worked diligently in creating *Small Wonder* to make all parts of her book, like the integrated parts of her belief system, into a single organism.

What Kingsolver achieves in the most complicated of her novels may in some ways be compared with the carefully precise drawings that Paul Mirocha created for both *High Tide in Tucson* and *Small Wonder*. So integral to the effects Kingsolver's 25 essays had created in the 1995 volume of essays, for the 2002 collection, *Small Wonder*, the author listed the Mirocha drawings immediately after the book's Table of Contents. The listing of drawings was entitled "Illustrated Catalog of Wonders" (Small Wonder xi–xii). That listing includes such poetic titles as "The bronze-eyed possibility of lives that are not our own," "*El que quiera azul celeste, que le custe*: If you want the blue sky, the price is high," "Jaguar consuming a human heart, stone panel from post-classical Chichen Itza," "When all at once there came a crowd," "April, the sexiest month: broad-billed hummingbird." It is interesting that the titles are not necessarily a part of the essay in which the illustration appears.

Rather than just inserting the drawings, usually at the start of an essay, in *Small Wonder* each drawing has its own title (which may have little to do with the essay in which it is placed). "The bronze-eyed possibility of lives that are not our own" captions a feline face prefacing "Knowing Our Place," probably to represent the "adolescent bobcat" Kingsolver feels looking over her shoulder as she sits before her computer screen. "When all at once there came a crowd" describes the single poppy-shaped flower bowl in the lushly imaged "Called Out"—the flowers during summer, 1998. "April, the sexiest month" captions the hummingbird on her tiny nest; the essay title, "A Fist in the Eye of God," suggests none of this. The Miroche drawings—no matter either their title or their placement—work delicately and insightfully to enhance *Small Wonder*.

One of the thrusts of Kingsolver's second essay collection is her explanation of the aesthetics of art. Her art being language, in *Small Wonder* (unlike *High Tide in Tucson*), a cluster of essays treats writing itself. Here she includes "Stealing Apples," the preface she wrote for the 1998 issue of the expanded poem collection *Another America/Otra America*. She also incorporates the essay that prefaced her edited volume, *Best American Short Stories, 2000*, entitled "What Good Is a Story?" In describing her personal toughness as a writing teacher, Kingsolver says,

> For me to love a work of fiction, it must survive my harpy eye on all accounts. It will tell me something remarkable, it will be beautifully

executed, and it will be nested in truth … I ask a lot from my reading—ask of it, in fact, what I ask of myself when I sit down to write, and that is to get straight down to the task and carve something hugely important into a small enough amulet to fit into a reader's most sacred psychic pocket. I don't care what it is about, so long as it's not trivial. (Small Wonder 212–13)

Here she combines her own aesthetics as writer with the work she faced in reading the stories to be included in the year's best stories volume, but as it turns out, the qualities that make something a good read align with those that make writing that piece itself effective. Kingsolver had written earlier, "The artistic consummation of a novel is created by the author and reader, together, in an act of joint imagination" (High Tide 253). In her address to the American Booksellers Association, she spelled this out in more detail:

You begin with the words on the page, put there by someone else, but you fill in the scene with pictures that are your own. You do it unconsciously, as you're reading, and the whole thing becomes very familiar and real to you.

Similarly, as she wrote in a current Web entry, elaborating on the importance of expert readers: "Writing and reading are the two best ways humans have invented to participate with the larger world … Writing is a kind of social networking in the way that it connects you with other people, but literature asks a bit more from you than Facebook, and offers more mature rewards. A great book can take you anywhere on earth, in the present or the past or the future. It's the only mode of communication we have that actually lets you *become another* person by living inside his head, experiencing his problems and hopes. Fiction is a sort of inter-human magic."

Written for this essay collection is the author's moving "Marking a Passage," her lament for the encroaching loss of the independent bookshop, as well as her lament for the usurpation of the discrete language of the sexual. She opens "Taming the Beasts with Two Backs" by saying

Readers, hear my confession. I have written an unchaste novel. It's a little shocking, even to me. In my previous books I mostly wrote about sex by means of the spacebreak. One reviewer claimed I'd written the shortest sex scene in the English language. I know the scene he meant; the action turns when one character notices a cellophane crackle in the other's shirt pocket and declares that if he has a condom in there, this is her lucky day.

The scene then proceeds, in its entirety:
He did. It was. {Spacebreak!} (Small Wonder 222–3)

Kingsolver's point here is far from comic. Just as she forced every iota of meaning from her scrutiny of the words "home" and "homeless," here she decides that the transformation of words normally associated with sex has not only cheapened the words, but perhaps the acts with which they are associated. But the dilemma remains the reader's, says Kingsolver: "here we are, modern Americans, with our heads soaked in frank sexual imagery and our feet planted in our puritanical heritage, and any novelist with something to say about procreation or the lordotic posture has to navigate those straights. Great sex is rarer in art than in life because it's harder to do" (Small Wonder 227).

The seriousness of the undertaking of fiction writing permeates much of Kingsolver's recent commentary about her art and its aesthetics. As she stated in "What Good Is a Story?" "The business of fiction is to probe the tender spots of our imperfect world, which is where we live, write, and read" (Small Wonder 213). Somewhat strangely, she does not include any mention in *Small Wonder*, the 2002 essay collection, of her newest aesthetic project, establishing the biennial Bellwether Prize for a first novel—the prize includes a cash award of $25,000 as well as the book's publication. The award is given for "Socially Engaged Fiction." Funded from the large advance Kingsolver had received for the contracting of *The Poisonwood Bible*, the prize has now been given to seven authors, and judges for the prize have included America's foremost fiction writers themselves—Toni Morrison, Ursula K. LeGuin, Barry Lopez, John Nichols, Ruth Ozeki, Anna Quindlen, Paula Sharp, Russell Banks, and others. Winners of the prize have been Donna Gershten (*Kissing the Virgin's Mouth*), Gayle Brandeis (*The Book of Dead Birds*), Marjorie Kowalsky Cole (*Correcting the Landscape*), Hillary Jordan (*Mudbound*), Heidi Durrow (*The Girl Who Fell from the Sky*), Naomi Benaron (*Running the Rift*), and—in the autumn of 2013—Susan Nussbaum (*Good Kings, Bad Kings*).

Early books were published by HarperCollins: more recent novels have been published by Algonquin, a division of Workman. The prize is now titled the PEN/Bellwether Prize for Socially Engaged Fiction. The novels have ranged from Benaron's novel about genocide in Rwanda to Nussbaum's descriptive (read, play-like) interaction of characters in a Chicago home for disabled children and adolescents, to Cole's account of strike activity in Fairbanks, Alaska and Durrow's poignant narrative of the child who remains after a parent's suicide, and the murders of her siblings, by being pushed off a building roof. Seemingly the essence of political in theme, these Bellwether winners also span the range of what might be considered socially engaged. In Kingsolver's words, "I don't consider a novel to be a purely recreational vehicle. I think of it as an outlet for my despair, my delight, my considered opinions, and all the things that strike me as absolute and essential, worked out in words. Art is entertainment but it is also celebration, condolence, exploration, duty, and communion" (High Tide 252–3).

In addition to this ongoing literary activism, Kingsolver donates proceeds from both readings and books to the causes she personally supports. For instance, when she undertook a reading tour after the publication of *Prodigal Summer*, she asked that the income from low-cost tickets be given to local conservatory projects; and in the case of *Small Wonder*, according to the prefatory notes, all royalties from that book's publication have been and are divided among Physicians for Social Responsibility, Habitat for Humanity, Environmental Defense, and Heifer International.

12

The Lacuna

There is a still place, a gap between worlds, spoken by the tribal knowings
of thousands of years … At times, when we are silent enough, still enough,
we take a step into such mystery, the place of spirit …

Linda Hogan, *Dwellings* 20

Even though Barbara Kingsolver said that she had been working on—
or, perhaps, toward—this novel for many years (dating its beginning to
February of 2002), reviewers often commented that it had been nine years
since *Prodigal Summer*. (That novel appeared in the year 2000, only two years
after *The Poisonwood Bible* was published in 1998.) Readers were not exactly
discounting her books since 2000—*Small Wonder*, *Last Stand*, and *Animal,
Vegetable, Miracle: A Year of Food Life*—but they still clamored for novels on a
more predictable basis. Clearly, Kingsolver's method of creating and writing
a novel needed explaining. As she recently wrote,

> I begin to plot out a story in which characters will face these questions
> [How do we balance the needs of the individual with the needs of the
> community, when they're in conflict? How does one make peace with
> the terrible things one country does to another, when we've profited
> from them but weren't responsible?] through some conflict or crisis.
> I write pages and pages of what this novel will be about, themes, plot,
> characters. I create life histories for the characters. I list the things I'll
> need to research, in order to tell this story. As scenes occur to me, I jot
> them down without worrying about chronology. The beginning and the
> resolution will come, once I understand the architecture of the story.
> (Web 2013)

To create a timeline of the work Kingsolver was doing toward the book that
in 2009 was published as *The Lacuna* is mere speculation. That work may
have begun as early as *Prodigal Summer's* appearance in 2000 because, as the
author has said, "I spend months or years thinking about the shape of a novel
and *earning the authority to write it*" (Web 2013, italics mine).

"Authoritative" voice and demeanor need not suggest only a buttressing of facts. Tempting as factual accuracy is for the historical novelist, a category into which Kingsolver had decided to move for this Mexican-North Carolina adventure, it will never provide a complete rationale for success. Although *The Lacuna* did win the Orange Prize, it received mixed reviews throughout its initial publication season. It may have been more seriously "researched" than any other of Kingsolver's novels, but despite her trips to Mexico and living in familial cultures there, it remained somewhat studied. Critic Maureen Corrigan called it "vacant," playing on the natural meaning of "lacuna" itself, stressing that "the thing unintentionally missing here is an engaging main character" (NPR 2009). Despite Liesl Schillinger's positive and comprehensive *New York Times* review, Kingsolver's novel posed problems: where would the author find the authority to tackle Mexican and Russian politics—along with those of the United States during World War II and the McCarthy years; the aesthetics of Frida Kahlo and Diego Rivera and the fictional Harrison Shepherd; the political battles of Leon Trotsky—leading to his murder; and the struggles of the closeted Harrison Shepherd as he becomes a significant novelist living in Asheville, North Carolina (complete with its tales of Thomas Wolfe, the Fitzgeralds, and the Biltmore estate).

Creating—that is, building—*The Lacuna* as she had her earlier larger novels such as *The Poisonwood Bible* and, perhaps, *Animal Dreams* posed no mysteries for Kingsolver's readers to grasp. They knew that this was the way she assembled materials from which she eventually would—or would not—draw her fiction. As she recently described *The Lacuna*, it is "a novel about memory, history, American political identity, privacy, celebrity, gossip, and truth. I had contemplated [it] for decades. It took years of research in libraries and archives, jungles, museums, and historic neighborhoods all over Mexico and the United States. It is without a doubt the most difficult and satisfying work I've done" (Web 2013).

The new aspect in the author's description of this process was its surprisingly personal element. *The Lacuna* is in part about the world's view of the *different* among us. Being an artist or a writer means automatic inclusion in that category. Diego Rivera and Frida Kahlo already carry visible traits, verifiable lives, that Kingsolver would (as an artist herself) respect. So too does being the leader of a political party, as is the character Leon Trotsky. Added to Harrison Shepherd's eventual fame in Asheville, North Carolina, as a writer (with many comparisons made to Asheville's own differently enabled Thomas Wolfe) was his homosexuality. These illustrations of the *different* human beings—*different* whether because of talent or brilliance or sexual preference—exist in Kingsolver's novel to limn the way modern day culture *persecutes* that difference. The last hundred pages of the novel create a chronology for such persecution—first achieved through deportation by the INS, persecution seemingly based on little but skin color—and then the full blown persecution growing from the FBI's Red hunts, leading quickly to the McCarthy trials.

Kingsolver began exploring the possibilities for the richness of *The Lacuna* soon after the "9/11" terrorist attacks and, as we have seen in the 2002 publication of her somewhat defensive essay collection *Small Wonder*, what she felt to be completely unwarranted attacks on her patriotism, and that of her family. When Harrison Shepherd receives unjustified hate mail after J. Edgar Hoover accuses him of being a Communist sympathizer and bans him from any work for the federal government (or receiving any pension for earlier work), the bitterly vituperative letters begin. Shepherd realizes in frustration that there is no way to answer these anonymous missives.

Some elements of *The Lacuna* exist as if in extended conversations with Kingsolver's earlier writings that both define "political writing" and lament some aspects of US politics. Nearly 20 years earlier, for example, in her *Los Angeles Times* review from 1991, she mourns the lack of interest in poetry here in the States. Not only can a poet make no living, he/she will never have influence. "It's a practical thing for poets in the U.S. to turn to fiction … Elsewhere, poets have the cultural status of our rock stars and the income of our romance novelists" ("Tex-Mex" 3). Some of this regret tinges her otherwise very positive address to the 1993 American Booksellers convention, where she claims that being a writer in the United States is a great career: "It's my opinion that the world is a wonderful and an awful place, and for all the quiet desperation out there, there is also a whole lot of joyful noise. I want to write about that … " She continues, expressing the seriousness of her definition of writing, which permeates her remarks; and— as she has done before—she begins with an excerpt from Ursula Le Gwin's essay about creating answers for the seriousness: "The novelists must say in words what cannot be said in words … "

Kingsolver's opening is followed by her realistic diminishment of that tone: "Somehow we have to find a way of getting across those truths that are too huge and maybe too terrible to say in simple language. Truths like 'If we don't pay attention to how we're wasting resources and fouling our habitat, our grandchildren will not get to live out their natural lives … Every single minute in this country, a child dies because of poverty.'"

In an essay titled "The Spaces Between," published in 1995 in *High Tide in Tucson*, Kingsolver lays out what she sees then as infringements on her authorial rights. She expresses one of her aims as author, "to write about the relationships between woman and man … I want to know, and to write about the places where disparate points of view rub together—the spaces between.

Not just between man and woman but also North and South; white and non-white; communal and individual; spiritual and carnal..." Fascinated as she is and always has been by what she calls "cultural difference," she adds that she has frequently been *warned* about writing about "the multicultural domain. I have been told explicitly, in fact, both that I should write *more* and *less* (or even *not at all*) about nearly every category of persons imaginable, including men, women, people with disabilities, Asians, Armenians, Native Americans..." To this caveat, she replies, "What seems right to me... is to represent the world I can see and touch as honestly as I know how, and when writing fiction, to use that variegated world as a matrix for the characters and conflicts I need to fathom" (High Tide 154–5).

In a 2013 Web posting, Kingsolver described *The Lacuna* as one story she had wanted to tell for a long time: "It raises questions I've wondered about for nearly as long as I've been a writer, starting with this one: Why is the relationship between art and politics such an uneasy one in the U.S.? Most people in other places tend to view these as inseparable. Mexico, for example, has historically celebrated its political artists as national heroes, but here that combination can make people nervous... We seem to have an aversion to national self-criticism in general. We began as a national of rabble-rousers, bent on change. But now, patriotism is often severely defined as accepting our country to be a perfect finished product.

"I suspected this internal shift might date to the mid-20th Century, a time when U.S. citizens were persecuted, lost jobs and could even be imprisoned for expressing dissident opinions. People were singled out not just for communism, but for supporting unions, women's rights or racial desegregation. Those times seem to have put a stamp on our national psyche that has never completely washed off. I always thought someday I should go sleuthing, to see if I could turn up something interesting: the end of World War II, the House Un-American Activities Committee, the blacklisting of artists...

In the autumn of 2001 after the September 11 attacks, I witnessed a ferocious backlash against people who raised questions about how we should respond. The mainstream media launched a lot of vitriol at any artist or public person identified as a dissident voice. It stunned me. The culture of fear is potent and terrible, something worth dissecting in order to understand. That was the push I needed." (Web 2013)

Placing *The Lacuna* into what was for Kingsolver a new literary category, that of the historical novel, meant that readers would question her about that kind of fiction. One of her theories as she answered was that these are "unusually challenging times. There's no recipe for how to fix a global economic collapse and climate crisis. Our news media don't always help, when they flood us with superficial glimpses of disaster, or lurid gossip about people we will never meet. It's not surprising that readers may be hungry to put our experience into a more useful context ... Historical fiction can be a part of that. As a case in point, when I was researching this novel I read a lot about World War II—not the battles abroad, but domestic life. I was amazed to learn how families adapted cooperatively to rationing ... Historical fiction carries that kind of useful context." (Web 2013)

Some critics tended to compare *The Lacuna* with Kingsolver's *The Poisonwood Bible*, but the uses of the historical were vastly different. Even as the author placed events in the correct chronology during the Congolese political debacles, she chose to tell the story through fictional people—the Price family (and the equally fictional Congolese characters who were never meant to suggest real people). The recognizable figures from history—such as Patrice Lumumba—provided only shadowy background. Contrastingly, in *The Lacuna*, the historical figures populate much of the novel, though the guiding consciousness throughout is that of the fictional Harrison Shepherd. Shepherd, like the Price family characters, fades in comparison to the real-life characters and events in these novels. For all of Shepherd's exciting boyhood and early manhood, he is most at home in the years he eventually spends in Asheville, North Carolina, a somewhat ghostly man whose only real presence is as a Henry James-like observer. Had he not hired the modest Violet Brown to become his secretary and assistant, the reader surmises that Shepherd's life—as well as his writing—would have, literally, come to nothing. As a protagonist, and as if in answer to Kristin Jacobson's wondering how Kingsolver reacts to the contemporary concept of "American exceptionalism," Harrison Shepherd *is ordinary*. No one would read him as exceptional. In Jacobson's words, as she reads through Kingsolver's *oeuvre*, "American exceptionalism becomes a misnomer or false landmark in the text's and hopefully the reader's cultural geography" (in Leder 194–5).

Perhaps "historical novel become fantasy" would better label *The Lacuna*. Just as the last hundred pages of the book describe US culture under the scrutiny of hostile politicians intent on finding and exposing Communism, so do the first hundred pages create the ocean island of Isla Pixol, as Harrison Shepherd at 12 goes with his mother (Salomé Huerta, "American Sally," Sally Shepherd) as she escapes from Harrison's boring American father in Virginia. Sally, herself a Mexican, leaves America to follow her Mexican lover, Don Enrique of the consulate in Washington. On Isla Pixol, isolated in luxury, she wears her beautiful clothes and worries that Enrique will not marry her. (He does not.) Surrounded by the clamorous howling monkeys, she and her son fantasize about the evil that impinges on their lives.

Between 1929 and 1931, when Sally takes her son on another escape, this time to Mexico City, the novel's narrative is a weirdly glamorous pastiche of 1920s international life. A few people do make contact with Harrison—the kitchen crew and the cook Leandro, whose young child dies of malnutrition. With unusual sympathy, Harrison leaves behind for him a valuable family watch.

It has been Leandro's attention to "the flutie boy from America" that made Harrison confident in the water. Leandro gave him a diving goggle, and the shy boy, then, "stood shivering in water up to his waist, thinking those were the most awful words in any language: *You will be surprised.* The moment when everything is about to change. When Mother was leaving Father... while you stand shivering in the corridor waiting to slip through one world into the next" (Lacuna 6).

Harrison eventually finds a lacuna as he swims in the ocean and—more importantly—as he learns, carefully, how to swim through the exploded space of unknown depths, left by volcanic activity, so that he can survive in extreme circumstances. The novel describes "Deep implacable holes... openings like mouths that swallow things" (Lacuna 35). Kingsolver widens that metaphor by pointing out that the word *lacuna* has multiple meanings; therefore, the novel is "about all the important things you don't know—the other side of the story, the piece of history that's been erased" (Web 2013). Kingsolver is at her best describing the smoky evanescence of the lacuna as it comes and goes, sometimes in places other than where Harrison expects it to be.

> This is how it feels when you are nearly drowned: the brain pounds like a pulse in red and black. The salt water burns your eyes, and you nearly go blind following the light until you come to the air, breathing. At the end of the tunnel the cave opens up to light, a small saltwater pool in the jungle. Almost perfectly round, as big across as this bedchamber, with sky straight up, dappled and bright through the branches... [Then...] This is where the bones were! Leg bones, wedged in the rocks. (Lacuna 44–5)

Coupled with the death of Leandro's child, as well as the sorrowful memory of his drowned brother, Harrison makes a will. To his mother, he leaves a curse. It is only to Leandro that he leaves his fragments of property.

Besides the ocean itself, Isla Pixol is only beaches and forests, the monkeys' habitat. In contrast, Mexico City offers urban loquacity and good-humored interchanges: here the world of the lacuna becomes the world of art, and the mysteries of art supplant those of nature. Here it is, also, that Harrison comes in contact with the first of Kingsolver's historical figures, Diego Rivera.

First, Rivera *is* his mural, and *only* the mural.

> "*Dios mio.* The paintings pull you right up the walls. Cienfuegos was right … The people in the paintings are larger than the men in the offices. Dark brown women among jungle trees. Men cutting stone, weaving cloth, playing drums, carrying flowers as big as brooms. Quetzalcoatl sits at the center of one mural in his grand green-feathered headdress. Everyone is there: Indians with gold bracelets on brown arms, Porfirio Diaz with his tall white hair and French sword. In one corner sketch, a native *escuincle* dog growls at the European sheep and cattle that have just arrived, as if he knows the trouble ahead … " (Lacuna 68–9)

The boy's contact occurs because Harrison can mix the plaster useful to Diego for his murals ("It was like mixing the flour for *pan dulce*," 71). In the Rivera household Harrison also works for Frida Kahlo, preparing and carrying her food to her, finding her beauty (and her art) inspiring. Known as "Sweet Buns," the young Harrison would likely have remained in stasis here, but then his mother takes him on a return trip to the DC area, enrolling him at Potomac Academy, where he both studies and boards.

Metaphoric as Kingsolver's titles often are, *The Lacuna* speaks for omissions, for black holes in a supposedly predictable tapestry. Whereas *The Poisonwood Bible* traced and described the province of the truly human, regardless of geography, *The Lacuna* describes the various provinces of art, regardless of people's interpretation of that art. Frida Kahlo admires and respects what Diego has accomplished; she tells Harrison, "Damn all other artists to hell, Diego *is* the cultural revolution … He's doing what nobody could do before him" (Lacuna 131). In contrast, she treats her own paintings wryly, as when she shows Harrison the bloody woman, stabbed (as recounted in a news story, by her lover) and titled "A Few Little Pokes" (Lacuna 140). If Kingsolver's readers had little trouble deciphering good and evil in the characters she drew for her African novel, they faced more complicated interpretations in *The Lacuna*.

Some of this difficulty stems from the fact that substantial parts of this 2009 novel are set in the United States. Some readers, at least, will remember the 1930s Depression, the House Un-American Activities Committee, McCarthyism, and the scathing descriptions of the bloody Bonus Army's eviction from Washington—so as Kingsolver sets political acts that could be sensitive to readers into the matrix that at first appeared to be exotic and other-worldly, she asks more and more from those readers' skills. (Not a difficulty that readers faced in processing either *The Poisonwood Bible* or *Prodigal Summer*, this *change* of venue becomes key to an unusually difficult text.) Somewhat like John Dos Passos's *USA Trilogy*, with its four-part system of narration, parts introduced at random, to tell the story of World War I and what follows, *The Lacuna* draws from historical excerpts taken from newspapers and magazines; it includes solid "archivist's notes" that are the words of Violet Brown as she assembles materials from Harrison's notebooks, an omniscient third person becoming the leading voice of the story—but a telling interrupted frequently by scenes in which Harrison and others (the fictional people as well as Rivera, Trotsky, Kahlo, others) speak in their own personae.

Kingsolver had long admired a novelist's ability to speak for characters other than himself/herself. She recalled the skills of, for example, John Steinbeck, whom she called a "virtuoso," because he could draw accurately "female," or "Mexican laborer" or "mentally retarded" from the inside (High Tide 155). Although none of her characters in *The Lacuna* was a true narrator, she forced readers to digest this difficult language composite so that they could, in turn, retell the Harrison Shepherd story. Very consciously crafted, this novel illustrates the power of revision, one of Kingsolver's favorite tactics (and principles of the advice she gives would-be writers).

> Pounding out a first draft is like hoeing a row of corn—you just keep your head down and concentrate on getting to the end. Revision is where fine art begins. It's thrilling to take an ending and pull it backward like a shiny thread through the whole fabric of a manuscript, letting little glints shine through here and there. To plant resolution, like a seed, into chapter one. To create new scenes, investing a character with the necessary damage, the right kind of longing. To pitch out boldly and try again. To work every metaphor across the whole, back and forth, like weaving. I love that word 'fabrication,' because making an elaborate fiction feels so much like making cloth. (Web 2013)

Tightly integrated, the result of the writer's usual painstaking methods, *The Lacuna* sets up a number of conflicts that all stem from various concepts of politics. In Meredith Sue Willis's recent essay about this novel's being a "political" work, she points to Kingsolver's emphasis on those who labor (and the vivid descriptions of that labor, as well as of communal marketplaces and other sites of interaction for lower class, working characters); on those who have political ideas—whether historically drawn or made up; and on scenes among the wealthy where they judge people economically, and often harshly. *Politics* does not accrue from whether or not someone believes in Communist doctrines. Instead, "in many different ways … Kingsolver uses politics in *The Lacuna*. Politics is part of the fabric of the novel, growing out of Kingsolver's concern and her choice of materials. The political is part of the warp and weft of her imagination and her art" (Iron 16).

Willis chooses to close her essay with a dynamic scene from *The Lacuna* that shows, she believes, how forceful Kingsolver can be in leading her readers to explore the tensile strengths of intricate language. She chooses the scene of Harrison Shepherd's imagining the way Trotsky was murdered, stressing the great Russian man's tendency to look for the best in everyone.

> They went in the house, he [Trotsky] probably asked Natalya [his wife] to make a cup of tea for the visitor, and then they must have proceeded to Lev's office. It's easy to picture: Lev sitting down, rooting out a clearing on his desk to set down the pages, collecting the patience to read it and make some tactful comment. The future waits. The world revolution waits, while Trotsky gives his full attention to a shallow-thinking but hopeful fellow, because nothing wondrous can come in this world unless it rests on the shoulders of kindness. (Lacuna 245)

What Willis says about this quotation is proof-in-fact of Kingsolver's skill: "Here we have an imaginary writer, Harrison, imagining an historical event in which a great revolutionary is kind to the man who is going to kill him; meanwhile, behind the imaginary Harrison and the character Trotsky is our very real … Barbara Kingsolver; imagining the writer who imagines. This is her art: the use of imagination to bring us closer to the reality of effecting change in the world" (Iron 17).

Before the novel's composition becomes so thoroughly a part of its *meaning*, however, Kingsolver early in the book creates the beauty of both the Mexican island and the city that embodies its country through the innocent eyes of the observant Harrison. Scatter-shot in some scenes, the preadolescent American boy eyes what he feels as difference with a combination of attraction and dismay. Nondisclosive, Harrison's amalgam of impressions (recorded in another of his valuable notebooks) reflect views that could be heterosexual as well as homosexual.

On the grounds of Enrique's estate, "The biggest *amate* tree had buttresses like sails reaching out from the trunk, dividing out little rooms furnished with drapes of fern and patchouli. A rooming house for dragonflies and ant thrushes, and once, a coiled little snake. Many trees in that jungle were as broad around their bases as the huts in Leandro's village, and held their branches too high to see" (Lacuna 16).

Of the estate itself, "The kitchen was connected to the house by the passageway of lime trees. It had low brick walls, planks for work counters, and was open all around to the sea air so smoke could escape from the firebox of the brick stove. Posts in the corners held up the roof, and the brick bread oven hunched in one corner. When Leandro came he would push the fire to the sides, keeping the heat away from the center of the heavy iron griddle. He mopped the griddle with a rag dipped in the lard jar so the tortillas wouldn't stick" (Lacuna 20).

Of the town's festival, "They stopped to watch the mariachis on the platform, handsome men with puckered lips giving long kisses to their brass horns. Trails of silver buttons led down the sides of their tight black trousers" (Lacuna 10).

"Earlier in the year the *Cristeros* had ridden into town wearing bullets strapped in rows like jewelry across their chests, galloping around the square to protest the law banning priests. The girls cheered and threw flowers as if Pancho Villa himself had risen from the grave and located his horse. Old woman rocked on their knees, eyes closed, hugging their crosses and kissing them like babies" (Lacuna 11).

Threaded throughout Harrison's descriptions are key mentions of his notebook, "the beginning of hope: a prisoner's plan for escape. Its empty pages would be the book of everything, miraculous and unending like the sea at night, a heartbeat that never stops" (Lacuna 18).

Still, seemingly with little order, Harrison's impressions crowd the pages of *The Lacuna*—as they intentionally move the narrative forward. Before Harrison has actually seen Diego Rivera, for instance, he overhears a conversation that describes the artist, the man who championed the workers' strikes. "He was as fat as a giant, and horribly ugly, with the face of a frog and the teeth of a Communist. They say he eats the flesh of young girls, wrapped in a tortilla. 'He's a cannibal. And from the look of her, I would say his little bride there might also eat children for lunch'" (Lacuna 66).

After moving to Mexico City, with Salomé using her various persuasions to capture Mr. P. T. Cash (a wealthy man who is unfortunately still married), Harrison finds himself enrolled in a mediocre school. His days there reinforce his attractions for the forbidden: "The shortest way home was to walk by the Viga canal, filled with floating newspaper pages and one dead dog, swelled up like a yellow melon" (Lacuna 65). It is after Harrison convinces Salomé that he could be of more benefit to her by finding a job that he is free to wander the city's streets, and learn about Rivera's art.

Eventually discouraged by her new lover's stinginess, Salomé takes Harrison on a five day-and-night train ride back to Washington, where his father meets them. It is at Potomac Academy that Harrison becomes the sidekick of one of the boys on scholarship, an association dependent on class.

> Bull's Eye smells like peeled potatoes, cigarettes, and the mop bucket. When the others go home on Saturday, he says, 'Hey-Pancho-Villa, you are cor-di-ally invited to assist me with my labors.' These include scrubbing the lunch mess, running with the wet mop in the commissary, jumping on it, and sliding across the floor between the long tables. And so forth. The assistant receives no pay except getting his head squeezed inside Bull's Eye's elbow and his hair scrubbed with knuckles. That is how boys touch here, Bull's Eye especially. (Lacuna 92)

Remiss in some ways in avoiding Harrison's descriptions of the Washington and Virginia areas in which he now lives, the novel begins to concentrate more on social and political events: Harrison's father is a mid-career hanger-on, with staid opinions about most of the political scene. He would not have protected the down-and-out veterans who comprised the Bonus Army once the American military set out to rid Washington of the protestors. Even as Liesl Schillinger praises "the music of its passages on nature, archaeology, food and friendship," she implants the reminder that *The Lacuna* gains its force through "its call to conscience and connection." She praises in particular Kingsolver's "*tableau vivant* of epochs and people" (NYT 9). But there are, as other reviewers have stated, comparative dead spots in the novel—and Harrison's time in Washington might count as one such interval. Once he drops out of the Academy and returns to Mexico City, and the narrative becomes the property, in fact, of Diego Rivera and his family, Harrison's descriptions come alive once more.

At this comparative still point, then, the novel hesitates. It seems to wander. According to one of Kingsolver's taut descriptions of the novel as a means of creating empathy—or of art as "the antidote that can call us back from the edge of numbness, restoring the ability to feel for another"—*The Lacuna* makes its return to Mexico none too soon (High Tide 231–2).

Late in 1935, Harrison is employed by the Rivera household. Frida is ill, in and out of hospital, but she and Rivera are at least united in the same living space. Then news arrives that Lev Davidovich and his wife Natalya are coming to live with them—Trotsky, wife, secretary, and guards enter Mexico City, and Harrison is asked to stop his writing in order to preserve Trotsky's safety (Lacuna 150). It is perhaps Trotsky's portrait that salvages the novel, and the man of great kindness (despite his brief affair with Frida) is described as being someone who is marked by "Delight." Inadvertently,

Lev Trotsky becomes a father to Harrison (he is the only man ever to call Harrison "son") (Lacuna 151, 153).

Everyone in the Rivera household is armed. Diego wears his gun and holster, and the household readies a machine gun. In Russia, Stalin plans an assassination: Trotsky is tried in absentia and then the purges of all his associates occur.

In the midst of this warning hysteria about Trotsky's safety, Harrison loses his mother, as she drives to the airport with her newest admirer, a journalist, to catch a glimpse of Howard Hughes. Salomé is 42; she does not survive the crash. Rivera pays for both her casket and the funeral. Harrison laments her sterile life and wonders "How could a life of such large hopes be so small in the end? ... If she had lived to be old, would she have resided in a teacup, to be sipped at intervals beneath some gray mustache?" (Lacuna 186–7). As Kingsolver said in her Diane Rehm interview, *The Lacuna* at times is about "the sadness, and smallness, of women's lives" (November 5, 2009).

The Lacuna shelters those women's lives, however. They exist in shadows, or perhaps only in Harrison's remaining notebooks: Violet Brown, in effect, becomes their spokesperson. At the present time, readers are torn between the glory of Rivera's murals, some of them placing white faces next to brown (as his Detroit paintings had, creating calls for erasure even as the auto unions allowed mixed-race membership. The Detroit Institute of Art protected the Diego Rivera paintings of the Ford Motor Company in the early 1930s— although it was rumored that those art works had been destroyed). Back in Mexico City, at the center of Rivera's Palacio Belles Artes mural was lodged the face of Lenin, leader of the Russian Revolution (Lacuna 141). On the political scene, the Dies Committee called Trotsky to Washington but then revoked his papers and his visa and declared that he was *never* to enter the United States (Lacuna 230).

A few days later, when a nondescript driver for a friend of Rivera's asks that Lev read some of his writing, there are no suspicions. Trotsky steels himself for the chore of making pleasant remarks about something he has yet to read: such a task is a famous writer's burden. Jacson Monard does not appear to be an assassin, but he is. As he killed Trotsky with "a strange small pickax with its handle cut short"—plunging the weapon 7 centimeters into Trotsky's brain—Harrison remembers "the roar. A scream or a sob but really a roar, indignation" (Lacuna 245). Years later, in his nightmares, Harrison records a different memory, "The white cuffs soaked like bandages, drops of blood falling on white paper." The writer adds, "Memories do not always soften with time; some grow edges like knives" (Lacuna 299). For the reader of the earlier novel *Animal Dreams*, this passage recalls the fragile Codi's belief that "memory runs along deep, fixed channels in the brain" (Animal 269).

Kingsolver shows her mastery of craft again and again in creating compelling scenes. It is the *tableau vivant* here and elsewhere that enlivens *The Lacuna*, and in many ways saves the narrative from the author's two difficulties—working with *the character of Harrison Shepherd* who is comparatively lifeless, and *inundating* readers with *a mix* of print journalism, Violet Brown's "archival" statements, and a narrative of novelistic length *that must push on against, and over*, these textual obstacles.

But first, here, she creates a significant bridge. One of the premises of *The Lacuna* is to show, in the author's words, that "The world shifts under our feet. The rules change" (Duke University). After Trotsky's murder and death, Harrison left Mexico City by train. Frida had given him money and a job: he was to be the "consignment marshal" for the eight paintings she was sending to the Museum of Modern Art in New York, for their exhibit of twentieth-century Mexican art. Charged with viable responsibilities, Harrison understood that his escape was insured although the police had ransacked his room and taken all papers. After the news stories that Trotsky knew would be in error, and Frida's being held two days and nights by the police (along with others from the household), Violet Brown recounts what Harrison had written in "The Train Station Notebook, August 1940."

Frida had packed a case of his remaining debris from the police station (he will not receive those materials until after her death; she describes them as "old clothes") and she gives him a painting she has made for him, packaged for travel with papers to get it through customs as if it were part of the MOMA transport.

Boarding the train, he thinks "The notebooks are gone. It must have been like this for Lev at the end, with his past entirely stolen." Harrison mourns as well his dreams of being a writer: "those hopeful hours of typing through the night shift ... be[ing] as tall as Jack London or Dos Passos" (Lacuna 258–9).

Under Violet Brown's signature as "Archivist," Harrison's words here change the novel from the historical recounting of Trotsky's life and death in Mexico to that of Harrison's own story. Part IV, dated 1941–1947, is set in Asheville, North Carolina: so too is Part V, which covers 1948 and 1949. The last pages of *The Lacuna* begin with another "Archivist's Note," which recounts Violet's shame at the town's gossip that makes her into Harrison's mistress, once he has become the famous novelist of Mexican history. Devoid of the Rivera–Kahlo–Trotsky characters, Kingsolver creates an eight-year political prolegomenon that takes the reader through the second world war and into the anti-Communist miasma that will upend the democratic principles previously so revered in the United States.

During World War II, Harrison (driving south and west in the car his father—unexpectedly dead by the time his son reaches Washington after delivering the MOMA paintings—has willed him) boards in one room in Asheville, North Carolina, and becomes the cook for Mrs. Bittle's rooming house. A genius at combining the stamps and tokens for rationed foods, Harrison earns his rent in this way—and makes a firm friend of Violet Brown, another of the boarders. When valuable art is going to be moved into the Biltmore mansion (so as not to be destroyed in attacks on east coast museums), Harrison is asked to oversee that work—eventually, he is able to buy a modest house in town. Having discovered that the "art" which Frida sent along with him on the train from Mexico is actually all his papers confiscated by the police, Harrison resumes his dream: he hires Mrs. Brown to become his secretary and assistant. Soon, he has finished the first of his historical novels and the book is published by a good New York house. "Asheville Writer a Mystery" in the words of several of the news stories Kingsolver includes as she imagines their headlines.

Busily involved in writing his second book, Harrison hardly notices the crumbling of the American freedoms. He earns profits enough from writing that he can buy a Philco radio (one of his dreams), but he seldom travels, and sees few people besides the townspeople who admire him. Literary fame brings him a cloak of near invisibility.

The last segments of the novel make clear Harrison's homosexuality, and accordingly make Violet Brown's loss of reputation a great irony. But for the townspeople of Asheville, it is Harrison's connection with the "radicals" of Mexico, in combination with his having lived with Trotsky, that damns him. His homosexuality (which would, of course, add to his damnation) comes through rarely, like slits in an artist's slashed canvass. And whereas it is Harrison's sexual energy that gives him the impetus to write his novels, in themselves those books are innocuous.

Kingsolver gives Harrison one stable and comparatively on-going love; he worked with Tom Cuddy during the war years when they were archivists together in New York. More recently Tom has resumed correspondence with him—and there are Harrison's visits to New York as well as Tom's visit to Asheville. A name-dropper of the first rank, Tom may also be an informer. In Harrison's words (in a dynamic scene when he first meets his lawyer Artie Gold), "this one [Cuddy] is all stars and stripes. We worked together in Civilian Service during the war, moving paintings into safe storage here for the National Gallery" (Lacuna 420).

In a scene rich with information, as Harrison meets Gold at the Swiss Kitchens for a meal, Kingsolver points to several significant qualities that are going to jeopardize Harrison's safety. Gold's role here is reassurance; he tells Harrison, "These crimes [of treason] are very difficult to prosecute," a statement that might have been truer in 1945 than it would be in 1948.

The first quality that might trigger suspicions is Harrison's speech. Artie tells him, "You have a manner of speaking... The first time we spoke on the phone, I heard it. Every word is perfect, but there is an accent. Like Gary Cooper. Not quite the regular apple pie." Harrison replies, "They tell me the same thing in Mexico—my Spanish has a faint accent. I am the permanent foreigner" (Lacuna 419).

The second is what Artie recognizes as his homosexuality, and in that context he inquires about Tom Cuddy (and his imagined loyalty). It is from Cuddy that Harrison has heard about the frightening arrests being made in New York. When he asks Gold about such happenings, his lawyer confirms what his friend has told him and goes on to reply, "Who needs crimes? The INS has a stable of witnesses, professionals. Very well paid, very talented, they can produce a testimony for any occasion. If a man is not a Communist, they'll prove he is" (Lacuna 422). Gold predicts that Communist party membership, as well as sympathy with party members, will be next.

Running parallel with the accurate historical milieu of suspicion about Communism is the difficulty of Kingsolver's having created, for this work, a male protagonist. In her fiction, there are few male characters who play the lead role in either stories or novels: Kingsolver is apparently much more comfortable with the voice, the language, and the situations that spring from women's lives. As she had written in 1995 (in her essay "Jabberwocky," about the ways fiction operates),

A novel works its magic by putting a reader inside another person's life. The pace is as slow as life. It's as detailed as life. It requires YOU, the reader, to fill in an outline of words with vivid pictures drawn subconsciously from your own life, so that the story feels more personal than the sets designed by someone else and handed over via TV or movies. Literature duplicates the experience of living in a way that nothing else can ... (High Tide 230)

Is the difficulty of getting inside Harrison Shepherd's life a gender problem? Surely, given the small bits of attention to his homosexuality, readers' reluctance to be absorbed within Harrison's own imagination—or, more simply, to absorb Harrison's character into their own imagination—is not a function of readers' sexual preference. Is this unusually *un*sympathetic protagonist an attempt to create the genderless writer figure, one who takes on the aesthetics of creativity and in that process loses many of his more apparent human traits?

Is Kingsolver's theme here that writers or painters or songwriters are never "like" other people? In *The Lacuna*, the *different* become central rather than lurking at the edges of narrative to enliven our day-to-day worlds. Can readers not identify with this *otherness* writ large? When the FBI investigates Harrison Shepherd, as they will many of the leading writers and artists of the United States in fact, they are bewildered by his randomly chosen life events.

> Why did his mother take him to Mexico?
> Why did he spend two years back in DC at the Potomac boarding school?
> Why did he live in the Diego Rivera household as a laborer before fleeing from Mexico just days after Trotsky's murder?
> Why did he live in an Asheville boarding house throughout World War II?

The non-normal life of the artist, a person called to pursue his own Difference over the human patterns possible—loving and being loved, maintaining a family, rearing children—is itself a decision that prompts curiosity, and curiosity unsatisfied does not lead to either acceptance or empathy. (Kingsolver answers what will later be the line of FBI interrogation in the scene of Harrison's meeting Artie Gold, the entertainment lawyer who is himself—being Jewish—another non-normal character. But even Artie is bemused by Harrison's life events.)

Taking Violet Brown on a trip to the parts of Mexico that have been important to him is meant as a gesture of thanks, of friendship. But after they return early in 1948, the Asheville *Star Herald* runs a story comparing the two of them to Thomas Wolfe and Aline Bernstein, making the point that Violet Brown is 17 years older than Harrison, just as Bernstein was much older than Wolfe. (The cultural assumption is that all people are heterosexual, 409.) From that time on, Violet Brown is literally hounded— even the FBI visits her at her home, making an offer of $5,000 if she will pass on to them Harrison's papers.

Kingsolver here includes the Zelda Fitzgerald death: when Tom Cuddy asks Harrison whether he knows Zelda, Harrison replies that his house is at the end of the street where the sanatorium is, and that two nights earlier, Zelda had died in the fire which, according to the author's lore, went from the kitchen up a dumb waiter shaft to Zelda's third story room (there are other accounts of the spread of the fire). Harrison's wise comment, to deflect any assumption of the woman's instability, is that "It could have been any of us in that hospital, Tom" (Lacuna 414).

The pursuit of a seemingly guilty Harrison Shepherd begins in earnest, with a photograph taken in 1930 at a party of supposed sympathizers (Harrison would have been 14, though it seems as if Jacson Mornard,

Tolstoy's killer, is there). On December 13, 1948, the letter from J. Edgar Hoover arrives, announcing that Harrison can no longer work for the federal government, nor can he be paid a pension for work he has already done. Although Violet Brown tries to protect him from the hate mail that follows, he realizes that there is a great deal of it. Soon, Lincoln Barnes, the publisher who has made so much money on Harrison's first two novels, suggests that his third book be published under a pseudonym (if it is published at all). Earlier, this publisher had attached to the book contract an affidavit of Anti-Communism, seemingly now a regular part of American business in 1948.

Another segment of actual history in the summer of 1948 was the polio epidemic in Asheville, "the worst epidemic in the nation, putting the whole town under quarantine"; in Kingsolver's words, the contagion of that horrific illness and its quick spread created what she called "the perfect, claustrophobic backdrop to the suspenseful narrowing down of choices for my protagonist" (Web 2013). For some months, Harrison's tactic of ignoring the political reality of the Red hunts had protected him from any real disturbance, but as 1948 moved on, he could no longer pretend that his life was as it once had been.

Plots thickened. Tom Cuddy disappeared from his life, after Harrison was labeled a more dangerous man than was Alger Hiss (the Asheville papers carried the headline, "Alger Hiss Verdict: Spy and Liar") (Lacuna 474). On March 7, 1950, Harrison is called up before the House Un-American Activities Committee. The novel proper ends with his unfrightened testimony, punctuated at several places with the Committee's warning that he will be held in contempt. Violet Brown and Artie Gold accompany him, as friends.

Kingsolver's fictional recreation of Harrison's hearing reads like the now-public transcripts of many other such interrogations. In Harrison's case, he did not take the Fifth Amendment because the committee members knew so little about him that their questions were far from personal. He was not afraid that he would incriminate others. Taking the oath, Harrison agreed that he was born on July 6, 1916, in Lychgate, Virginia ("facts" later given in error in his obituary). The longest series of questions concerned his possible membership in the Communist party. Harrison answers truthfully, if flippantly:

> Mr. Ravenner: Did you or did you not at that time believe membership in the Communist Party was inimical to the interests of the United States?
> Mr. Shepherd: To be honest, sir, I didn't think one way or another about it. I never met any Communist Party members in this country.
> Mr. Ravenner: Can you give me an answer "Yes" or "No"?

Mr. Shepherd: Does a citizen have a right to be uncertain until further informed?

Mr. Ravenner: Let me inform you. A member of the Communist Party is a person who seeks the overthrow of the government of the United States by force and violence in this country. Is that something you approve of?

Mr. Shepherd: I've never sought to overthrow the United States. Is that an answer?

Mr. Ravenner: It is a form of answer. Now, I understand that you were born in the United States, but chose to spend most of your life in another country. Is that correct?

Mr. Shepherd: "My mother was Mexican. We moved back there when I was twelve. She threatened to leave me by the tracks if I put up a fuss. So yes sir, I chose to go …

In the interim, committee member Richard Nixon has entered the hearing. When Ravenner moves to question Harrison about working for Trotsky, this is the lengthy interchange:

Mr. Ravenner: Just answer the question. Did you work for this Trotsky?

Mr. Shepherd: Yes.

Mr. Ravenner: In what capacity?

Mr. Shepherd: As his cook, his secretary-typist, and sometimes cleaner of rabbit cages. But usually the Commissar preferred handling the manure himself.

Mr. Wood: Here, I'll have order!

Mr. Ravenner: You say you were his secretary. Do you mean to say you helped prepare documents whose purpose was to arouse a Communist insurrection?

(The witness did not answer.)

Mr. Velde: Mr. Shepherd, you may take the Fifth Amendment if you wish.

Mr. Shepherd: I don't know how to answer, when you say "helped prepare documents." I was a typist. Sometimes I could hardly understand the words in those documents. I don't have any expertise in politics.

Mr. Nixon: Is the welder of a bomb casing innocent of the destruction it causes, just because he doesn't understand physics?

Mr. Shepherd: It's a very good question. Our munitions plants make arms we sell to almost every country. Are we now on both sides of all the wars?

Mr. Ravenner: Mr. Shepherd you are instructed to answer "yes" or
"no" to all further questions. One more outburst will land you
in contempt of Congress. Did you help prepare Communist
documents for this Trotsky, a leader of the Bolshevik revolution?
Mr. Shepherd: Yes.
Mr. Ravenner: And are you still in contact with Comrade Trotsky?
(Very long pause.)
Mr. Shepherd: No ... (Lacuna 484–5)

The hearing continues, with another of Nixon's smart jokes, and the reader's understanding that even though Communism is the evil in the room, the men representing loyalty to the United States know nothing about that evil—even the fact of Trotsky's murder.

The rest of the Harrison Shepherd story occurs in the "Afterward," written in 1959 and then sealed for the requisite 50 years (hence, the story's publication in 2009). Violet Brown has salvaged all his papers and correspondence; she only pretended to burn his possessions. She also accompanied him back to Mexico, after Gold had told Harrison to leave the United States while he still had a passport. Planning to return home after the full moon in June, 1951, Harrison in actuality swims deep in the ocean off the shore of Mexico City, while Violet Brown reads on the beach. He does not surface.

The obituary in the Asheville papers gives Harrison's age as 34; his birthday as July 16, 1916; and the cause of his death as drowning.

Before taking the trip, Harrison made his will with Gold—leaving Violet Brown everything except one last wired bequest of money to Frida. He also left a letter for Violet in which he spoke of their great love for each other, his for her, and her immense support in his writing life. He also left the small stone image that had served as a talisman for 20 years, the ancient god that fit inside a person's hand, the representation of the other worldliness of the lacuna that he had used to cross over into the next existence. Jolly, rotund (like Diego Rivera), indestructible—Violet Brown guarded the stone figure as she did every fragment of Harrison Shepherd's existence and bequeathed his story to a less skeptical posterity.

The reader again faces the complexity of the book—a historical novel with the fantastic overlay of creativity/imagination/lacuna/passage to unknown worlds. *The Lacuna* ends with Violet Brown's observant words, "My heart pounding because of that cave he found under the water. And his business with the moon, learning to wait for a day the tide would help him push through to the other side, without his drowning first. That was him all over. That patient study" (Lacuna 504).

The evolution of the "story" through Violet Brown's diligence, and her craftiness of keeping Harrison's papers away from either the FBI or the later would-be archivists trying to study the political situation in the early 1950s, means that the reader is thrown back into the various dimensions of Kingsolver's title.

The Lacuna remains a book about creating the unknowable, which gives us the successful art—the painting, the novel, the song. Mysterious as the process of creation is, it comes without guarantees. For every novel published, a hundred others repose in unopened desk drawers, or have been relegated to ashes. The process is almost impenetrable: "Fiction is all about the re-imagined life," Kingsolver noted a decade before she finished *The Lacuna* (Off the Beaten 19). In her 2013 Web comments about fiction, she says more directly,

A novel is like a cathedral, it knocks you down to size when you enter into it.

13

Flight Behavior, Our Bildungsroman

Nonfiction can be whatever it is, but literature that seems political to people often strikes a suspicious nerve. I keep getting asked … why I choose to write political fiction, as if I had a choice in the matter … I think about character, and theme, and imagery. I think about making this the best piece of literature I can create, and part of that, naturally, is ensuring that it contains questions and conflicts that I believe are important … to write about civic interactions.

Kingsolver in Fisher 28

Flight Behavior shows itself to be another of Kingsolver's expert fictions because, in part, it surrounds the reader with handfuls of weather. "When the storm broke, the world was changed. Flat rocks dotted the pasture with their damp shine, scattered on a hillside that looked like a mud finger painting. The receding water left great silted curves swaggering down the length of the hill, pulled from side to side by a current that followed its incomprehensible rules" (Flight 134). No matter where readers have lived, they have experienced hard rains, rains which had the potential to cause surprising damage.

Flight Behavior demands that the reader adjust to this weather. *Flight Behavior* follows *The Lacuna* in a simple pattern that emphasizes *no* mystery except the natural, no world stage filled with a Shakesperian fulsomness: there is no Trotsky, there is no Diego Rivera. There is only Dellarobia and Cub, Preston and Cordie (our own Cordelia), leading a life that slogs up and down those Tennessee hills where every day mandates rubber boots. There is *nothing* magical or mysterious about the setting for *Flight Behavior*.

This current paradigm suggests Kingsolver's earlier alternation—when she moved so rapidly from the historically based African book (*The Poisonwood Bible*) to *Prodigal Summer*, the lush weather-filled Virginia trilogy. The first important and sometimes bewildering novel appeared in 1998; the simpler "homeplace" novel followed that blockbuster in 2000. Just as the reviewers of *Prodigal Summer* often began their commentary with a reference to *The Poisonwood Bible*, so did reviewers of Kingsolver's 2012 *Flight Behavior* sometimes refer to her 2009 *The Lacuna*. (One does not win

England's Orange Prize for every work although *Flight Behavior* was a short-listed finalist for the same award.) *The Lacuna*, so difficult in its convoluted interstices, comes into the discussions that *Flight Behavior* prompts. There seems to be a kind of *resonance* that follows—from *The Poisonwood Bible* to *Prodigal Summer*, and now, correspondingly, from *The Lacuna* to *Flight Behavior*.

The difference in the second novel of each of these pairings is more unsettling than just its weather.

The second novel, in each case, is *realistic*. When Kingsolver moves back into those Southern Appalachian hills, she gives us characters we can identify. As she said years ago, "I was stunned to discover the world knows almost nothing about 'hillbillies' and respects them even less. An undercurrent of defensiveness about this has guided my writing and my life, I think, as I've tried to seek out the voices of marginalized people" (Snodgrass 13). Less staged than the story of Harrison Shepherd and his entourage, less forbidding than the odyssey of Nathan Price, the characters in both *Prodigal Summer* and *Flight Behavior* (regardless of their gender) are suitably nondescript. Kingsolver once issued orders to a fiction writing class about how an effective short story should work: "The trick is to construct a story readers will want to believe, with all their hearts, and to play it out in a world so detailed and appealing that they're prepared to pack their bags and move in" ("Widows at the Wheel").

The writer's art does not depend entirely on her fiction, however. Before *The Poisonwood Bible* was published, Kingsolver had brought out not only *Homeland and Other Stories*; she had also published her poem collection and, most significant, *High Tide in Tucson*, her first book of essays (many of which had already appeared elsewhere). Readers who already knew the Barbara Kingsolver who had given them Taylor Greer (of *The Bean Trees* and *Pigs in Heaven*) as well as Codi and Hallie Noline of *Animal Dreams*, were hungry to read more from this movingly personal author.

The same kind of pattern occurred just before *The Lacuna* was published in 2009. Kingsolver's second essay collection, *Small Wonder*, appeared in 2002, inserting this author into a meaningful, if difficult, post-"9/11" dialogue. As if deflected by various controversies, Kingsolver published two of her most important ecological treatises, the prose passages in *Last Stand, America's Virgin Lands*, with its marvelous photographs by Annie Griffiths Belt, and the idiosyncratic and yet surprisingly powerful *Animal, Vegetable, Miracle: A Year of Food Life* (2005 and 2007).

This configuration of books seems to suggest that Kingsolver has moved further away from musing about the past injustices of Western history (including issues of race and gender) in order to focus her keen knowledge on a global dilemma—and attempting as she changes this focus to help save elements of the natural world. In effect, Kingsolver has relinquished the political realms of Patrice Lumumba and Leon Tolstoy for the scientific worlds of biodiversity, Monarch butterflies, and a previously unknown scientist, Ovid Byron—a man not so unknown that he has been awarded one of the MacArthur Genius grants.

Another way of placing Kingsolver's work into a meaningful chronology might be to consider how often her characters are marked by *trauma*. Part of the seriousness of her fiction stems from the readers' acknowledgment that characters are faced with unusually tough problems: nothing Kingsolver writes is "chick lit" in that the problems are inconsequential. In *Animal Dreams*, for example, Codi Noline is haunted by the somewhat inexplicable memory of her mother's body being carried away by helicopter—followed by the painful memory of her miscarriage when the fetus is nearly six months along. Those losses are exacerbated by the kidnapping and murder of her beloved sister Hallie, volunteering in Nicaragua as an agricultural worker. Much of Codi's lack of conscious, and self-conscious, behavior stems from the unacknowledged misery of these personal losses: trauma trails years of anguished memory in its wake.

Trauma can also be occasioned by *threats* of loss. Taylor Greer is motivated throughout two books by the worrisome conditions that her illegal adoption of Turtle causes; this trauma is underscored by threats of harm to the abused Indian child, repeated within *Pigs in Heaven* even though introduced in *The Bean Trees*—as well as the habitual losses that Angie experiences when Lucky Buster, her mentally retarded child/man, takes off on his own. By the time of *The Poisonwood Bible*, Kingsolver floods the text with threats of all kinds, many of them natural, culminating in the death of Ruth Ann from snakebite. Impacting her mother and sisters, Ruth Ann's death barely reaches to the egomaniacal father, Nathan Price. Whereas Leah's family's living under threat, especially after the assassination of Patrice Lumumba, is more remote, none of the Price women ever forgets the loss of their youngest sister.

The death of Cole Widener in *Prodigal Summer* does not have a similar impact. Lusa moves into a central role within the Widener family, adopting the orphaned children after their mother's death. In this novel, which presents a contradiction to the themes of trauma and loss, even the animals live.

Lev Trotsky's assassination in *The Lacuna* dominates Harrison Shepherd's consciousness for the next years; memories of the man's anguished, angry outcry and blood-soaked cuffs are inescapable. The extension of the loss of Trotsky extends into the history of political persecution in the United States, culminating in Harrison's hearing before the House Un-American Activities Committee. More quietly and even ironically, Harrison's loss of his mother—Salomé—at the young age of 42, underscores his isolation from any kind of human community. Similarly, although given less physical space, the effect of Harrison's own loss by drowning (or living, if he escapes through the lacuna) dominates Violet Brown's later years.

The losses in *Flight Behavior* seem nominal, in comparison to these catastrophic events. Just as Cub is readying his mind to accept the separation Dellarobia insists upon, he may have lost her in fact. The losses that Kingsolver intends to parallel this great one—the loss of their first child, commemorated by Dellarobia in her remarks to Preston; as well as the hidden loss of Hester's illegitimate baby, with Bear's mandate to silence her even in the midst of the woman's grief—seem unnecessarily remote.

In the world of Kingsolver's fiction, it seems clear that trauma itself changes. If the assassination of Leon Trotsky marks the height of political vengeance, then the presumed death of Dellarobia Turnbow has *no* political effect at all. It is Kingsolver, in one of her 1995 *High Tide* essays, who stated, "one of the extremely valuable things to be done with the power of fiction is the connection of events with their consequences" (High Tide 253). The distance between philosophies in 1995 and here in 2014 is wider than readers might predict. As Timothy Clark, quoting Ulrich Beck, states, "We live in an age of unintended consequences" (Clark 1). As the natural and political worlds change, so too will the worlds of aesthetics and literature.

The worlds Kingsolver creates have also changed, and this set of changes is not just a progression from the author's focusing on her fictional characters to focusing on the world that provides both setting and interesting narrative for them. It may be said that in the twenty-first-century world, where all human concerns are likely to be global ones, this *change*, or *shift*, or *re-emphasis* makes whatever Kingsolver attends to seem new, pertinent, and even prescient. Therefore, her writing today has even more appeal, as well as a wider base of readers.

Classifying the uses Kingsolver makes of trauma for her characters, and isolating those traumatic experiences, makes the readers come down hard on the feminine side of loss. The deaths that the author presents as most traumatic are those of family members, and mostly female family members—mothers, children (sisters), and unborn children. With the exception of Lev Trotsky, Harrison Shepherd, Patrice Lumumba, and Cole Widener (and the almost unacknowledged loss of Nathan Price, whose whereabouts in the Congo remains a mystery), the losses within the Kingsolver *oeuvre* are either mothers or children.

It looks to readers as if *Flight Behavior* will follow that pattern, although the death of Dellarobia's mother is mostly unmourned. But in some ways *Flight Behavior* becomes an *ironic* novel. In fact, it could be said that the book's characters exist primarily to further the plot: the plot becomes not the Turnbow family's existence but rather the narrative of the Turnbow family's *land*.

Dellarobia herself, for example, is barely characterized. Caught as she was in the accidental pregnancy that dating Cub Turnbow had led her to, she exists for much of the book in a condition one might call "pre-feminist." To compare Dellarobia with Taylor Greer, for instance, shows the true dimensions of the former's entrapment. Whereas Taylor believes she can both support and care for her adopted Turtle, Dellarobia has lived as a stay-at-home mom, chafing at her dependence on Cub and his father but doing nothing to change that status. Once her first pregnancy ended in miscarriage, she worked at waitressing—but she did not attempt to go to college.

Kingsolver's emphasis in *Flight Behavior* is on the characters' attitudes toward both education and work, and, implicitly, toward the myth of the American dream. In *Pigs in Heaven*, Jax had told Taylor that the ideology of personal economic success no longer validated individual effort (regardless of gender). Twenty years after Kingsolver's 1993 novel, her description of Dellarobia's attitudes shows only a faint glimmer of the young mother's hope of escaping her all-too-conventional life.

Even in the most positive reviews of *Flight Behavior*, there is little comment about Dellarobia. Judging from reviews, it would seem that Kingsolver's eighth novel remains strangely unpopulated.

When Elinor Lipman, writing in *The New York Times*, calls *Flight Behavior* "a marvelous novel," she shies away from discussing characters. Her attention instead falls on moments of comedy, on what she calls "smaller-scale, deliciously human moments." She explains that the novel is filled with "line after line that can be at once beautiful, casual, wry, offbeat." Lipman's emphasis is on the written work as a whole, and one of her primary concerns seems to be whether or not "global warming and intimations of doomsday tax the storytelling at times" (she admits that the answer is Yes) (November 18, 2012).

Categorizing *Flight Behavior* as a part of the new literary genre known as "cli-fi" (for *climate fiction*), Angela Evancie is absorbed with a similar thematic emphasis, and quotes the author's query, "Why do we believe or disbelieve the evidence we see for climate change?" (NPR, April 20, 2013). In an earlier *Time* interview, Kingsolver tried to deflect this omnipresent theme by stressing that "I wanted to write about why humans have stopped listening to each other. It was important not to take sides in this novel. I feel profound sympathy for everyone in this novel. That includes the people who come down on both sides of this culture war ... Disagreement should be a healthy thing and instead in the modern era, disagreement has become debilitating. Particularly on the subject of climate change. Particularly on any subject that is informed by science" (November 8, 2012).

Perhaps Kingsolver needed to say more herself about Dellarobia. If she has seemingly changed the nature of the novel (where *is* the protagonist we are watching for?), perhaps readers would have profited from some direction. In the case of our speculative pairing a few pages ago, suggesting that some *resonance* from *The Lacuna* would spread toward *Flight Behavior*, any reader might be puzzled at having to move interests that are largely historical, based on factual twentieth-century happenings, over to this apparently pastoral novel, a book with a theme that is anything but pastoral.

On the author's current Web site, she describes herself as a *novelist*, emphasizing some of the finesse with language which Elinor Lipman had described. This is Kingsolver: "As a literary novelist, I spend my days testing the insides of words, breathing life into sentences that swim away under their own power, stringing together cables of poetry to hold up a narrative arc. I hope also to be a fearless writer: examining the unexamined life, asking the unasked questions."

Given that global climate change may no longer be labeled an "unasked" question, it remains a vexing one. As Kingsolver writes,

At least half the population of this country has not been educated to understand basic, thoroughly documented phenomena like climate change, or even to grasp evolution through natural selection, which has now been the cornerstone of all biological sciences for two centuries. When a population this uninformed tries to steer environmental policy, it is like asking a five-year-old to drive the car: we might fully expect calamity. I've noticed that very few people even know that *ecology* is a field of science—the theoretical study of how living populations interact with one another. (Many have a vague idea that it means 'the environment.') It's a difficult science, involving a lot of advanced math and computer modeling, but the principles it gives us are literally matters of life and death. (Web 2013)

Even Jackie McGlone, writing in the Scottish *Herald* and trying diligently to make Dellarobia important, succumbs to the novel's all-consuming thrust. Although the review positively descries the woman's working with Ovid Byron ("Every day she rose and rose to the occasion of this man"), the reviewer concedes that "it is the impact of climate change on a community, an eco-system and a species that is the fulcrum of this ambitious book, with its profound religious subtext, which wears its learning lightly yet is full of amazing facts about the world of science."

To illustrate the accuracy of this comment, McGlone includes a number of the author's remarks. She agrees, for instance, that writing *Flight Behavior* took an immense amount of research, "everything from the life cycle of the monarch butterfly—'an insect as small as a paperclip, with a brain the size of a pin, which migrates thousands of miles to alight on the same tree where its grandmother was born'—to physics, chemistry, biology, psychology and cognitive behavior." She also gives McGlone a different term for the categorization of *Flight Behavior*, calling that "a peculiar genre of a novel." "It's not science fiction, nor is it magical realism. It is realism based firmly in real science, but it's about something that has not happened but *could*. I need readers to trust that this *can* happen" (Herald July 26, 2013).

The one question McGlone asks Kingsolver—about future "adventures" that Dellarobia might have—meets with a definite negative answer. There will be no more Dellarobia. Even given the sense of *Flight Behavior*'s conclusive ending, the author does not scold the reviewer, but rather accepts the query as a compliment to her beautiful young character.

Any reader who has been following the bevy of Kingsolver's women characters, starting with Taylor Greer's appearance in *The Bean Trees* (1988), would run, helpfully, to salvage Dellarobia Turnbow. Thinking of the critics who have—for several decades now—posited ways these women characters might find health and hopefulness, one remembers the work of Marianne Hirsch, Marilyn Yalom, Priscilla Leder, Krista Comer, Sheryl Stevenson, Magali Cornier Michael, Sandra L. Ballard, and especially Rinda West. In the latter's *Out of the Shadow*, she summarizes a major theme in Kingsolver's *oeuvre*, "exploring the relationships among psychological growth, intimacy with place, and political activism. Activism requires narratives of hope, both personal and political" (West 151).

In keeping with Kingsolver's explorations of characters in relation to place (and especially with what West terms *wilderness*), this critic describes the successful female characters

who find in wilderness a way out of the constraints of cultural expectations. Wilderness offers them an encounter with something authentic and Other, a site where they can strengthen the ego in order to begin to allow shadow material to come to light. In addition, these characters gain access to nonrational ways of knowing. Thus, wilderness has a vital function in psychological life, most crucially at times of transition. Protecting the wilderness is essential to healing the disconnect that has resulted from the estrangement of humans from the natural world. (West 122)

If Kingsolver had made Dellarobia just a bit more dissatisfied with her life on the Turnbow farm. *If* she had made her move to take some college courses, or do some volunteer work, or show any tendency to explore the life she was living—then West's suggestions about coming to full psychological health might suggest ways of implementing her growth. The problem with the author's introduction of, and development of, Dellarobia in *Flight Behavior* is that it prefigures any push toward personal change. In a career laden with prizes, successful books, and a myriad of shorter pieces—filled with immense numbers of works that result from sheer hard labor, Kingsolver has here herself slighted the rules of drawing character. She has given us Dellarobia, in those uncomfortable, second-hand boots, making the decision to walk up the mountain to meet the handsome young stranger: but when Dellarobia sees the glowing fire of the unexpected Monarchs, she *stops*, and so does her development.

Dellarobia Turnbow is no Codi Noline, and she is far from being her sister Hallie. She is also no kin to Leah Price (or Adah), nor does she bear any resemblance to either Deanna Wolfe or Lusa Widener. She is, rather, a woman who has not slept away from her small house "for a single night in ten-plus years of marriage … The wide-screen version of her life since age seventeen" (Flight 2). Pity does not usually motivate many readers.

On sheep-shearing day in the following chapter, Kingsolver creates Dellarobia's interchange with Cub, her husband who is dejected because his father does not ever talk with him. Alarmed that his father fears bankruptcy, puzzled because he has already made plans to cross cut the forest, Cub still cannot criticize his parent.

"Well, hon, it's money we need," Cub tells Dellarobia.
"I know. Let's all sing the redneck national anthem: Settle for what you can get."
"I'm sorry you see it that way, but I don't see where we have a lot of choice."
He looked sorry all right. It made her want to punch something, all that *sorry*. She wished he would get mad. Instead he sat pulling threads of fleece from his jeans in a slow, passive way that made her blood boil. With occasional exceptions in the bedroom, Cub did every single thing in his life in first gear. It could take him forty minutes to empty his freaking pants pockets. (Flight 43)

Spirited in her criticism of her young spouse, Dellarobia empathizes with him in his frustration, but she does not figure *herself* into any of the Turnbow equations. She does still not see a means of becoming an effective part of the family's life; she exemplifies that "redneck national anthem" in her earlier reference.

The irony of evaluating the Dellarobia character according to Rinda West's injunction that she find herself in the wilderness is, simply, that Dellarobia *is* positioned to do that. Instead, making the trip up mountain which she has not done since before her children were born stalemates her. Rather than showing her how to avoid cultural expectations that stifle women's lives, her junket mires her in both religious and cultural constraints; she becomes "Our Lady of the Butterflies."

Eventually, under the guidance of Ovid Byron and his graduate students, Dellarobia *does* learn. But even her personal thirst for knowledge is given to her; she does not know how to hunger for a change in her circumstances, or how to enact anything that resembles change.

The reader thinks, perhaps, that Dellarobia's experiences while she learns in *Flight Behavior* will save her. We love her kindly relationship with the old-for-his-age Preston, her kindergarten son, and her hoydenish younger child Cordie. Yet, just when the reader has happily read what she is telling Preston—that she is going to college, that she is leaving their father in order to become *herself* instead of the accidentally pregnant mother she has spent her adult life growing into—Kingsolver adds the last, irretrievable chapter. The land floods. Dellarobia, like the butterflies, has no more choices. While the reader does not know how much of her family dies in the flooding, it seems clear that Dellarobia does not survive. And in the blending of the natural world with the human, the novel makes its sadly realistic point: *extinction* is the plotline for the butterflies.

Kingsolver states clearly in her *Time* interview that the novel's title is about much more than Dellarobia's fate. As she explained,

"there are a lot of things, a lot of strikes against us as human animals. It's very hard for us to believe in things we don't see. We don't see the effects of climate change, we don't see that melting sea ice. It's hard for us to believe that the world under our feet could ever be any different than how it's always been. I think the human animal has a fundamental trust in certain kinds of continuity. It's hard to convince ourselves that that's not the case. But most of all we're wired to fight or flee. That's the title of this novel. It's *Flight Behavior*. Every cell in our body wants to run away from the big scary thing. So this is a novel about flight behavior, all the ways that all of us are running away from scary truths." (Time November 8, 2012)

Kingsolver says on her 2013 Web site, "My life surprises me daily." In her plans for the writing she is now doing—"at work on a new novel, a poetry collection, a screenplay, and whatever the farm requires of me today"—and for the continuation of her attempts to meet the stringent demands of her aesthetic life, the novelist remains steady and, perhaps more important, steadfast in her writing objectives. Still winning a plethora of prizes (in 2011 the Dayton Literary Peace Prize for her *oeuvre*, and that same year the Duke University LEAF award for her lifetime of work), she will create new protagonists, new questions, and new novels for her readers to revere.

Bibliography

Primary (Books)

Kingsolver, Barbara. *Animal Dreams*. New York: Harper Perennial, 1990.

———. *Animal, Vegetable, Miracle: A Year of Food Life* (Coauthored with Steven Hopp and Camille Kingsolver). New York: HarperCollins, 2007.

———. *Another America/Otra America*. 2nd ed. 1998. Spanish Trans. Rebeca Cartes. Seattle, WA: Seal Press, 1992.

———. *The Bean Trees*. New York: Harper & Row, 1988.

———. ed. *The Best American Short Stories 2001*. Boston, MA: Houghton Mifflin, 2001.

———. *Flight Behavior*. New York: HarperCollins, 2012.

———. *High Tide in Tucson: Essays from Now or Never*. New York: HarperCollins, 1995.

———. *Holding the Line: Women in the Great Arizona Mine Strike of 1983*. 2nd ed. 1996. Ithaca, NY: ILR Press, 1989.

———. *Homeland and Other Stories*. New York: Harper & Row, 1990.

———. *The Lacuna*. New York: HarperCollins, 2009.

———. *Last Stand: America's Virgin Lands* (with Photographs by Annie Griffiths Belt). Washington, DC: National Geographic, 2002.

———. *Pigs in Heaven*. New York: Harper Perennial, 1993.

———. *The Poisonwood Bible*. New York: HarperCollins, 1998.

———. *Prodigal Summer*. New York: HarperCollins, 2000.

———. *Small Wonder: Essays*. New York: HarperCollins, 2002.

(Selected Stories, Essays, Reviews, Articles, Poems)

———. "Albert Uplifts Anything." (Review of Clyde Edgerton's *The Floatplane Notebooks*). *New York Times Book Review* (October 8, 1989). 10.

———. "An Address from Barbara Kingsolver—Delivered at the 1993 American Booksellers Conventions." http://www.readinggroupguides.com/guides/poisonwood_bible-author.asp

———. "Barbara Kingsolver, Authorized Web." 2013.

———. "Barbara Kingsolver, Dear Mom." *I've Always Meant to Tell You: Letters to Our Mothers/An Anthology of Contemporary Women Writers*, ed. Constance Warloe. New York: Pocket Books, 1997. 248–61.

———. "Between the Covers." (Review of John Irving's *A Widow for One Year*). *The Washington Post* (May 24, 1998).

———. "*Brazil.*" (By John Updike). *New York Times Book Review* (February 6, 1994). 1, 26–7.

———. "Deadline." (Poem). *A Map of Hope: Women's Writings on Human Rights, An International Literary Anthology.* ed. Marjorie Agosin. New Brunswick, NJ: Rutgers University Press, 1999. 70–1.

———. "Desert Heat: *So Far From God* by Ana Castillo." *Los Angeles Times Book Review* (May 16, 1993). 1, 9.

———. "Dialogue: Barbara Kingsolver." *Barbara Kingsolver.* New York: HarperCollins, November 2000. Web. July 5, 2008.

———. "Downscale in Topanga Canyon." (Review of T. Coraghessan Boyle's *The Tortilla Curtain*). *The Nation* 261.9 (September 25, 1995). 326–7.

———. "Ear to the Ground." (Review of E.O. Wilson's *Anthill*). *New York Times Book Review* (April 9, 2010).

———. "Everybody's Somebody's Baby." *New York Times Magazine* (February 9, 1992). 20, 49.

———. "FAQ." *Barbara Kingsolver.* HarperCollins. Web. July 5, 2008.

———. "Fish Fall From the Sky for a Reason: The Stones of Eva Luna." (By Isabel Allende). Trans. Margaret Sayers Peden. *New York Times Book Review* (January 20, 1991). 13–14.

———. "A Forbidden Territory Familiar to All." *New York Times* (March 27, 2000). E1.

———. "A Good Farmer." *The Essential Agrarian Reader.* ed. Norman Wirzba. Lexington: University Press of Kentucky, 2001. 11–18.

———. "How Poems Happen." *The Beacon Best of 1999: Creative Writing by Women and Men of All Colors.* ed. N. Shange. Boston, MA: Beacon, 1999. 252–4.

———. "How to Be Hopeful." (Poem). *Iron Mountain Review* 28 (Spring 2012). 5.

———. "How to be Hopeful." 2008 Commencement Address, Duke University. May 11, 2008.

———. "How to Shear a Sheep." (Poem). *Iron Mountain Review* 28 (Spring 2012). 4.

———. "Introduction." *Off the Beaten Path: Stories of Place.* New York: North Point Press, 1998.

———. "Journeys." *Paris Review* 153 (Winter 2000).

———. "Local Foods That Please the Soul." *New York Times* (November 22, 2001).

———. "A Metaphysics of Resistance." (Review of Maria Elena Lucas's *Forged Under the Sun*). *Women's Review of Books* 11.5 (February 1994). 25–6.

———. "Mexican Torture Victims Face Trial." *Militant* (July 25, 1980). 5.

———. "Mormon Memories, Angeleno Enigmas." (Review of *The Chinchilla Farm* by Judith Freeman). *Los Angeles Times Book Review* (November 19, 1989). 1.

———. "My Father's Africa." *McCall's* (August 1991). 115–23.

———. "Night Time Losing Time." (Review of Novel by Michael Ventura). *New York Times Book Review* (April 2, 1989).

———. "Not in Their Backyard." (Review of A.G. Mojtaba's *Called Out*). *New York Times Book Review* (June 19, 1994). 4.

———. "Notes from Underground." (Review of Priscilla Long's *Where the Sun Never Shines: A History of America's Bloody Coal Industry*). *Women's Review of Books* 7.9 (June 1990). 21–2.

———. "Once on This Island." (Review of T.C. Boyle's *When the Killing's Done*). *New York Times Book Review* (February 18, 2011).

———. "The Other Sister." (Review of Karen Joy Fowler's *We Are All Completely Beside Ourselves*). *New York Times Book Review* (June 6, 2013).

———. "Poetic Fiction with a Tex-Mex Tilt." (Review of *Woman Hollering Creek and Other Stories* by Sandra Cisneros). *Los Angeles Times* (April 28, 1991).

———. "The Prince Thing." *Woman's Day* (February 18, 1992). 26, 28, 110.

———. "Reconstructing Our Desires." *The Progressive* (December 2010/January 2011). 36–7.

———. "River of Traps: A Village Life" (By William deBuys and Alex Harris). *New York Review of Books* (September 23, 1990). 33, 50.

———. "Secret Animals." *Turnstile* 3 (1992).

———. "Snow Day." (Poem). *Iron Mountain Review* 28 (Spring 2012). 6.

———. "Some Can Whistle" (By Larry McMurtry). *New York Times Book Review* (October 23, 1989). 8.

———. "Survival of the Fittest." (Review of Cathleen Schine's *The Evolution of June*). *New York Times Book Review* (October 11, 1998). 13–14.

———. "The Way We Are. A Parenting Special Report." *Parenting* (March 1995). 74–81.

———. "Tribute to Edward Abbey." *Tucson Weekly* 6.7 (April 1989).

———. "Where Love is Nurtured and Confined: A Review of *Me and My Baby View the Eclipse* by Lee Smith." *Los Angeles Times* (February 18, 1990). 2; Collected in *Friendship and Sympathy: Communities of Southern Women Writers*, ed. Rosemary M. Magee. Jackson: University Press of Mississippi, 1992. 255–7.

———. "Whipsawed in Washington." (Review of Annie Dillard's *The Living*). *The Nation* 254.20 (May 25, 1992). 692–4.

———. "Widows at the Wheel." *Los Angeles Times* (October 1, 1989). 1.

———. "Women on the Line." With Jill Barrett Fein. *The Progressive* (March 1984). 15.

———. "World of Foes." (Review of *Endless Enemies: The Making of an Unfriendly World* by Jonathan Kwitny). *The Progressive* (December 1984).

———. "Worlds in Collision." (Review of Linda Hogan's *Mean Spirit*). *Los Angeles Times Book Review* (November 4, 1990). 3.

Secondary

Adams, Noah. Interview with Barbara Kingsolver. "All Things Considered." Washington, DC: National Public Radio, October 23, 2000.

Anderson, Lorraine. "New Voices in American Nature Writing." *American Nature Writers*, vol. 2, ed. John Elder. New York: Scribner's, 1996. 1157–72.

Anon. "Briefly Noted." (Review of *Flight Behavior*). *New Yorker* (December 24–31, 2012). 139.

————. "History Lesson." (Review of *The Lacuna*). *USA Today* (November 12, 2009). D4.

————. "Little Big Voice: New Essays." (Review of *Small Wonder*). *The Economist* (May 11, 2002). 363.

————. "*The Poisonwood Bible*." *Publishers Weekly* (August 10, 1998). 366.

————. "Serendipity and the Southwest: A Conversation with Barbara Kingsolver." *Bloomsbury Review* (November–December 1990). 3+.

————. "Where the Wild Things Are." *The Economist* (December 16, 2000). 8.

Aprile, Dianne. "Kinship with Kingsolver: Author's Characters Long to Belong, Something That Touches Readers." *The Courier-Journal* (July 25, 1993). 11.

Aulette, Judy and Trudy Mills. "Something Old, Something New: Auxiliary Work in the 1983–1986 Copper Strike." *Feminist Studies* (Summer, 1988). 251–68.

Austenfeld, Anne Marie. "The Revelatory Narrative Circle in Barbara Kingsolver's *The Poisonwood Bible*," in Austenfeld. 246–59.

Austenfeld, Thomas, ed. *Critical Insights: Barbara Kingsolver*. Pasadena, CA: Salem, 2010.

Bakopoulos, Paul. "Prodigal Summer." *Progressive* 64.12 (December 2000). 41.

Ballard, Sandra L. "'Disclosing the Heart of the Form': An Appreciation of Barbara Kingsolver's Nonfiction." *Iron Mountain Review* 28 (Spring 2012). 18–25.

Banks, Russell. "Distant as a Cherokee Childhood." (Review of *Homeland and Other Stories* by Barbara Kingsolver). *New York Times* (June 11, 1989). 16.

Bargreen, Melinda. "Characters Are Saving Grace of 'Prodigal Summer,'" *Seattle Times* (November 5, 2000).

Barker, Elspeth. "With Buster the Hermit Crab." (Review of *High Tide in Tucson*). *The Independent on Sunday* (London) (June 23, 1996). 36.

Battista, Christine M. "Cultivating Our Bioregional Roots: An Ecofeminist Exploration of Barbara Kingsolver's *Prodigal Summer*," in Austenfeld. 52–68.

Beattie, L. Elisabeth, ed. "Barbara Kingsolver Interview." *Conversations with Kentucky Writers*. Lexington: University of Kentucky Press, 1996. 150–71.

Bell, Millicent. "Fiction Chronicle: *The Poisonwood Bible*." *Partisan Review* 66 (1999). 417–30.

Bennett, Barbara. *Scheherazade's Daughters, the Power of Storytelling in Ecofeminist Change*. New York: Peter Lang, 2012.

Berry, Wes. "Earthbound Rhetoric and Praxis: Authentic Patriotism in a Time of Abstractions," in Leder. 199–210.

Birch, Carol. "The Missionary Imposition." *The Independent* (London) (February 6, 1999). 14 ("Features").

Birnie, Sue. "*The Poisonwood Bible*." *National Catholic Reporter* 37.32 (2001). 16.

Bolton, Matthew J. "The Gothic and the Ethnic in Barbara Kingsolver's *The Bean Trees*," in Austenfeld. 69–84.

Bouton, Katherine. "In Lab Lit, Fiction Meets Science of the Real World." (Review of *Flight Behavior*). *New York Times* (December 4, 2012).

Bowdan, Janet. "Re-placing Ceremony: The Poetics of Barbara Kingsolver." *Southwestern American Literature* 20.2 (Spring 1995). 13–19.

Brandmark, Wendy. "Kinship with the Earth." (Review of *Homeland and Other Stories*). *Times Literary Supplement* (January 24, 1997). 22.

Brinkmeyer, Robert. *Remapping Southern Literature*. Athens: University of Georgia Press, 2000.

Bromberg, Judith. "Review of *The Poisonwood Bible*." *National Catholic Reporter* (March 19, 1999). 13.

Browning, Dominique. "The Butterfly Effect." (Review of *Flight Behavior*). *New York Times Book Review* (November 11, 2012).

Buell, Lawrence. *Writing for an Endangered World: Literature, Culture, and Environment in the United States*. Cambridge: Harvard University Press, 2001.

Butler, Jack. "She Hung the Moon and Plugged in All the Stars." *New York Times Book Review* (April 10, 1988). 15.

Carpenter, Mackenzie. "Kingsolver's Essays Stumble on U. S. Guilt for Sept. 11," *Pittsburgh Post-Gazette* (April 13, 2002). B-7.

Charles, Ron. "Review of *Prodigal Summer*." *Christian Science Monitor* 92.230 (October 19, 2000). 20.

Ciolkowski, Laura. "Review: *Small Wonder*," *New York Times* (May 5, 2002).

Clark, Timothy. *The Cambridge Introduction to Literature and the Environment*. New York: Cambridge University Press, 2011.

Clifford, James. *Routes: Travel and Translation in the Late Twentieth Century*. Cambridge: Harvard University Press, 1997.

Clinton, Hillary. "On Kingsolver." *Oprah* ("Bookshelf"). (July–August 2000). 224.

Cockburn, Alexander. "The Execution of Ben Linder." *Nation* 245 (October 17, 1987). 402–3.

Cockrell, Amanda. "Luna Moth, Coyotes, Sugar Skulls: The Fiction of Barbara Kingsolver." *Hollins Critic* 38.2 (2001). 1–15, in Austenfeld. 173–91.

Cohen, Robin. "Wild Indians: Kingsolver's Representation of Native America," in Leder. 145–56.

Comer, Krista. "Sidestepping Environmental Justice: 'Natural' Landscapes and the Wilderness Plot." *Breaking Boundaries: New Perspectives on Women's Regional Writing*, eds. Sherrie Inness and Diane Royer. Iowa City: University of Iowa Press, 1997. 216–36.

———. *Landscapes of the New West: Gender and Geography in Contemporary Women's Writing*. Chapel Hill: University of North Carolina Press, 1999.

Cooke, Carolyn. "Review of *Animal Dreams*." *Nation* 251.18 (November 26, 1990). 653–4.

Corrigan, Maureen. "'The Lacuna,' Kingsolver's Vacant Return." NPR (November 3, 2009).

Cox, Bonnie Jean. "The Need in Us All: A Caring Dynamic Connection with the Past." *The Lexington Herald-Leader* (September 16, 1990). F6.

Cronon, William. "The Trouble with Wilderness; or, Getting Back to the Wrong Nature." *Uncommon Ground: Rethinking the Human Place in Nature.* ed. William Cronon. New York: Norton, 1995. 69–90.

Cryer, Dan. "Gladdening Stories of Hope and Strength." *New York Newsday* (June 26, 1989). 6.

———. "Talking with Barbara Kingsolver/The Good Book." *New York Newsday* (November 15, 1998). B11.

———. "An Unexpected Miracle and a Conflict of Roots." *New York Newsday* (June 21, 1993). 46.

———. "You Can Go Home Again." *New York Newsday* (August 26, 1990). 19.

Cusick, Christine. "Remembering Our Ecological Place: Environmental Engagement in Kingsolver's Nonfiction," in Leder. 213–32.

Daurio, Beverly. "A Rare, Bracing Tonic for a Cynical Age." (Review of *Pigs in Heaven*). *Globe and Mail* (Toronto) (July 10, 1993). C16.

DeMarr, Mary Jean. *Barbara Kingsolver: A Critical Companion.* Westport, CT: Greenwood Press, 1999.

———. "Mothers and Children in Barbara Kingsolver's *The Bean Trees.*" *Women in Literature: Reading through the Lens of Gender.* eds. Jerilyn Fisher, Ellen S. Silber, and David Sadker. Westport, CT: Greenwood Press, 2003. 26–8.

De Reus, Lee Ann. "Exploring the Matrix of Identity in Barbara Kingsolver's *Animal Dreams.*" *Reading the Family Dance: Family Systems Therapy and Literary Study.* eds. John V. Knapp and Kenneth Womack. Newark, NJ: University of Delaware Press, 2003. 93–108, in Austenfeld. 152–72.

Dinnerstein, Dorothy. *The Mermaid and the Minotaur.* NY: Harper and Row, 1976.

Doenges, Judy. "The Political Is Personal—Barbara Kingsolver's Novel Measures Tragedy in the Congo in Terms of Intimate, Individual Costs," *Seattle Times* (October 29, 1998).

Donahue, Deirdre. "Interview." *USA Today* (July 15, 1993). F3.

Douthat, Ross. "Kumbaya Watch: Barbara Kingsolver's America." *National Review* (September 26, 2001).

Doyle, R. Erica. "Barbara Kingsolver: The Bellweather Prize." *Ms* (June/July 2001).

Dunaway, David King. "Barbara Kingsolver," *Writing the Southwest.* Albuquerque: University of New Mexico Press, 2003. 93–103.

———. "Foreword" to *Barbara Kingsolver* by Linda Wagner-Martin, 2004. ix–xiv.

Eckhoff, Sally. "Scents and Sensibility." *Wall Street Journal* (October 20, 2000). W10.

Eisele, Kim. "The Where and Why of Literature: A Conversation with Barbara Kingsolver." *You Are Here* 2.2 (Fall 1999). 10–15.

Epstein, Robin. "Barbara Kingsolver." *Progressive* 60.2 (February 1996). 33–7.

Evancie, Angela. "So Hot Right Now: Has Climate Change Created a New Literary Genre?" *NPR* (April 20, 2013).

Fagan, Kristina. "Adoption as National Fantasy in Barbara Kingsolver's *Pigs in Heaven* and Margaret Laurence's *The Diviners*." *Imagining Adoption: Essays on Literature and Culture*. ed. Marianne Novy. Ann Arbor: University of Michigan Press, 2001. 251–66.

Fisher, Stephen L. "Community and Hope: A Conversation." *Iron Mountain Review* 28 (Spring 2012). 26–32.

Fitzgerald, Karen. "Review of *The Bean Trees*." *Ms* (April 1988). 28.

Flairty, Steve. "Barbara Kingsolver—Kentucky's 'Polite Firebrand' Author," *Kentucky Monthly* (February 2002). 12–15.

Fleischner, Jennifer, ed. *A Reader's Guide to the Fiction of Barbara Kingsolver: "The Bean Trees," "Homeland and Other Stories," "Animal Dreams," "Pigs in Heaven."* New York: HarperPerennial, 1994.

Fletcher, Yael Simpson, "History Will One Day Have Its Say: New Perspectives on Colonial and Postcolonial Congo." *Radical History Review* 84 (2002). 195–207.

Fox, Stephen D. "Barbara Kingsolver and Keri Hulme: Disability, Family, and Culture." *Critique: Studies in Contemporary Fiction* 45.4 (2004). 405–20.

Frucht, Abby. "'Saving' the Heathen Barbara Kingsolver's Missionary Goes into Africa, but He Just Doesn't Get it." *Boston Globe* (October 18, 1998). K1.

Frye, Bob J. "Nuggets of Truth in the Southwest: Artful Humor and Realistic Craft in Barbara Kingsolver's *The Bean Trees*." *Southwestern American Literature* 26.2 (Spring 2001). 73–83.

Gates, David. "The Voices of Dissent." *Newsweek* (November 19, 2001). 66–7.

Gergen, David. "Interview: Barbara Kingsolver." *U.S. News and World Report* (November 24, 1995).

Giles, Jeff. "Review of *Prodigal Summer*." *Newsweek* 136 (October 30, 2000). 82.

Godfrey, Kathleen. "Barbara Kingsolver's Cherokee Nation: Problems of Representation in *Pigs in Heaven*." *Western American Literature* 36.3 (Fall 2001). 259–77.

Goldstein, Bill. "An Author Chat with Barbara Kingsolver." *New York Times* (October 30, 1998).

Goodman, Ellen. "Books for Many Tastes." *Boston Globe* (July 18, 2000).

Gray, Paul. "Call of the Eco-Feminist." *Time* (September 24, 1990). 87.

———. "On Familiar Ground: Barbara Kingsolver Returns with Another Novel of Strong Women, Noble Issues and Love of the Land." *Time* (October 30, 2000). 90.

Greene, Gayle. "Independence Struggle." *Women's Review of Books* 16.7 (April 1999).

Gussow, Joan. "Calling Across the Fence." *Green Guide*, 93 (November/ December 2002). 4.

Heffernan, Nick and David A. Wragg, eds. *Culture, Environment and Ecopolitics*. Newcastle Upon Tyne: Cambridge Scholars, 2011.

Himmelwright, Catherine. "Garden of Auto Parts: Kingsolver's Merger of American Western Myth and Native American Myth in *The Bean Trees*," in Leder. 27–46.

Hirsch, Marianne. *The Mother-Daughter Plot: Narrative, Psychoanalysis, Feminism*. Bloomington: Indiana University Press, 1989.

Hogan, Linda. *Dwellings, a Spiritual History of the Living World*. New York: Norton, 1995.

Holt, Karen. "Review of *The Bean Trees*." *San Francisco Chronicle* (March 6, 1988). 1.

———. "Metamorphosis." (Review of *Flight Behavior*). *Oprah* (November 2012). 135.

Houston, Lynn Marie and Jennifer Warren. *Reading Barbara Kingsolver*. Santa Barbara, CA.: ABC-Clio, Greenwood Press, 2009.

Hughes, Kathryn. "Kathryn Hughes Finds a Chronicle of Living Off the Land Is Saved from Being Preachy by Glorious Wit." (Review of *Animal, Vegetable, Miracle*). *The Guardian* (London) (July 7, 2007). 8.

Hussein, Aamer. "Interview with Barbara Kingsolver." (By Lisa See). *Publisher's Weekly* (August 31, 1990). 46–7.

———. "Daughters of Africa." *Times Literary Supplement* (February 5, 1999). 21.

Jackson, Jason Baird. "The Opposite of Pow-wow: Ignoring and Incorporating the Intertribal War Dance in the Oklahoma Stomp Dance Community." *Plains Anthropologist* 48.187 (2003). 237–53.

Jacobs, Naomi. "Barbara Kingsolver's Anti-Western: 'Unraveling the Myths' in *Animal Dreams*." *Americana: The Journal of American Popular Culture 1900 to the Present* 2.2 (2003): Web. July 8, 2013.

Jacobson, Kristin J. "Imagined Geographies," in Leder. 175–98.

———. "The Neodomestic American Novel: The Politics of Home in Barbara Kingsolver's *The Poisonwood Bible*." *Tulsa Studies in Women's Literature* 24.1 (2005). 105–27.

Jones, Suzanne W. "The Family Farm as Endangered Species: Possibility for Survival in Barbara Kingsolver's *Prodigal Summer*," *Southern Literary Journal* 39.1 (Fall 2006). 83–97, in Austenfeld. 283–300.

Kakutani, Michiko. "The Poisonwood Bible: A Family Heart of Darkness," *New York Times* (October 16, 1998). 45.

Kappala-Ramsamy, Gemma. "Barbara Kingsolver: 'Motherhood is so Sentimentalized in Our Culture.'" *The Guardian (The Observer)* (London) (May 11 2013).

Karbo, Karen. "And Baby Makes Two," Interview with Barbara Kingsolver. *New York Times on the Web*. (June 27, 1993).

Karpen, Lynn. "The Role of Poverty, Interview with Barbara Kingsolver." *New York Times Book Review* (June 27, 1992). 6.

Kentoff, Maureen Meharg. "They Live Deliberately: Feminist Theory in Action in *High Tide in Tucson*," in Leder. 47–69.

Kerr, Sarah. "The Novel as Indictment." *New York Times Magazine* (October 11, 1998). 52–6.

King, Casey. "Books in Brief: Nonfiction." *New York Times* (October 15, 1995).

Klindienst, Patricia. *The Earth Knows My Name: Food, Culture, and Sustainability in the Gardens of Ethnic Americans.* Boston, MA: Beacon, 2006.

Klinkenborg, Verlyn. "Going Native." *New York Times Book Review* (October 18, 1998). 7.

Knickerbocker, Scott. *Ecopoetics: The Language of Nature, the Nature of Language.* Amherst: University of Massachusetts Press, 2012.

Krasny, Michael. "Interview: Barbara Kingsolver, Author, Discusses Her New Book." *Talk of the Nation* (NPR) (December 13, 1999).

Kummer, Corby. "My Year of Vegetables." (Review of *Animal, Vegetable, Miracle: A Year of Food Life*). *New York Times Book Review* (May 27, 2007).

Kunz, Diane. "White Men in Africa: On Barbara Kingsolver's *The Poisonwood Bible.*" *Novel History: Historians and Novelists Confront America's Past (and Each Other).* ed. Mark C. Carnes. New York: Simon & Schuster, 2001. 285–97.

Lang, John. "The Editor's Page" (On Barbara Kingsolver). *Iron Mountain Review* 28 (Spring 2012). 2.

Leder, Priscilla. "*Prodigal Summer*: A Narrative Ecosystem." *Critical Insights, Nature and the Environment.* ed. Scott Slovic. Ipswich, MA: Salem, 2012. 302–15.

———. ed. *Seeds of Change: Critical Essays on Barbara Kingsolver.* Knoxville: University of Tennessee Press, 2010.

Le Guin, Ursula K. "The Fabric of Grace." (Review of *Animal Dreams*). *Washington Post* (September 2, 1990). 1+ (*Book World*).

Lehmann-Haupt, Christopher. "Community vs. Family and Writers vs. Subject." *New York Times* (July 12, 1993). C16.

Leonard, John. "Kingsolver in the Jungle, Catullus and Wolfe at the Door." *The Nation* 268.2 (January 11–18, 1999). 28.

Lezard, Nicholas. "Believe in Evil." *The Guardian* (London) (January 8, 2000). 11 (*"Guardian* Saturday Pages").

Lipman, Elinor. "A Visitation of Butterflies to a Town and to a Life." *New York Times* (November 19, 2012).

Litovitz, Malca. "Huck Finn, Barbara Kingsolver, and the American Dream." *Queen's Quarterly* (Winter 1998). 3–12.

Lubiano, Wahneema, ed. *The House That Race Built, Black Americans, U.S. Terrain.* New York: Pantheon, 1997.

Lyall, Sarah. "Termites Are Interesting but Books Sell Better." *New York Times* (September 1, 1993).

MacEoin, Gary. "Nature Triumphs in Novel Buzzing with Life." *National Catholic Reporter* (November 9, 2001). 19.

Magee, Richard M. "Reintegrating Human and Nature: Modern Sentimental Ecology in Rachel Carson and Barbara Kingsolver." *Feminist Ecocriticism, Environment, Women, and Literature*. ed. Douglas A. Vakoch. New York: Lexington, 2012. 65–75.

Malinowitz, Harriet. "Down-Home Dissident." *Women's Review of Books* 19.10–11 (July 2002). 36–7.

Marshall, John. "Fast Ride on Pigs." (Review of *Pigs in Heaven*). *Seattle Post-Gazette* (July 26, 1993). 1.

Maslin, Janet. "Three Story Lines United by the Fecundity of Summer." (Review of *Prodigal Summer*). *New York Times* (November 2, 2000).

———. "Because It's Good for You, That's Why." (Review of *Animal, Vegetable, Miracle: A Year of Food Life*). *New York Times* (May 11, 2007).

McDowell, Linda. *Gender, Identity and Place: Understanding Feminist Geographies*. Minneapolis: University of Minnesota Press, 1999.

McGee, Celia. "'Bible' Offers Two Good Books in One." *USA Today* (October 22, 1998). 6D.

McGlone, Jackie. "Barbara Kingsolver's Flight of Fancy for the Real World." *The Herald/Scotland* (Sunday) (June 1, 2013).

McKie, Robin. "Review." (*Flight Behavior* by Barbara Kingsolver). *The Observer* (London) (November 10, 2012).

Mendes, Guy. "Messing with the Sacred: An Interview with Barbara Kingsolver." *Appalachian Journal* 28.3 (Spring 2001). 304–24.

Mesic, Penelope. "Earth Mother." (Review of *Small Wonder*). *Book* (May–June 2002). 70–1.

Messman, Robert. "Review of *The Bean Trees*." *English Journal* 79.6 (1990). 85.

Metteer, Christine. "*Pigs in Heaven*: A Parable of Native American Adoption Under the Indian Child Welfare Act." *Arizona State Law Journal* 28.2 (1996). 589–628.

Michael, Magali Cornier. *New Visions of Community in Contemporary American Fiction: Tan, Kingsolver, Castillo, Morrison*. Iowa City: University of Iowa Press, 2006.

Montgomery, Isobel. "Mission Impossible." *The Guardian* (London) (February 13, 1999). 6. ("*Guardian* Saturday Pages").

Murphy, Patrick D. "Nature Nurturing Fathers in a World Beyond Our Control." *Eco-Man: New Perspectives on Masculinity and Nature*. ed. Mark Allister. Charlottesville: University of Virginia Press, 2004. 196–212.

Murrey, Loretta Martin. "The Loner and the Matriarchal Community in Barbara Kingsolver's *The Bean Trees* and *Pigs in Heaven*." *Southern Studies: An Interdisciplinary Journal of the South* 5.1–2 (1994). 155–64.

Myszka, Jessica. "Barbara Kingsolver: 'Burning a Hole in the Pockets of My Heart,'" *DePauw Magazine* 5.2 (Spring 1994). 18–20.

Neuhaus, Denise. "On Dependable Ground." (Review of *Homeland and Other Stories*). *Times Literary Supplement* (September 7, 1996). 956.

Newman, Vicky. "Compelling Ties: Landscape, Community, and Sense of Place," *Peabody Journal of Education* 70.4 (Summer, 1995). 105–18.

Nizalowski, John. "The Political Is Personal: Sociocultural Realities and the Writings of Barbara Kingsolver," in Austenfeld. 17–35.

Norman, Liane Ellison. "Review of *The Poisonwood Bible*," *Sojourners* 28.2 (1999). 59.

Novy, Marianne. "Nurture, Loss, and Cherokee Identity in Barbara Kingsolver's Novels of Cross-Cultural Adoption." *Reading Adoption: Family and Difference in Fiction and* Drama. Ann Arbor: University of Michigan Press, 2005.

Ognibene, Elaine R. "The Missionary Position: Barbara Kingsolver's *The Poisonwood Bible*," *College Literature* 30.3 (2003). 19–36.

Owens, Louis. *Mixedblood Messages: Literature, Film, Family, Place.* Norman: University of Oklahoma Press, 1998.

———. "As if an Indian Were Really an Indian: Native American Voices and Postcolonial Theory." *Native American Representations: First Encounters, Distorted Images and Literary Appropriations.* ed. Gretchen Bataille. Lincoln: University of Nebraska Press, 2001. 11–25.

Parsell, DL. "New Photo Book an Homage to Last U.S. Wildlands." *National Geographic News* (October 29, 2002).

Pence, Amy. "Barbara Kingsolver." *Poets & Writers* 21.4 (July–August 1993). 14–21.

Perry, Donna. "Interview with Barbara Kingsolver." *Backtalk: Women Writers Speak Out.* ed. Donna Perry. New Brunswick, NJ: Rutgers University Press, 1993. 143–69.

Pitcaithley, Dwight T. "Barbara Kingsolver and the Challenges of Public History." *The Public Historian* 21.4 (1999). 9–18.

Pollan, Michael. "In Conversation" with Adam Platt. *New York* (April 22, 2013). 32–37, 87.

Price, Catherine. "The Man Who Changed the Way We Think about Food." *Oprah* (April 2013). 172–8.

Quick, Susan Chamberlin. "Barbara Kingsolver: A Voice of the Southwest—An Annotated Bibliography." *Bulletin of Bibliography* 54 (1997). 283–302.

Quinn, Judy. "Book News: HarperCollins Gets to Keep Kingsolver." *Publishers Weekly* (February 10, 1997). 19. See also Kingsolver's Response, "Kingsolver Clarifies." *Publishers Weekly* (April 7, 1997). 11.

Randall, Margaret. "Foreword." *Another America* by Barbara Kingsolver. xi–xiii.

———. "Human Comedy." *Women's Review of Books* 5.8 (May 1988). 1, 3.

Regier, Amy M. "Replacing the Hero with the Reader: Public Story Structure in *The Poisonwood Bible*." *Mennonite Life* 56.1 (March 2001).

Rehm, Diane. *Interview with Barbara Kingsolver.* Washington, DC: WAMU, American University, November 5, 1988.

———. *Interview with Barbara Kingsolver.* Washington, DC: WAMU, American University, May 14, 2002.

Rosenblum, Jonathan D. *Copper Crucible: How the Arizona Miners' Strike of 1983 Recast Labor-Management Relations in America.* Ithaca, NY: ILR/Cornell University Press, 1995, 1998.

Rosenfeld, Megan. "Novelist in Hog Heaven; 'Pigs' Brings Home the Bacon While Its Author Writes Her Heart Out." *Washington Post* (July 14, 1993). D1.

Rubenstein, Roberta. "Homeric Resonances: Longing and Belonging in Barbara Kingsolver's *Animal Dreams*." *Homemaking: Women Writers and the Politics and Poetics of Home*. eds. Catherine Wiley and Fiona R. Barnes. New York: Garland, 1996. 5–21.

Ryan, Maureen. "Barbara Kingsolver's Low-fat Fiction." *Journal of American Culture* 18.4 (Winter 1995). 77–82.

Schillinger, Liesl. "Artists and Idols." (Review of *The Lacuna*), *New York Times Book Review* (November 8, 2009). 9.

Schoeffel, Melissa. *Maternal Conditions: Reading Kingsolver, Castillo, Erdrich, and Ozeki*. New York: Peter Lang, 2008.

Schuessler, Jennifer. "Men, Women and Coyotes." *New York Times Book Review* (November 5, 2000). 38.

Scigaj, Leonard. *Sustainable Poetry*. Lexington: University of Kentucky Press, 1999.

Seaman, Donna. "*The Poisonwood Bible*." *Booklist* (August, 1998). 1922.

See, Lisa. "Interview with Barbara Kingsolver." *Publisher's Weekly* (August 31, 1990). 46–7.

Shapiro, Laura. "A Novel Full of Miracles." *Newsweek* (July 12, 1993). 61.

Shilling, James. "Animal Instincts." *London Times* (December 23, 2000). 25.

Shuffleton, Frank. *A Mixed Race: Ethnicity in Early America*. New York: Oxford University Press, 1993.

Shulman, Polly. "Wild Lives/Human Fortunes Are Rooted in the Fate of the Chestnut Tree—and Other Flora and Fauna—in the Ecological Romance." *New York Newsday* (October 29, 2000). B9.

Siegel, Lee. "Review of *The Poisonwood Bible*." *New Republic* 220.12 (March 22, 1999). 30, 37.

Skow, John. "Hearts of Darkness: Matters of Race, Religion and Gender Collide as a Missionary Family Moves to the Congo in 1959." *Time* 152.9 (November 9, 1998). 113.

Slovic, Scott, ed. *Critical Insights, Nature and the Environment*. Ipswich, MA: Salem, 2013.

Smiley, Jane. "In One Small Town, the Weight of the World." *New York Times Book Review* (September 2, 1990). 2.

Smith, Lee. "Mountain Music's Moment in the Sun." *Washington Post* (August 12, 2001). G1.

Smith, Wendy. "Talking with Barbara Kingsolver: Reality with a Punch Line." *New York Newsday* (August 8, 1993). 34.

Snodgrass, Mary Ellen. *Barbara Kingsolver: A Literary Companion*. Jefferson, NC: McFarland, 2004.

Stegner, Page. "Both Sides Lost." (Review of *Holding the Line*). *New York Times* (January 7, 1990).

Stevenson, Sheryl. "Trauma and Memory in Kingsolver's *Animal Dreams*," in Austenfeld. 123–51.

Stobie, Mary. "Kingsolver Sequel Emphasizes Importance of Family Roots." *Rocky Mountain News* (July 4, 1993).

Strehle, Susan. "*Chosen People: American Exceptionalism in Kingsolver's The Poisonwood Bible*." *Critique* 49 (2008). 413–28.

Swartz, Patti Capel. "'Saving Grace': Political and Environmental Issues and the Role of Connections in Barbara Kingsolver's *Animal Dreams*," *Interdisciplinary Studies in Literature and Environment* 1.1 (1993). 65–79.

Thomas, P. L. *Reading, Learning, Teaching Barbara Kingsolver*. New York: Peter Lang, 2005.

Tischler, Barbara L. "Holding the Line: Women in the Great Arizona Mine Strike of 1983." *Labor Studies Journal* 17.1 (Spring 1992). 82–3.

Trachtman, Paul. "High Tide in Tucson." *Smithsonian* 27.3 (June 1996). 24.

Wagner-Martin, Linda. *Barbara Kingsolver*. Philadelphia, PA: Chelsea House, 2004.

———. *Barbara Kingsolver's "The Poisonwood Bible": A Reader's Guide*. New York: Continuum, 2001.

———. "'Keeping an Eye on Paradise': The Exuberance of *Prodigal Summer*," *Iron Mountain Review* 28 (Spring 2012). 7–11.

Walsh, Bryan. "Barbara Kingsolver on *Flight Behavior*." *Time* (November 8, 2012).

Warren, Colleen Kelly. "Family Tragedy Plays Out in Congo." *St. Louis Post-Dispatch* (October 18, 1998). C5.

———. "Literature, Biology Fuse in Kingsolver's Novel About Life." *St. Louis Post-Dispatch* (October 15, 2000). F10.

Wenz, Peter S. "Leopold's Novel: The Land Ethic in Barbara Kingsolver's *Prodigal Summer*." *Ethics and the Environment* 8.2 (2003). 106–25.

Wertheimer, Linda. "Interview: Barbara Kingsolver Discusses Her Latest Novel, 'Prodigal Summer,'" *All Things Considered* (NPR) (October 23, 2000).

West, Rinda. *Out of the Shadow: Ecopsychology, Story, and Encounters with the Land*. Charlottesville: University of Virginia Press, 2007.

Wilder, Katherine. *Walking the Twilight: Women Writers of the Southwest*. Flagstaff, AZ: Northland, 1994.

Willis, Meredith Sue. "Barbara Kingsolver, Moving On," *Appalachian Journal: A Regional Studies Review* 22.1 (1994). 79–86.

———. "Barbara Kingsolver's *The Lacuna* as a Political Novel," *Iron Mountain Review* 28 (Spring 2012). 13–17.

Wirzba, Norman, ed. *The Essential Agrarian Reader: The Future of Culture, Community, and the Land*. Lexington: University Press of Kentucky, 2001.

Wittenberg, Judith Bryant. "*Go Down, Moses* and the Discourse of Environmentalism." *New Essays on Go Down, Moses*. ed. Linda Wagner-Martin. New York: Cambridge University Press, 1996. 49–71.

Woods, Gioia. "Barbara Kingsolver." *Twentieth-Century American Western Writers*: First Series. *Dictionary of Literary Biography*. vol. 206. Detroit: Gale, 1999. Literature Resources Center. Web. April 11, 2009.

———. "Together at the Table: *Animal, Vegetable, Miracle* and Thoreau's *Wild Fruits*," in Leder. 263–76.

Wrede, Theda. "Barbara Kingsolver's *Animal Dreams*: Ecofeminist Subversion of Western Myth," *Feminist Ecocriticism, Environment, Women, and Literature*. ed. Douglas A. Vakoch. New York: Lexington, 2012. 39–64.

Wright, Charlotte M. "Barbara Kingsolver." *Updating the Literary West*, eds. Max Westbook and Don Flores. Ft. Worth, TX: Texas Christian University Press, 1997. 504–11.

Yalom, Marilyn. *Maternity, Mortality, and the Literature of Madness*. University Park: Pennsylvania State University Press, 1985.

Young, Elizabeth. "Review of *Pigs in Heaven*." *The Guardian* (London) (November 23, 1993). 9.

Index